AROUND THE WORLD IN 575 SONGS

TRADITIONAL MUSIC FROM ALL THE WORLD'S COUNTRIES

VOL 1: EUROPE

NICK WALL

ISBN 978 1999631 406

British Library Cataloguing in Publication Data.
A catalogue record for this book is available from the British Library.

Printed and bound in Great Britain by 4edge Limited
Typeset in 11pt Minion Pro by Troubador Publishing Ltd, Leicester, UK

MUSIC IS POWER. MUSIC IS A LANGUAGE. MAYBE FOR ME, THE FIRST LANGUAGE. WE CAN USE IT TO DEVELOP LOT OF JUSTICE AROUND THE WORLD.

Youssou N'Dour

CONTENTS

SERIES INTRODUCTION

I n 2013 I set myself the task of collecting songs from every country in the world. It's taken up five years of my life, but the results of my labours can now be heard on this website – https://aroundtheworldin575songs.com/

and can be seen in the four volumes of this book. The book is your guide to the song list. In its volumes I will introduce all the selected songs, tell you stories about many of the artists, and give you some insight into the cultures that they represent. Please browse the website, listen to some of the streamed songs, and above all be adventurous! If I can lead people to discover new music and take inspiration from it, then this book will have served a purpose.

I'm going to be straight with you: this isn't quite the book that I had sketched out in my mind when I began this project. In fact, it's become a lot bigger. So what happened?

This is a project that began with a love of global rhythms and a desire to share some of this music with as many people as possible. To make the list more accessible and interesting I wanted to write about all the songs that I'd be selecting. The idea of a book immediately suggested itself, but the book I intended to write was something closer to a guide to the songs themselves. It's hard to say exactly when this changed. Was it when I first heard from Xavier Fethal about how rising sea levels are threatening to destroy his people's way of life on their Pacific island home? Or when Mariem Hassan told me of a life spent in refugee camps and in exile, dreaming of the day when Saharawi people would be able to live in peace in their homeland? To do justice to Xavier Fethal and Mariem Hassan, as well as telling their stories I would have to write something about their people and their culture.

What had begun as a search for culturally distinctive music from 200 countries had taken on new dimensions. We live in a world that's becoming less culturally diverse, more homogenised. The Eurovision Song Contest is a prime example: it's anything but a celebration of diversity. The songs are mostly pop-oriented, produced in ways designed to appeal to an international audience; and in 2017 no less than 35 of the 42 songs in the final were sung entirely in English. In this world it can sometimes take courage to stand up and say what is most valuable in our culture is what makes us unique. So it's been very interesting to look at artists who've adopted that standpoint, to see what motivates them and what they've been able to achieve.

As well as new insights, the expanding project raised certain questions in my mind. Why do we see so many struggles to establish a national or ethnic identity in every part of every continent in the 21st century? The world has changed so much in the last 100 years; you might say that in many ways it's moved on: is it still meaningful even to talk about unitary national identities? What, if any, are the benefits to humanity of reconnecting with our cultural roots? What's music's role in all this? Should it be left to musicians themselves to rekindle the flame of their cultural heritage, or should the state be supporting them to a lesser or greater extent?

But let's take a step back. I guess the first question that I need to answer is how did I ever end up doing this?

BEGINNINGS

I love compiling music lists. It's a bit of a hobby, but what makes it more rewarding than ever before is that there are so many more ways of sharing music now that billions of people have access to the internet.

In the spring of 2013 I put out this message:

Calling all folk music enthusiasts!

I'd like your help please in compiling a list of the most loved folk songs. What I need you to do is to decide on your 25 favourite folk songs (or a smaller number if you prefer), and send these to me by email.

I'll leave the question of what is a folk song essentially up to you. The songs may be in any language, or instrumentals, and they can be old or new.

I want the artist name and song title. If the song's been recorded by different artists, just choose your favourite version.

I didn't get as many responses as I hoped for, but some of the ones I got were very interesting. Fingal Folk Club polled their members and sent in a combined list (so they only got one vote!). The bulk of the songs nominated were Irish, but about a third were American standards. There may well be a few Americans living in the west of Ireland, but I had a notion that this was more to do with the influence of American music. I saw the same thing with some of the other lists. So even Colin MacDonald, who works for the Glasgow-based Celtic Music Radio, devoted 40% of his list to American singers.

There was something else too. The songs being chosen, whether traditional or modern, were nearly all in the English language, and in the main performed by white artists, though a few blues numbers by the likes of Leadbelly and Mississippi John Hurt did make the final list. There were no mentions for Chile's Violeta Parra, or for Zimbabwe's Thomas Mapfumo. This was not unexpected: after all, I'd been soliciting responses mainly from among people who'd attended folk clubs; this demographic is overwhelmingly white and English speaking; and most of the folk songs that they know and sing in the clubs are from the British, Irish and American traditions.

Such reflections kindled in me the desire to delve into the stock of fabulous music from around the world which I'd been quietly accumulating. In the late 1980s I was an occasional listener to Andy Kershaw on BBC Radio 1 and Charlie Gillett on Capital Radio, and riffling through my old vinyl collection I'm surprised to find quite how much African music I was buying at that time, though my interests were by no means limited to African music: Le Mystère des Voix Bulgares was often on my turntable, and one of my most memorable concerts was seeing Nusrat Fateh Ali Khan at the Hackney Empire. Twenty-odd years later, I now had a healthy collection (or so I thought) of world music on iTunes, and an urge to share some of it.

The time was ripe for a new project.

And then one morning when I was in the shower the idea grabbed me to collect songs from every country in the world. Straightaway I knew that this was a challenge that I couldn't turn down.

How the songs were selected

One trouble with a list that covers 200 countries is that it risks upsetting people from 200 countries.

So let me be clear what this list is not. It is not intended to be a reflection of what music is most popular in any particular country. And it's not a comprehensive guide. I am limited on numbers. I can't represent each and every region, or ethnic group, and I certainly can't represent every artist of importance. What I'm offering you is a small sampler of each country's music, it's a personal selection, and while I'm interested to know what you would have chosen, I hope that you won't be too hard on me for what I've left out.

The Countries

There are currently 193 member states of the United Nations. I have included these 193, plus two 'observer states' (Vatican City and Palestine) and five others: Kosovo, Kurdistan, Puerto Rico, Saharawi and Taiwan. By including these five, and not others, I'm not trying to make any case for which countries are most deserving of recognition as nation states. I hope that it's clear from the narratives that I am supportive of the rights of self-determination of all geographical entities and self-defined populations. In my song choices I seek to represent not only the countries, but also, when I can, a few of the main population groups and cultures within those countries, so while there is no separate chapter on Scotland for example, Scottish music is represented and discussed in the book. Of these five countries Taiwan and Kosovo are recognised by most of the world as independent nation states, while Kurdistan, Saharawi and Puerto Rico all have compelling stories to tell about establishing a sense of identity which seemed deserving of separate chapters.

Number of songs per country

Fifty-nine countries have one song, 47 have two, 29 have three, 20 have four, 20 have five, 21 have six, three have seven (USA, UK and France) and one has eight (India).

There was no fixed formula. The only way to eliminate all argument would be to have one song per country, but in my view a list which gave the same space to France as to Monaco and to Spain as to Andorra would be of limited value. The decision whether to select one or six songs, or somewhere in between, was based on the amount of music available, and the minimum number of songs that I felt I needed to properly represent that country's music and to do justice to all the cultures and musical genres in which I had an interest.

The subjective element made planning the book more difficult as, while I had a set of targets for numbers of songs to include, these would often have to be modified upwards or downwards as I researched each country in turn and found that some surpassed my expectations while others fell short.

Who qualifies? – Issues of nationality

There's probably no question that you can think of which I haven't had to answer when compiling this list. Let's take Iraq. Who qualifies as an Iraqi artist? Do they have to have been born in Iraq? Or hold an Iraqi passport? Or identify as being Iraqi? Many Iraqi musicians have been forced into exile at one time or another as a result of political repression and war. Should I be giving precedence to music recorded locally, or music recorded in Europe on international labels where the headline artist will often be backed by a band put together of musicians from several countries?

Saleh and Daoud Al-Kuwaity were Jewish brothers born in Kuwait to an Iraqi father, who spent the best part of their lives and careers in Iraq before packing their bags and going to live in exile in Israel. Which country would you place them in, if you had to pick one?

Rahim AlHaj, who was born in Baghdad, fled Iraq in 1991, when he was a young man. He's lived for many years now in New Mexico and is a US citizen. He aims through his music to bridge the gap between western audiences and Arab musical tradition, describing it as "a conversation between East and West". How confident would you be that the music he plays typifies Iraqi culture?

I never laid down hard and fast rules. However, there were plenty of artists who I decided to exclude because they were born in another country, or lived in another country, or because their work was defined by collaborations with musicians from different countries and traditions. To fully appreciate the reasons for this, you have to understand the nature of the project. I wasn't interested in music that happened to have been made by Iraqi artists but could equally have been made in any Arab country. I wanted to find that music which spoke to me most eloquently of the particularity of a musical heritage over 1,000 years old.

Living permanently in another country has a tendency to affect the music that you make. I have observed this on so many occasions that I believe it to be a fact. You're suddenly exposed to a wide range of new musical influences; perhaps you have opportunities to work with musicians from other cultures. You're performing in front of audiences who have completely different expectations from audiences in your home country, who may not even understand the language in which you sing. All these influences and pressures may change your musical direction. That's not a crime, it's through interaction such as this that music continually renews itself and new genres and traditions are born. Salsa music is a case in point: a musical genre created in New

York, predominantly by Puerto Rican immigrants, which was exported to Latin America where in a number of countries it's become part of the cultural fabric. Just because you live abroad doesn't mean that you can't contribute to the way in which people in your home country make music and add a new strand to their sense of national identity. Sivan Perwer had an immense influence on Kurdish music in Turkey despite spending most of his adult life in exile in Europe. So I am by no means excluding musicians who live in exile, but unless I can see that their music has a continued influence and relevance in their home country it's unlikely to be selected.

What type of music?

I have preconceived ideas. I want to find music that's rooted in a country's past heritage and culture, music that employs traditional instruments. I prefer to steer clear of songs that employ electronic instruments and I'm not interested at all in beat-heavy pop, R&B, hip hop and reggae: the globalised culture in which past traditions become meaningless.

I want to give a sense of cultures at their best and most vibrant. In some cases that will lead me to write about the music of the 1970s, '60s, '50s, or even earlier. I also want to give a sense of how those cultures are faring today, what current artists we should be paying attention to and what the future holds. Where there is a lot of current music that's of interest, I will focus on that rather than on the stars of the past.

There's no guaranteeing where all of this will take me. With each country that I look at, the journey that I take is different. In some cases, the direction of travel is fairly obvious. So it would be inconceivable to write about Mongolia without discussing throat singing, or Georgia without celebrating its tradition of polyphonic song. But what of South Africa? In the 1980s whenever you went to an anti-apartheid rally you could rely on hearing beautiful singing, and there were many great artists whose names will be forever associated with the movement. It would have been easy to use up the whole chapter just writing about Hugh Masakela, Miriam Makeba, Johnny Clegg, Ladysmith Black Mambazo, Mahlatini, etc. But there's another story here, and it's one that needs to be told: about how in post-apartheid South Africa the synthesiser has largely replaced traditional instruments, about how the youth of today no longer listen much to the music of these past giants which they see as a little dated, and about those traditionalists like Dr Thomas who are trying to fight against the tide.

I talk a lot in this book about traditional music. Probably more than I should, because it's one of these terms that mean different things to different people. The term is useful in that it can be applied to any pre-existing culture, while terms like 'folk music' and 'volksmusik' are more culture-specific. Is the term still meaningful though if applied to a song that wasn't passed on by oral tradition, and which the singer performs in their own manner, without reference to how it would originally have been performed? If 'traditional' is used in its general popular sense of something that is rooted in past tradition then we can, but we may feel that we need to make further distinctions, for instance between 'recovered tradition' which tries to reconstruct how music was originally performed, and 'reinvented tradition' – newly composed music that evokes past tradition without trying to imitate it.

An important reason for using the term 'traditional music' is to distinguish these songs from 'world music'. While there is some crossover there is a difference which may be explained in this way: 'world music' is aimed at a global audience, while 'traditional music' is primarily aimed at people from a specific region or ethnic group. World music glories in multiculturalism, and celebrates successful cross-cultural collaborations and fusions of beats and genres from diverse origins. Traditional music, on the other hand, is focused on a particular culture and suggests an unbroken relationship with the past.

WHICH SONGS?

The secret to compiling a good song list is very simple. The more candidate songs that you discard and don't use, the more confidence you can have that the finalised list is as good as it can possibly be.

With every artist on the list, I've had to consider which song to pick and from which of their albums. The choices were mine, though I've tried to accommodate any record companies, managers and agents who wanted me to promote a particular song. The one non-negotiable criterion for inclusion is that it has to be a song that I genuinely like and would be happy to own on iTunes. I'm not a linguist; where I can I've done some research into non-English-language songs to find out what they're about and this has helped guide me in my choice of songs. Where I'm unable to translate the lyrics or decipher a song's meaning I judge it on how it sounds to the ear, also taking account of the instruments used.

HOW TO LISTEN

This is a celebration of difference, an affirmation of the fact that in the globalised world that we live in, where kids in Mombasa and Mumbai can keep up with the latest musical craze in New York City, real music, the music of the people, still exists in thousands of different forms, and in every country there are people who recognise this and care passionately about holding on to what they can of the diversity of past musical tradition.

There will be pieces of music here which are unlike anything that you've ever heard before. You might find something that changes your life. You may equally hear things that leave you grabbing for the mouse so you can skip to the next track – songs that grate on your ear.

Much of this music is traditional in origin. Reflect on what that means. The earliest commercial jazz recordings only date back 100 years. Before that, music performance was limited to certain contexts: you had the elite culture such as western classical music and opera; folk music as would be played in communities, places of work and places of leisure; and music associated with religious rituals and ceremonies. For much of human history forms of unaccompanied singing were far more important than they are now. Musical instruments were not mass-produced, and examples of regional variants of a particular instrument are rife. Folk dancing was integral to many cultures, and entire musical genres and sub-genres were originally associated with particular types of dance. Genuinely traditional music is music that once had a reason for existing.

Besides this, be open to the strange and the new. Listen out for all the differences just in music that originates from the same country – such as Senegal, home to Youssou N'Dour's band and its soulful music, father to Malick Pathe Sow and Bao Sissoko with their gentle, intricate duets, yet also capable of producing the raw and raucous sound of Aby Ngana Diop. Above all, if you find something that you like, follow the links, check out the artist and buy their music.

Music and the Search for Identity

Written music has existed since ancient times, but prior to the 20th century its use was the preserve of a privileged educated few. As for folk musicians, village singers, travelling players, gypsies, klezmorim, bards, griots, Bauls – none of them had ever learned to read music. Oral tradition was the means by which they gained their knowledge of music and passed it on to the next generation. It wasn't a pure science. Every time that a song was passed on a line or two would get changed here and there, and perhaps the young would stamp their own character on the song. So even a song like The Parting Glass which has survived remarkably well for over 400 years has undergone innumerable changes, has been known under many different titles, and so on.

Oral tradition extends beyond music. It underpins the transmission of culture – through language, sayings, storytelling, and the construction of myth and legend. By the late 19th century it was already becoming obvious to many observers that oral tradition was dying. This was happening not just in one country but all over the world, and everywhere the causes were the same: rapid urbanisation, large-scale migration, industrialisation and increasing literacy. In the 20th century the process of social change accelerated, while at the same time the emergence of modern mass media such as radio, television and the internet had a very damaging effect on traditional culture, effectively killing off oral tradition altogether except in a tiny number of isolated pockets.

This matters, fundamentally, to all of us. We are all a product of our past: not just our immediate ancestors, but the communities in which they lived, the cultures in which they grew up. We can choose to discard that past and take on new identities. But for many people, that's not an option. Language, religion, culture and tradition are the only things that are truly theirs, that establish who they are. Mass media can never replace this. So if you're someone who's been ripped away from your roots, you feel no special sense of kinship with the people living in your neighbourhood, you have a nagging sadness that part of you has been lost, what do you do, where do you turn?

Musicians have not been the only ones trying to provide

answers. Political and religious movements have done so too. And the linkage of traditional music with nationalist politics or organised religion takes us into sensitive territory. Earlier on I wrote glowingly about the close relationship of South African musicians with the anti-apartheid struggle back in the 1980s. During the same period though – unbeknownst to me at the time – in Croatia, Franjo Tudjman was evoking folk music as a means of stirring up support for his reactionary and dangerous brand of nationalism. Not every folk group joined Zlatni Dukati in performing at Tudjman's election rallies. Nonetheless, this was more than just a piece of opportunism by Tudjman. Half a century earlier, a whole folklore movement had been built up in Croatia linked to the centre-right Croatian Peasant Party which based itself on a sanitised, romanticised version of traditional peasant culture.

Some of my friends on the left view attempts to revive traditional music with suspicion, or even hostility. Their creed is internationalism, workers' unity; multiculturalism is their idea of what the world should look like. So music that looks back to the past, that is tied to a specific culture/ethnic group and that can be harnessed by nationalist movements, spells danger.

I'm all for multiculturalism, but denigrating certain music for not being multiculturalist enough is generally not a good idea. There's nothing reactionary in itself about studying, and celebrating, past history. Let's take the case of Croatia. Croatia has many traditional dances, and traditional costumes, which are associated with particular regions. Why so? Well, it probably has much to do with the area's complex history which has seen empires rise and fall, waves of immigration, battles over areas of land. Across the border, Serbia has its own complex mix of regional culture. But look at what's been taking off in Serbian music: Balkan brass band music, played by Roma musicians. This too is rooted in history. The brass band tradition goes back to the time when Serbia was part of the Ottoman Empire, over 200 years ago. Brass band music gave rise to the Cocek dance, and the music and dance was largely kept alive by Roma people who passed it on from one generation to the next. This is by no means untypical. Studying past tradition doesn't negate multiculturalism, but rather reinforces it, by revealing to us the varied mix of cultural influences which contribute to the making of a particular musical style.

Yugoslavia was a multi-ethnic state built on the aspiration that the constituent ethnic groups would move toward a unified Yugoslavian national culture. From our knowledge of the violent way in which Yugoslavia was ripped apart and ethnic rivalries asserted themselves, one might easily conclude that this was a utopian aspiration. I don't subscribe to this: the goal was perfectly reasonable, the problems stemmed from the method of getting there.

No one is born a patriot. Nations are political entities where people of different origins coexist. So every nationalism is a created narrative, a story that people are invited to buy into. It's also just one route to dealing with questions of identity. The past offers up many narratives; the challenge is to come up with a narrative that resonates with people's lived experience. Tito and the founders of the Yugoslav state failed this test when they assumed that ethnic rivalries would wither away. During World War II many thousands of Croats had fought with the Ustaše who sided with the Germans against Tito's Partisans. What proportion of the population they represented is unclear, but atrocities were committed; there was no reconciliation, leaving a toxic legacy of hatred and distrust.

The divisions that civil wars leave behind are the hardest to heal. Such divisions demand a response that goes beyond simple nationalism or anti-nationalism – the development of a different kind of narrative that celebrates diversity while also recognising and celebrating the specificity of individual cultures. Music, which is always connecting people across cultural divides, is integral to this whole idea. Yugoslavia's communists didn't see the progressive potential in traditional culture, understandably so perhaps, given the extent to which it had become identified with the political right in much of the country. Culture though is never completely static and unchanging. All cultures are fluid, they can change when people are influenced by new ideas, and at particular times in history this process can be accelerated. The state has to trust musicians and artists to navigate the process, and respect their artistic choices: the consequence of crude state intervention is likely to be that more and more artistic activity is driven underground. What the Communist state could have done though is what other states around the world have done, often to their benefit, which was to facilitate the study and practice of traditional culture, effectively opening the field up to greater numbers of young people who support the multicultural state.

The search for cultural identity in the 21st century is a reclaiming of lost values: like pride in one's region (the idea that 'local is beautiful') and in the language of one's ancestors. There's very often a political dimension to this. The growing reach of supra-national institutions such as the EU and NAFTA makes many people feel disempowered and disenfranchised. They see such institutions as bureaucratic and serving the interests of others, not their own. On both sides of the political spectrum you can find people who've reacted against this by embracing the politics of localism. Localism typically focuses on such things as regional promotion and investment, and greater local democracy. What it's not is a charter for secession. Secessionist movements gain critical mass for different kinds of reasons – because of wars, because of extreme economic disparities between regions, because the rights of one or more population group have been denied.

What makes music and dance so important to so many groups in their search for identity? It's a living link to the past. Being at a festival, a concert, dancing and applauding, you're bringing traditional culture into your life. It's very accessible. Learning to play an instrument to a basic level of competence is easier and, dare I say, more fun than learning a language. And that's the third point: music can be taught, can be passed on. This is vital to any culture that wants to renew itself.

THE TORCHBEARERS

There are many heroes in this book, but pride of place has to go to the torchbearers. It wasn't planned that way, I'm not a fanatical traditionalist by any means. But this project has really taught me to appreciate how vital a lot of the work done by folklorists of one kind and another can actually be – this is work that can change history, can affect the cultural life of a whole nation.

Torchbearers are those who pass on knowledge of traditional music to future generations. Traditionally, as we've seen, this would have been done by oral tradition – father to son, mother to daughter, and so forth. Oral tradition was part of a way of life that has largely disappeared. Today's musicians are very unlikely to be part of a community where cultural practices have continued over many generations. More likely it is that they'll see old languages being forgotten, they'll see young people growing up ignorant of their own musical roots and unfamiliar with traditional instruments. It's an existential threat, one that's prompted a good many musicians to look for bigger and bolder responses. And it's been inspiring to see some of the things that they've done.

For some, the starting point has been the realisation that there can still be found authentic tradition bearers, people who remember the time when there was a village community life, who remember the songs that family members used to sing. So they did what John and Alan Lomax and other folklorists have done before them: they travelled with their recording equipment, sought out those who had knowledge of old music coursing through their veins and invited them to sing. In every case this was a labour of love – an activity funded where possible by universities or grants from heritage organisations, with little or no hope of commercial reward. Some activists set up their own record labels, taking the view that this was the only way of getting this supposedly non-commercial music recorded and released to the widest possible audience. Ketebul Music in Kenya, Tao Music in the Philippines, Asasi Records in the Maldives, Amarrass Records in India, Wantok Musik in Oceania and Stonetree Records in Belize all have one thing in common: a mission to preserve traditional indigenous music. Then there are whole projects dedicated to making field recordings and publishing them online: Vincent Moon with his Collection Petites Planètes; Laurent Jeanneau (Kink Gong); the Singing Wells project of which Ketebul Music is a co-sponsor; the UK-based Song Collectors Collective. Sam Lee, who founded the Song Collectors Collective, is also very much a working musician who's won great acclaim for his reinterpretations of traditional songs. Other musicians who've wrestled with the question of how best to perform songs learned from field recordings include Russia's Sergei Starostin, Serbia's Svetlana Spajic and the Belarus ensemble Rada. They all want to honour the original recordings, but in each case the decision on how much to rework it comes down to an individual artistic decision.

Just as important as preventing the loss of old singing traditions is saving musical instruments from extinction. Nothing gives more character to a country's music than its native instruments and homegrown variants of instruments seen in other countries. And as the number of instrument makers becomes fewer and fewer, and instruments are being lost to the world because nobody plays them anymore, we are losing some of the precious diversity that once existed in our music. There are many examples of instruments being revived following a lengthy period of declining popularity, but the most striking stories are those where only the singlemindedness of individuals has rescued instruments from extinction. In Iceland we will meet Bára Grímsdóttir and Chris Foster: no one had played the fiðla for so many years that no recordings of the instrument existed, so having had one made they then had to figure out ways of playing it, relying on nothing more than their musical experience and instincts. Alan Stivell was a nine-year-old boy when he picked up the clarsach made by his father and tried to play it. He had tuition, but there were some things that could not easily be taught: no one really knew then what a Breton harp playing Breton music should sound like. Stivell not only mastered the instrument, but later through his recordings revived the fortunes of the Celtic harp, helping it along from virtual extinction to the icon that it is today.

In many of the world's poorest countries the state has very little money to spend on culture of any kind. They have other priorities, it's understandable. And yet these are often the countries where music education could have the greatest social benefit. It can give kids a skill, a purpose to their lives, a sense of being part of a wider community, thus helping to create the fabric of future society. The organisation Musicians Without Borders was established to "use the power of music to bridge divides, connect communities and heal the wounds of war" – they've been running successful programmes in places like Rwanda, El Salvador, Palestine and Northern Ireland.

Beyond this, formal education may be the only way to keep knowledge of certain traditional instruments and musical forms alive.

So it's very good to see the work that the Aga Khan Development Network is doing in Central Asia, setting up music schools, training teachers and mentoring of talented musicians. In Bhutan the singer Jigme Drukpa has set up the country's first private music school, while in Gambia Sona Jobarteh has opened the country's music school dedicated to traditional music. While the Bhutan school gets enough money from student fees to cover its costs, the Gambian school seeks to offer scholarships to students from poor backgrounds, and needs grants and donations to cover this.

Such initiatives are normally small-scale, but Ahmad Sarmast had a big vision: to improve the state of music education in Afghanistan. Very impressively, he was able to secure funds from the international community and support from the beleaguered Afghan government, and in 2010 the Afghanistan National Institute of Music came into being. There is still much to do to realise Ahmad Sarmast's vision, but in the chapter on Afghanistan you can read about some of the work that they've been doing.

These are the forgotten heroes. It's become like a mantra of music writers that we're always quick to praise the innovators, the creators: those who take music in new directions or successfully combine different musical forms. The assumption is that we should be looking to the future, not to the past. But as a great man once said, "in this bright future you can't forget your past". Identity matters, because who we are is also about our beliefs, our values, what we hold dear. Who we are can shape who we can become, adding purpose to our future.

Research Methods

The information in this book has been largely obtained from research done on the internet. As a rule I have tried not to rely on a single source, but to verify facts from an independent source or sources. It's inevitable in a book of this scope that there will be some factual errors, and I take full responsibility for these.

I have had to access foreign language websites throughout the last four years, and I am much indebted to Google Translate, without which the book would have been the poorer. Needless to say though, the responsibility for any poor translations, or misunderstandings arising from clumsy translations, is entirely mine.

With names and words in languages such as Arabic which have their own alphabet, there are often alternative spellings. I won't bore you with the difficulties that this causes trying to google Arabic names, but suffice to say that where choices were available I have opted to use what appears to be the most commonly accepted spelling.

Artist interviews are quoted frequently throughout this book. I'm enormously grateful to those who took time to speak to me and write to me, despite the language barriers that sometimes presented themselves. Interview snippets have also been taken from newspaper and magazine articles, TV shows and documentaries, etc. As well as being a valuable source of information about the artists and their music, these interviews also document from time to time the views of the artists on wider cultural and social questions to do with their countries. These voices are at the heart of the book; because they are speaking of things that have touched their lives their insight and perspective is that much more penetrating. At times what they have to say may be combative, may get under the skin of some people. These words have not been chosen out of any lack of respect for the country or its peoples – quite the reverse. I could have just told you that Aaron Bebe Sukura plays a wooden xylophone called a gyil, and that would have been true, but it wouldn't have given you a full picture of what's happening with traditional music in Ghana. Aaron Bebe's sharp words about the lack of government support for traditional music come from the passion that he has about his culture, and I would be doing him a disservice if I failed to address the issue.

You may or may not recognise your own country in these pages. Each chapter is just a series of snapshots, and there are innumerable other stories that could equally be told. I hope that at least I have portrayed the artists accurately and fairly, and that the range of artists featured gives some sense of the uniqueness and diversity of a country's music. Among them are many brave and inspiring people, and great musicians, and while there may be some who feel that I've not represented their country as they would wish, one point I would make is that for me what makes a country is the people who reside there. Throughout this book, I avoid referring to national stereotypes, because I believe that countries thrive out of the diversity of their people, cultures and human experiences. So I invite you to celebrate not only the countries, but the artists and their music, which can be heard on the website that accompanies this book. Prepare yourself to be enthralled!

II. INTRODUCTION TO VOLUME 1

I grew up in the 1960s and '70s a few miles from Liverpool, a city whose music was then famous throughout the world. Any pride that this gave me was intellectual rather than emotional: it didn't feel part of who I was. Perhaps it might have been different if I'd started out singing Beatles songs on my mother's knee, but my only experience of Merseybeat was as a movement whose time had come and gone. Nor did Merseybeat groups claim any particular continuity with an established local culture: they were a collection of bands who'd evolved along similar lines, moving from skiffle to American rock'n'roll.

My initiation to folk came from listening to the music of Bob Dylan. For years my perception of English folk music was of something arcane and stilted, a poor relation of Celtic folk music. The route that I took may have been my own, but my experience was a common one: like a great many Europeans alive today I have no compelling sense of belonging to a particular local culture. (One such is Björk, who we will later encounter telling the South Bank Show that "it's very hard to start from complete scratch with no tradition whatsoever".) A recurring theme of these chapters is the many different ways in which modern-day musicians have tried to instil a form of cultural identity through music.

In some respects the UK is in a fortunate position thanks to the enduring strength of its folk club movement. But for all the dedication of so many individual folk club goers, the movement as a whole lacks any overarching sense of purpose. Thus it was that, already back in the 1960s, Shirley Collins found that all too often floor singers would sing American folk songs rather than researching the song tradition of their own patch of land, a practice repeated in many folk clubs today.

Liverpool group The Spinners moved from skiffle to sea shanties, in which they found a tradition that they could recognise and identify with. For a really strong regional culture though you have to look north of the border, where the revival of traditional instruments such as the Highland bagpipe and of the Scottish Gaelic tongue have contributed to something of a cultural and national renaissance. Another example that I explore is the Czech Republic, where the folklorist Leoš Janáček had documented a rich Moravian folk culture. Many years later Moravian music reasserted itself through the rise of the cimbalom band, and Moravian musicians played an important part in the country's folk revival.

More often than not, the older traditions will be specific to a region, a district, a minority ethnic group, rather than a country. Some of these traditions are locked in archives or in the heads of dwindling populations of tradition bearers. It's been a real education to learn how the dedicated work of isolated folk enthusiasts can bring about the most astonishing revivals – as in Sweden where Eric Sahlström brought back the nyckelharpa, or Alan Stivell and his Breton harp, or in Ireland where the uilleann pipes were rescued from near-extinction. The success of these revivals depends on bringing on board musicians who feel a connection to the culture, then building from the ground up, spreading knowledge of how to manufacture and play the old instrument, and organising concerts and festivals.

There are no shortcuts. Occasionally an album may be

released – like Le Mystère des Voix Bulgares – which brings a long-neglected area of folklore to international attention. But the world music industry has its own agenda, its own commercial logic. Its stock-in-trade is music that's both exotic and instantly accessible. Social and historical context becomes less important than beats which people can dance to, or headline-grabbing collaborations. Across much of Western Europe – the Benelux countries and France and Germany particularly come to mind – world music labels and festivals operate as an alternative to indigenous folklore, helping to build new Celtic music scenes while regional traditions are dying through lack of support. In many ways it's cause for celebration that young people in Europe are more open to different cultures than ever before, are comfortable listening to African music. The other side of the coin though is all the cultures that are in danger of being lost, sometimes very close to home.

Folk clubs aren't the only model. In various countries like Switzerland, Austria, Slovakia and Slovenia, folklore is a jealously guarded cottage industry steeped in nostalgia. Former Soviet Bloc countries inherited a state-controlled folk scene with all the restrictions that came with this. Following the breakup of the Soviet Union significant numbers of artists in Lithuania, Latvia and Belarus have developed new musical modes of expression derived from ancient Pagan folklore. Elsewhere, attempts have been made to develop a folk tradition that is more informal, accessible and inclusive with the Irish and Scottish ceilidh, the French Fest Noz, the Hungarian tánchaz and the Polish Dom Tanca. Each of these had traditional roots, but was essentially a reinvented tradition.

Some of the biggest success stories in these chapters raise the question of how far folk musicians need to adapt and change for their art not just to survive but to thrive. In the 21st century we've grown to know and love the Roma brass band as exemplified by Taraf de Haïdouks (Romania), Boban i Marko Marković Orkestar (Serbia) or Kočani Orkestar (Macedonia). But this is gypsy music that's been repackaged and gone through a series of changes aimed at satisfying the demands initially of urban audiences and latterly of international audiences. Even the idea of a gypsy brass band is a modern conception. Portuguese fado music has enjoyed a surge in popularity in recent years, but for good or ill the new fado is not the same as the old fado, it's become more commercialised and heavily produced. The other story, of course, is that of Ireland, a place where traditional and largely unadulterated music continues to enjoy an astonishing degree of success.

ALBANIA

Environmentalists are joining forces as I write this in a battle to save the Vjosa river.

The Vjosa is one of the last great wild rivers of Europe, freeflowing the full length of its 270 kilometres, and unencumbered by large cities or heavy industry. As it leaves Greece and flows across Albania it cuts its way through extensive forests of oak, beech, fir and pine. As it nears the Adriatic coast it opens up to wetlands which are an important gathering place for migratory birds. The Vjosa itself is home to otters and to impressive numbers of fish species, including the endangered European eel. The Albanian government is looking to build several hydropower plants along the river, two of which are already under construction. In May 2015, the European Parliament renewed a call to Albania to review these projects which would encroach on existing national parks and disrupt the balance of some of the Balkans' most valuable ecosystems.

One might also say that the river has, over the centuries, helped to enrich human culture in the region. If you had a picture in your mind of the people of this small nation united by common characteristics, prepare to jettison it now. Albania is a patchwork of peoples speaking in different dialects, sometimes

DJEPI QE TUNDI JANINE   *Polyphonie de Lapardha*
KABA KURBETI   *Aleks Xhelili*

separated by mountains, rivers and wetlands, and with a strong sense of their regional/ethnic identity. The Shkumbin river demarcates the territory of the Ghegs who live to the north of the river and the Tosks whose land is to the south; more broadly it's a geographic faultline between the very different musical and cultural traditions of the north and south of the country. Likewise the Vjosa stands as a barrier between Toskeria to the north and Laberia to the south.

Southern Albania is famed for its iso-polyphonic singing tradition. Polyphony is a form of choral singing where two or more melodies are sung or chanted simultaneously. In iso-polyphony a drone (the continuous sounding of a single note) replaces one of the melodies. So in its simplest form, a lead singer will begin chanting, then a few seconds later a group of backing singers will join in, singing or humming the continuous drone sound which acts as a counter-melody. It's a living tradition: in 2005, Unesco found that "most of the villages and towns have an iso-polyphony band", and that the music was "performed at a wide range of social events, such as weddings, funerals, harvest feasts, religious celebrations and festivals such as the well-known Albanian folk festival in Gjirokastër." [1] It comes in many variations. The

Tosks and the Labs use different drone sounds. But according to Albania's leading musicologist, Professor Vasil Tole, there are other variations too: "The Toskeria iso-polyphony includes two-voice and three-voice songs while the Laberia iso-polyphony consists of two, three and four-voice songs." [2] Four-voice songs are where you have three singers, all with different functions, and the drone chorus. The overlaying of these four separate melodic lines makes for a very complex harmonic structure, one which is only found in Lab culture.

There's a lot going on in the featured track **DJEPI QE TUNDI JANINE**, which is perhaps why I've chosen it: vocal lines coming in and out, and different kinds of sounds, all elaborately layered and interwoven. It's also a small miracle that this CD – Albanie: Polyphonies de Lapardha – was ever made. South east from Vlorë, Lapardha is the tiniest of villages, overlooking the river Shushicë, a tributary of the Vjosa. In Laberia jobs and opportunities for young people are scarce, particularly in the rural areas. Many men have left to find work in Tirana, or in the European Union. Between 1989 and 2011 Albania's population fell by over 10%, mainly due to external migration. I think I'm beginning to understand why some Albanian politicians want to build hydroelectric plants in the south of the country, even if the policy still seems shortsighted.

The man responsible for the album is Francis Corpataux, a musicologist from Quebec. For a quarter of a century he's travelled to dozens of countries recording traditional songs performed exclusively by children. One of the products of this project is a series of CDs, Le chant des enfants du monde. While he was gathering material for his Albanian CD (number 16 in the series), he met with Mohamed Tartari, a school teacher from Vranisht: "Mr Tartari brought together a group of children to do polyphonic singing and this encounter led me to contact Mr Çelaj who is the director of the youth group." [3] The result of these discussions was a one-off album, performed by five 'young singers', including three members of Mr Çelaj's family.

Elsewhere it seems getting young people to take up this centuries-old tradition is a real problem. Yzeir Llanaj is founder and director of the Albanian Polyphony Cultural Association. Poylphony today, he says, is "practised only by older generations". [4] He speaks of the need for a music academy where the polyphonic arts can be taught, and calls on the Ministry of Culture to provide greater funds and backing.

The historic town of Permet lies many miles up the Vjosa river, toward the Greek border. Once part of the Ottoman Empire, in modern times it's been home to one of the largest enclaves of Greek people in this predominantly Albanian-speaking country. In the Balkan War of 1912–13 it was part of a region seized by the Greek army. After the war ended a settlement was reached under which 'Northern Epirus' would become a self-governing autonomous region within Albania. The settlement failed to hold, and by the 1920s it had lost all special status. Only 10,000 people live there today, but it attracts a steady stream of tourists, drawn by its mountain setting, its history, its food, its homemade raki and its music. Two of Albania's greatest musicians, the clarinetists Laver Bariu (1929–2014) and Remzi Lela (1937–95), were both natives of Permet.

A saze is an iso-polyphonic music ensemble in southern Albania. A key part of a saze is the clarinet, and the clarinet really comes into its own in the kaba. Kaba is a form of instrumental music unique to the region; apparently it's a form of mourning tune. It has two sections, the first one slow and free moving, and the second at a more regular tempo. The lead instrument (clarinet or violin) is improvisational and emotionally expressive; other instruments are used to create a steady background drone.

Vasil Tole has written extensively about Laver Bariu: this self-taught musician, he believes, has elevated the status of clarinet playing in the country, and his music embodies the spiritual values of Albanian music. In May 2014, after Bariu's death, he organised a festival in Permet honouring the musical traditions that Bariu had done so much to preserve. Bariu's music can be heard on an album originally released in 1995, Songs From the City of Roses (the city of roses being a reference to Permet).

Time seems to stand still as I listen to the rippling music of the clarinet on **KABA KURBETI.** This kaba is performed by Aleks Xhelili (born 1964), a clarinetist from the Kolonjë region not far from Permet. It's taken from Cry You Mountains, Cry You Fields: Traditional Songs and Instrumental Music From SE Albania, which is one of two compilations of Albanian music made by Chris Johnston for Saydisc. The sound of Xhelili's clarinet opens and closes the album; on another track he plays accordion. The recording was made in 1996, but Xhelili is still performing today.

The main cultural centre in the south east is Gjirokastër, an old town on the Drino river and a World Heritage site. It was the birthplace of the former Stalinist ruler of Albania, Enver Hoxha, but don't hold that against it. The citadel of Gjirokastër Castle overlooks the town where it's stood since the 12th century. It's seen a lot of rebuilding and more than a few political changes – during the Hoxha years it was used to house political prisoners. The castle is the venue for Albania's premier folklore festival, held there roughly every five years since 1968 (2015 was the 10th season). It's a showcase for music, costume, dance, arts and crafts, not just from Albania but from its international neighbours. More than half of ethnic Albanians live outside of Albania, and it's important to people in Albania that this wider shared heritage is recognised and celebrated.

NOTES

1. http://www.unesco.org/new/en/member-states/single-view/news/
   safeguarding_albanian_folk_iso_polyphony_a_unesco_masterpie/
2. http://www.southeast-europe.eu/index.php?id=1569
3. http://association-albania.com/Interview-de-Francis-CORPATAUX.
   html?lang=fr
4. http://shekulli.com.al/56756/

ANDORRA

If you're going to Andorra, your main concern will probably be how to pack all your skiing gear. The mini-state sits high in the Pyrenees on the border between France and Spain, and Andorra la Vella is Europe's highest capital city (if city's the right word for a place with a population of 22,000). It's unlikely that you'll have given much thought to its culture, and why would you, when Barcelona's just a couple of hours' drive away.

As a place to live it has its upside: there are no taxes, crime is low and most people live to a ripe old age. But it doesn't have a lot of culture that it can call its own, beyond what you might expect to find in any similar mountain community. Catalan is the official language, native Andorrans also identify as Catalans, and the Andorran contrapàs circle dance is related to the Catalan sardana.

Lluis and Gerard Claret are twins whose Catalan parents fled to France during the Spanish Civil War. "Actually, they met in France," recalls Lluis.

"And it is there that my father became very good friends with Pablo Casals, because Casals was part of a group of important Catalan artists, poets and writers exiled in

the South of France and my father was in that group too. When the 2nd World War ended, my parents went to live in Andorra, which was the closest place to Catalonia where they could go, because they were not allowed to enter Spain. That's where I was born with my twin brother and my father asked Casals if he would accept to be the godfather of one of the two twins. The lucky draw fell on me." [1]

The significance of this is that Casals was a very eminent cellist, and Lluis's connection with Casals may have been the decisive factor which meant that Lluis ended up playing cello and Gerard the violin.

In the early 1960s it was pretty unusual for Andorran kids to take up music. There were no music schools, and teachers weren't easy to find, though for a friend of Pablo Casals there was always a way. With Lluis showing promise, his father interceded with the French cellist Maurice Gendron, who agreed to give some private lessons. Later Pablo's brother Enric Casals took Lluis under his wing, and although not a cellist himself Lluis is quick to acknowledge how valuable Enric's support and advice proved at the start of his career.

And so the boy from Andorra la Vella went on to become one of Europe's most respected classical cellists, performing with symphony orchestras in several countries. He may not be living there now, as he does some teaching in Barcelona, but Andorra remains part of his identity. He once recorded a tribute CD to his earliest musical inspiration, Pablo Casals. For a number of years Lluis and Gerard performed together in the Barcelona Trio. They both take satisfaction from the fact that there is now an Institute of Music in Andorra la Vella – though at first, Lluis says, standards were poor, now he sees professional musicians emerging from Andorra.

CANT DELS OCELLS is Catalan for birdsong. Which seems an incongruous title for this brief peaceful, melodious cello instrumental; but I suppose that it's all in the imagination.

NOTES

1. http://www.opuscello.com/lluis-claret/

ARMENIA

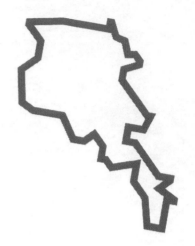

"What music on earth is unmixed and pure? Only that of
animals... there is no nation that remains isolated from
such merging of idioms. Each nation appropriates a thing
it does not possess from one that does and integrates it into
its national style. Any nation's language and literature
assimilates elements of language from other nations as
it develops. But, if a nation has a unique language and
literature, it has a unique music as well.

... Poor Armenian people! A nation you are, as unique
as other nations; nobody can deny that. Yours is a distinct
tongue: you speak. You have a distinct mind: you judge.
You have a distinct physiognomy, through which you are
distinguished from other nations and their physical make.
But your heart, which is the source of your feelings, is
allegedly not yours, it is merely Assyro-Byzantine and Indo-
Persian." – Komitas [1]

In Julius Caesar's day Armenia was a large and powerful state that
extended far beyond its present-day borders. Armenian people
lived in what is now eastern Turkey, northern Iran, Lebanon
and Syria – all areas that still have Armenian populations today.

A COOL WIND IS BLOWING   Djivan Gasparyan
ANUSH KNIK   Hasmik Harutyunyan
ADANA   Vardan Hovanissian and
Emre Gültekin

Since then, it's had a convoluted history, seeing borders in flux and empires come and go, as control of the region has been contested for large parts of the last 2,000 years. Throughout this time Armenians have spoken their own language, which has its own unique alphabet, and have stayed loyal to the Armenian Church. So while Armenian culture bears the marks of the many civilisations who've rubbed shoulders with them over the years, history has also worked to preserve an identity and a sense of continuity with an ancient past.

There is no finer way of experiencing what it means to be Armenian than to listen to the unhurried, infinitely expressive music of the duduk. But the duduk music that's played today is very much a reinvention of past tradition.

Komitas (1869–1935), the author of the passage quoted above, was an Armenian, but he was born and grew up in western Turkey. He became an orphan at the age of 11 when his father died, but his father had left him a valuable legacy: his love of singing. Some months later, a local prelate went to Echmiadzin in Armenia to be consecrated a bishop. He was asked to take one orphaned child to be educated at the Echmiadzin seminary, and the sweet-voiced Komitas was selected from 20 candidates to make the long journey. A decade later, he was ordained a priest, and according to tradition he took on a new name; so it was from here that he adopted the name Komitas. He set up and conducted a monastery choir; meanwhile he was also beginning to show an aptitude for music research. He got the chance to travel to Berlin, where he spent a few years studying under distinguished German tutors. On his return, he threw himself into work on music, and travelled round the region collecting thousands of songs – Armenian, Kurdish, Persian and Turkish. During these years of intense activity he wrote several music research papers and began to establish himself as a composer.

This promising career was to be derailed by tragedy. April 24th 1915 is a date engraved in the memory of every Armenian: they know it as the start of what they call the Armenian genocide. Komitas himself had been living in Constantinople since 1910. In April 1915, the Ottoman police came knocking on his door. He was rounded up along with other prominent Armenians, thrown in a jail cell, then sent on a terrifying train journey. He saw men being abused and murdered. He was allowed to return to Constantinople a few weeks later, but he returned to a changed city where Armenians lived in terror and every week new outrages were committed as fears were stoked up that Armenians were collaborators with the enemy. Hundreds of thousands were to die in the months and years ahead. Komitas suffered from acute stress, survivor guilt and PTSD. His symptoms weren't properly understood or diagnosed, and he was to spend most of his final years in psychiatric institutions and asylums.

Komitas never fulfilled his desire to open a music conservatory in Armenia. But in 1921, a music studio started up in Yerevan which became the Yerevan State Conservatory and then from 1946 the Komitas State Conservatory.

Armenia's most celebrated folk musician, Djivan Gasparyan, was largely self-taught and for a long time was unable to read music. Born in 1928, his first experience of duduk music was as a small kid, hearing it performed in a Yerevan movie theatre at a time when silent movies were always accompanied by live ensembles. Here's Djivan's own account of his first meeting with the duduk players:

> *"After it was over, I went up to the players and asked them if I can have lessons. Well, one of them told me, you are too young, and besides you must buy a duduk. How are you going to afford it? I asked them whether they would give me lessons if I had a duduk, and they said yes. So for the next month, I would save up money by collecting bottles for which the owner of a restaurant who knew me would pay. Eventually when I had collected enough I went back to the players, who were so surprised by my devotion that they said such a boy could not fail to become a great duduk player. So I was given free lessons." [2]*

The version of the story that's more commonly told is that Djivan was given his first duduk on such an occasion by the great musician Margar Margaryan. Whatever the truth of this, to me the notion that he had to work for it is more compelling.

Barely out of his teens, Djivan auditioned for Tatul Altunian's Armenian Song and Dance Ensemble. He was taken on as a soloist and stayed with the ensemble for 25 years. At the age of 52, having collected numerous awards, he began studying music at the Komitas Conservatory. After graduating he became a teacher of the duduk and later a professor at the Conservatory.

Meanwhile his career as a performer was moving on by leaps and bounds. **A COOL WIND IS BLOWING** is the lead track on an album first released in 1983, I Will Not Be Sad In This World. The music is spellbinding: beautiful and poignant, with the haunting sound of the duduk set against soft drone effects. This was the first Gasparyan album that Brian Eno was able to find after seeing the master performing in Moscow in 1988. Eno immediately set about obtaining the rights to release the album on his own label. While he was doing this, a devastating earthquake hit Armenia on 7th December 1988. So when the album was rereleased a few months later, it was dedicated to the earthquake victims. And on the next album there was a mournful track with rare vocals by Djivan simply entitled 7th December 1988.

Djivan grabbed with enthusiasm the opportunity to perform in other countries: quite simply he wanted more than anything to take Armenian heritage and duduk music to the wider world. Nor did he confine himself to playing the big stages: his music became part of the soundtrack of several Hollywood films. And while writing this chapter I learned that his own life is shortly to be the subject of a film. Called Bitter Apricot after the apricot wood that's used to make duduks, Eva-Luise Volkmann's film focuses on the relationship between the octogenarian Djivan and his grandson who bears the same name. Djivan Junior had been living in Los Angeles since his early teens, but now he had returned to Yerevan intent on learning what he could from his grandfather and carrying on his legacy.

ANUSH KNIK is an Armenian lullaby. Hasmik's voice is beautifully clear, ringing out over the sparse and sombre instrumentation (there's no duduk on this track, though it does make an appearance elsewhere on the album). According to the press release, the collection of lullabies that are on the album had been gathered by Hasmik herself, "from old women who had emigrated from Anatolia to eastern Armenia before or during the Armenian massacres of 1915, as well as from their descendants and old song collections." [3] She tries to keep it faithful to how the songs would have been sung in the past, right down to the regional accents.

Born in 1960, Hasmik's career began during the Soviet era when she was working as a soloist for the Agoonk Ensemble on Armenian National Radio. Independence came in 1991, and with it many hopes and expectations. Hasmik's dream was to connect with the roots of Armenian culture. She joined a band, the Shoghaken Ensemble, who played traditional instruments and tried to revive knowledge and interest in Armenian folk song.

In fact, says Hasmik, "things got harder" for folk musicians after independence. [4] State support for folk ensembles dried up. It was next to impossible for an outfit like Shoghaken to get to do concerts or to appear on the broadcast media. Anxious to ensure that children in Yerevan should be made aware of their heritage, Hasmik formed the Hayrig Mouradian Children's Traditional Song and Dance Ensemble (named after her former teacher), and acted as its artistic director. Shoghaken were, however, able to release a number of albums in the international market which got plenty of glowing reviews; and they appeared at several festivals abroad.

Vardan Hovanissian well-remembers how difficult it was to be a musician of any kind in Armenia after independence: "the economy was on its last gasp, many people couldn't even get electricity or gas in their home, culture was at the very bottom of the list of needs… for musicians there was hardly any work." [5] While Hasmik stuck it out, he decided to emigrate. He now lives in Brussels, where he loves the multicultural feel of the city and the opportunities to collaborate with artists from other genres.

Like many duduk players, Vardan first learned to play the shvi flute before moving on to the duduk. He's played in several ensembles in Armenia and also in Belgium. Among the musicians whom he met along the way was a Belgian-born Turkish saz player called Emre Gültekin. A chasm of difference still exists between Turkish and Armenian people, but Vardan and Emre were determined to do a musical project that would also be a symbol of reconciliation. So on 24th April 2015, the centenary of the Armenian genocide, they released an album called **ADANA**. Musically it was like a natural coming together of two cultures that had much in common. There's no saz on the title track; we hear in turn the double bass, the duduk, the tanbur (Kurdish stringed instrument) and Emre's voice: it's a poignant expression of grief at the tragedy that befell the city of Adana, but also of hope that people of the region can learn to live together.

For Vardan this is no abstract hope. He owes his existence to the fact that Turkish citizens gave refuge to his grandfather at the time of the genocide. [6]

NOTES

1. Taken from the Virtual Museum of Komitas website – http://www.komitas.am/eng/folk_music.htm
2. Andy Nercessian – The Duduk and National Identity in Armenia (Scarecrow Press, 2001), p36
3. http://traditionalcrossroads.com/epages/79bbb619-3828-417a-8326-55a761667bd1.sf/en_US/?ObjectPath=/Shops/79bbb619-3828-417a-8326-55a761667bd1/Products/%22CD%204321%22
4. http://hetq.am/eng/news/57258/hasmik-harutyunyan-world-renowned-folk-singer-believes-in-the-power-of-pure-music.html
5. http://www.brusselnieuws.be/nl/nieuws/vardan-hovanissian-dudukspeler-de-duduk-en-diepe-droefenis
6. http://www.mo.be/interview/ons-album-wil-turken-en-armeni-rs-verzoenen

AUSTRIA

The single most famous Austrian song, Edelweiss, is in fact an American take on Alpine music, written by Rodgers and Hammerstein for the score of The Sound of Music.

For authentic Austrian music you need to go back a few years earlier, to a British film shot in Vienna called The Third Man.

The film's director, Carol Reed, first saw Anton Karas playing his zither for tips in a Viennese tavern during a break in shooting for the film. A few days later he got in contact with Karas and persuaded him to make a recording. Reed took the recording back to London and it was here while he edited the footage that he decided he wanted Karas to provide the score for the whole film. There was only one problem.

Karas's love affair with the zither had begun when he came across the fascinating instrument in the loft of his grandmother's house when he was aged 12. The son of a factory worker, he began an apprenticeship as a toolmaker at the age of 14, but he managed to find the pennies to enrol on an evening course at a local music school. When Reed found him he was in his 40s, earning an honest living playing zither. He told Reed that he wasn't much of a composer, and he wasn't that keen on leaving his family for

THE HARRY LIME THEME — Anton Karas
WURZHORNER — Alma

weeks on end to go and work with Reed in London. Besides, he didn't speak any English. Eventually Reed persuaded him to do it.

For three months in 1949, Karas worked in a makeshift studio in Reed's London home. When the film came out it was a sensation. Everyone agreed it was a good film, but the music elevated it to another level. Using a single instrument to record a complete film soundtrack was novel and daring, but it worked like a dream. It brought the Viennese street scenes to life: you felt like you were in another place and another time. THE HARRY LIME THEME is named after the character played by Orson Welles: in the USA it was released as The Third Man Theme. It topped the Billboard singles chart for 11 weeks, becoming the best-selling film tune of the age.

The tune is a folk dance, an addition to the traditional repertoire. Behind its apparent simplicity though there is great skill. The arrangement is magical, and it's a hard piece (so I'm told) to perform well. Karas played around with the tuning and worked hard on getting the best sound out of his instrument. The rest of the soundtrack is wonderful too, but this is the melody that really lodges in your brain and refuses to go away.

When Karas returned to Austria after his first world tour he was greeted as a hero. But he had no desire for stardom, and never sought to follow up on the success of the film soundtrack. He opened his own wine bar which he called Der Dritte Mann, and Orson Welles was among his clientele. On his death in 1985, he was buried in Sievering Cemetery in Vienna under a headstone which is inscribed in gold with the opening bars of the Harry Lime Theme.

Volksmusik is the generic word for traditional folk music, while Volkstümliche Musik refers to commercialised folk-pop. The distinction is not always obvious. Volksmusik has long lost any semblance of homespun rural charm. The dances are still the same – ländler, polka, waltz, zwiefacher. Typically though when you hear them played it will be in a relentlessly cheery style in a major key without a lot of scope for expressiveness. Volksmusik may still be popular enough, but it's not very cool, and it's not taken very seriously by music critics. It wasn't always this way, and don't take my word for this, listen instead to the recent compilation Schrammelmusik – Music from Old Vienna/ Recordings 1908–35.

In recent decades a number of artists have tried to reclaim volksmusik and give it a contemporary makeover. Though their music doesn't fit into any one genre it's been described as neue volksmusik and as world music. Most revolutionary of all was the artist widely credited with kicking it all off – the 'Tyrol Zappa', Werner Pirchner. His 1973 album, Half a Double Album, was extraordinary: a freakish, surreal head-spinning journey. He was a free spirit, a musician well versed in jazz and classical music but who was passionate about artistic freedom of expression. After Half a Double Album, Pirchner moved on to other projects, other challenges; the album though continued to enjoy cult status and helped give other artists the strength to do their own thing.

Two bands who've recently emerged as flagbearers of neue volksmusik are Alma and Federspiel. They know each other well: Julia Lacherstorfer, violinist with Alma, and Simon Zöchbauer, who plays trumpet, flugelhorn and zither with Federspiel, are a couple who've also performed together in a third band, Ramsch & Rosen. Federspiel was formed in 2004 by seven male students at Vienna's University of Music and Performing Arts and the Vienna Conservatoire. They're a brass band ensemble who love being able to surprise and challenge their audiences. Theirs is a cosmopolitan folk, mixing elements from the Austrian folk tradition with musical styles from other countries in a spirit of creativity and playfulness.

Julia Lacherstorfer and her sister Marlene are from a small spa town called Bad Hall, which means 'salt bath'. They grew up with folk music, encouraged by their grandfather who was an accordion player, their mother who played double bass, and their father, "a passionate bagpiper and hurdy-gurdyist, a circumstance that caused one or the other rather ungentle morning for me and my sister Marlene." [1] A family band was formed: Lacherstorfer Soatnkråtzer. "This roughly translates as Lacherstorfer String-Scratchers – and the name was not too far-fetched, I'm afraid." Julia went to Vienna in 2003 to study music and it was in the capital in 2011 that her bands Alma and Ramsch & Rosen were formed.

In Alma, Julia is joined by Marlene on double bass and harmonium, Marie-Theres Stickler on accordion and two other violinists, Evelyn Mair and Matteo Haitzmann. The band are united by a love and respect for Alpine folk tradition, though they're not constrained by it. Transalpin, the title of their second album, released in 2015, is a signal that the album's roots may be found across the Alpine region and beyond. Two thirds of the pieces are original compositions; traditional tunes have been thoroughly rearranged. The one I was most drawn to is **WURZHORNER**, a traditional yodelling number from the Styrian region. The basic structure and melody of the yodel has been left and allowed to breathe while the violins add an emotionally intense, haunting quality.

"The generations before us have paved our way," says Julia, "and now it's easy for us to reset it." [2] By allowing themselves the freedom to tinker with the rules, to improvise and use their imagination, while remaining grounded in a knowledge and understanding of volksmusik, bands like Alma have shown that Alpine folk music can still be relevant and exciting.

NOTES

1. http://www.julialacherstorfer.at/wp/en/about-me/
2. http://www.tagesanzeiger.ch/kultur/pop-und-jazz/Nirgends-ist-die-Musik-so-frei-wie-in-der-Neuen-Volksmusik/story/11907517

AZERBAIJAN

On 27th December 2008, Baku's International Mugham Centre was opened by President Ilham Aliyev. It's a dramatic piece of architecture situated on the city's waterfront. Two adjacent buildings are designed to form the shape of a tar, an ancient stringed instrument. Inside, a long glass corridor facing the main entrance doors is lined with busts of distinguished artists. There's a 350-seat concert hall, conference rooms, recording studio and restaurant. This modernist building is the flagship in the young country's campaign to revive a 1,000-year-old musical heritage.

To retrace the history of mugham music is akin to learning the history of Azerbaijan and its people. It's a history that spans three continents and many centuries, full of questions that may never be satisfactorily resolved. Even the origins of the word are a matter of dispute. Suffice it to say that it's a classical modal music which is strongly associated with this turbulent region of the Middle East, and which requires performers to have a comprehensive knowledge of the repertoire and the rules, and an impressive vocal range. To become a true mugham master though, according to the great Alim Qasimov, takes something else, something that can't be learned by rote:

MUGHAM BAYATI SHIRAZ	*Gochag Askarov*
KÖCHARI YALLY	*Abuzer Gülaliyev*
UZUNDERE	*Nadir Talibov*
TOFIG GULIYEV ILK BAHAR	*Imamyar Hasanov*

"Mugham is an elite art. It's for a select group, for people who have some kind of inner spirituality, who have their own inner world. These days 'elite' refers to something more commercial than spiritual – for example, to the kind of people who can buy a new car every year. But that's not what I have in mind. An elite person is one who knows how to experience, how to endure, how to feel, how to listen to mugham and begin to cry. This ability doesn't depend on education or upbringing, nor on one's roots. It's something else. It's an elite of feeling, an elite of inspiration." [1]

A mugham ensemble normally has three instruments: tar, kamancha and gaval. The long-necked tar is often used as the lead instrument: the Azeri version has 11 strings. The kamancha, or spiked fiddle, is a stringed instrument with a bowl-shaped resonating chamber played using a bow. Completing the trio is the gaval, a type of frame drum.

Soviet cultural policy – urging artists to create art 'socialist in content and national in form' – undermined the mugham tradition. How, you may well ask, does one introduce socialist content to classical poems that are centuries old? And that was not all. Imamyar Hasanov tells us that "during World War II, the government controlled which mughams should be played. There are seven main mughams and they express different feelings, from sad to hopeful. During the war, the government banned the sad music but promoted the cheerful music for propaganda." [2]

It was in this environment that Uzeyir Hajibeyov (1885–1948) laid the foundations of modern Azeri music. Before the birth of the Soviet Union he'd written several operas – all in a radical new style, using Azeri folk instruments alongside western orchestral instruments. In 1920, he helped to found the Baku Academy of Music. He was an advocate for composed music and insisted that mugham music be set down in note form. He also documented hundreds of Azeri folk songs. In the late 1920s, there were calls to ban traditional instruments such as the tar, but Hajibeyov never wavered in his defence of them. In 1931, he set up Azerbaijan's first orchestra using only folk instruments, and he also introduced the tar, kamancha and zurna into symphonic orchestras. This, according to his contemporary Ramazan Khalilov, "was a very bold experiment and even Stalin noticed it. This synthesis was an entirely new way, a new approach to music." [3] After his death, other Azeri composers continued the search for a fusion of mugham and western classical music.

A graduate of the Baku Academy of Music, Alim Qasimov's career was just taking off when independence was declared in 1991, and very soon he was receiving a series of accolades at home and abroad, and getting people interested again in the largely forgotten mugham music. Qasimov didn't belong to the classical school: his music was based on improvisation, it wasn't capable of being written down, and it was vocal rather than instrumental. He wasn't just a populariser of his art: he reinterpreted mugham music, adding new instruments and drawing new inspiration from the music of Pakistani qawwali singer Nusrat Fateh Ali Khan. Since the late 1990s, he's been working professionally with his daughter Ferghana Qasimova, now also an acclaimed singer.

My featured track though is from another exciting young mugham artist, Gochag Askarov. Gochag was born in 1978 in the mountainous region of Nagorno-Karabakh. After the breakup of the Soviet Union, Azerbaijan and Armenia went to war over control of this territory. At the age of 15, Gochag volunteered for battle. In the fighting he got an eye wound and his Azeri family were driven from their homes, while Nagorno-Karabakh became an autonomous state with close relations with Armenia. Gochag ended up in Baku, where he put his troubles behind him and embarked on his musical studies.

In February 2007, Gochag made his international debut at a concert in London. Diz Heller from the UK-based world music label Arc Music was at the concert, and he asked Gochag to sign a record deal. While still in London, Gochag was also invited to appear on the BBC's World Routes radio show, where he was to make a strong impression. The Arc Music album was released under the name Sari Gelin Ensemble. Since then, though, a couple of albums have come out on Felmay under Gochag's own name. The chosen track is a sample of **BAYATI SHIRAZ**, one of the seven classic mugham modes. Each mode has an emotional mood associated with it, so Bayati Shiraz is meant to be melancholic, but Gochag's moving rendition seems appropriate to the meaning – a tale of unrequited romantic love.

Two world music labels have released a multi-CD series of traditional Azerbaijani music. The first one wasn't originally planned as a series. Alim Qasimov gave a series of concerts in France and Switzerland in 1989, which resulted in a couple of live CDs on Maison des Cultures du Monde's Inédit label. After independence other Azeri artists started to come and perform in France, and the producers decided that they wanted to do something more than put out the occasional CD. Anthologie du Mugam d'Azerbaïdjan was to run to nine volumes and bring home to people the richness of the Azeri mugham tradition.

The Felmay series, by contrast, is just four volumes to date, but it's very well conceived and each CD reveals an important side to Azeri music. Mugham is represented by the Gochag Askarov CD, Sacred World of Azerbaijani Mugham. Poetry and music of ashiqs highlights Azerbaijan's most important and distinctive folk music culture. Then there's Azerbaijani Love Songs, a collection of folk and popular songs, many of them written by mugham singers and ashiqs. My personal favourite though is Rhythms of Azerbaijani Dances, which has 17 tracks covering an amazing variety of folk instruments and folk dance traditions.

There are dozens of Azeri folk dances, many of them specific to particular regions. Most male dances are very different in character to female dances: for the men, a lot of fast foot movement, standing up on tiptoe and kneeling down, while the women's movements are more sensual, more expressive. The Yalli is a popular dance involving both sexes, either separately or together:

"Its roots lie in ancient customs. Over 240 types of the Yalli are known, of which only 120 have survived. The dancers form a circle, holding each other with open arms or entwining their little fingers. The dance consists of two parts. It begins solemnly with loping steps. Gradually the tempo increases, ending with rapid, technically complex 'jumping' movements. One person holding a scarf - a 'yallibasi' - follows at the head of the dancers. He is the initiator in the dance." [4]

On **KÖCHARI YALLY** the Yalli is performed on zurna, accompanied by the naghara drum. This is how it's normally performed at weddings. I'd love to see how the wailing sound of the zurna goes down at an Azeri wedding, because it's certainly something of an acquired taste. There are several different types of zurna, but basically it's a small conical wooden horn that generates a riot of noise, not unlike the sound of a bagpipe.

An atmospheric, evocative track, **UZUNDERE** features balaban and naghara. The balaban is a wind instrument with a somewhat mournful sound: in Armenia it's known as the duduk, and in Turkey, the mey. Uzundara is a dance from the Karabakh region. Originally a bride's dance, it's characterised by slow, graceful movements and can be performed solo or with a group of female dancers.

On Bakhtavari and Reyhani we get to hear the garmon, a Caucasian button accordion, smaller than the traditional European accordion, but popular in Azerbaijan and well suited to folk dances. While researching the instrument I was struck by a quote from garmon player Rahim Shahriyari, who says that "at a typical [Azeri] wedding, I often play for eight hours – about 150 different songs." [5] Choban Bayati & Sevinji begins with a whistling melody ringing out in the clear air: this is the high-pitched sound of the tutek (shepherd's pipe).

Uzeyir Hajibeyov used to have a particularly high regard for the kamancha, emphasising its similarity to the human voice. The instruments with their beautiful designs are played sitting down using a bow. Imamyar Hasanov has known the kamancha all his life, having started playing it at the age of seven. Like so many before him, he studied at the Baku Academy of Music, which in 1991 had been renamed Hajibeyov Baku Academy of Music. At the turn of the millennium, now in his mid-20s, he emigrated to the USA where he revelled in the opportunities that he found to work with musicians from different cultures and backgrounds.

The feature track **TOFIG GULIYEV ILK BAHAR** shows the kamancha's expressive range. It's from a 2005 album, Undiscovered Treasure: The Kamancha of Azerbaijan, on which Imamyar Hasanov is accompanied only by Iranian drummer Pezhham Akhavass. Projects since then have included The Sound of My Soul, a collaboration with another Iranian, Pejman Hadadi, billed as "a selection of the instrumental music of some of the great Masters of Azeri music"; and Persian Azeri Project – From Shiraz to Baku with Hadadi and sitar player Hamid Motebassem.

The young country remains in buoyant mood, boosted by years of dizzying economic growth and rising standards of living. But there are clouds on the horizon. The country is still reliant on oil, and when oil prices fell in 2014/15 the economy stumbled and the central bank devalued the currency by 34% in February 2015. The status of Nagorno-Karabakh is an open wound that shows no sign of healing, and while no one wants to see a return to war there is much hostility and distrust toward Armenians. [6] I began this chapter by talking about the Aliyev government's support for mugham music, which has meant that mugham is now taught in schools at every level. The commitment to mugham music is like a ray of light amid the gathering clouds. Mugham is a music that has the power to affect people at a deep personal level. For Ferghana Qasimova the improvisation and the unspoken communication between singer and musicians and between artist and audience which takes place during a performance is a spiritual thing: it's part of a search for the divine. [7] And being music, it's also inclusive: it's not necessary to have a particular belief system in order to fully appreciate it.

NOTES

1. Liner notes to Music of Central Asia, Vol. 6 http://media. smithsonianfolkways.org/liner_notes/smithsonian_folkways/SFW40525.pdf
2. https://azerbaijanmusic187.wordpress.com/2013/06/06/interview-with-imamyar-hasanov/
3. http://hajibeyov.com/bio/bio_life/khalilov_ramazan/khalilov_ramazan_eng/khalilov_ramazan.html
4. http://regionplus.az/en/articles/view/2319
5. http://www.azer.com/aiweb/categories/magazine/91_folder/91_articles/91_shahriyari.html
6. In a 2009 household survey, 97% of Azerbaijanis were opposed to friendship with Armenians.
7. http://www.thejustice.org/article/2015/03/azerbaijani-artist-in-residence-performs

BELARUS

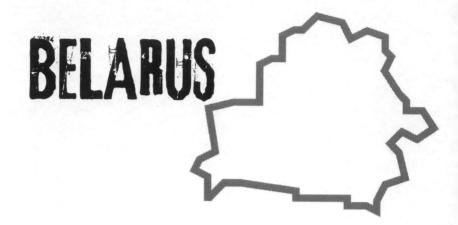

The idea of a Belarusian national identity is modern: it doesn't go back much more than 100 years. In the course of the 19th century a number of Polish writers had taken a deep interest in Belarusian folklore, raising awareness of its existence as a separate culture and laying the foundations of a Belarusian literature. But the growth of political and cultural organisations didn't start until the beginning of the 20th century. Since then the collective consciousness of the people has been shaped on the one hand by the genocide inflicted by the Nazis on the country's population after 1941, and on the other hand by the decades of Soviet rule. There is general support for sovereignty; however, pinning down what national identity means in Belarus is no easy task. There are far more Russian speakers than Belarusian speakers, and the Russian language is completely dominant in public life. (It took me a while to realise that I could learn more about Belarusian culture on Russian language websites than on sites in Belarusian!) Belarus is not a particularly religious country, and a glance at its main religions suggests a possible reason why: the Orthodox Church is strongly linked with Russian culture and language, while the Catholic Church has associations with Polish culture and language.

I TUDY GARA   *Rada*
STRALA   *Osimira*

Belarusians do appear, though, to have real affection for their folklore. One of their favourite festival days is Kupala Night: a midsummer solstice celebration, named after a pagan deity. The Christian Church have now adopted this day as their own, but that doesn't deter young people from marking the occasion in distinctly unchristian ways – young girls collect flowers and plants to make wreaths which supposedly have magical properties; the practice of jumping over bonfires is also laden with superstition. Belarus is also the only country in the world which still observes the ancient Slavic feast of Dziady. On this day people visit the graves of their ancestors, not just to leave flowers, but to invite the souls of their ancestors back into their homes, where special ritual meals will be cooked and plates left out for the dead. In 1988, Dziady was the occasion of the first mass demonstration in Belarus against Soviet rule, and ever since then protest marches have been held on this day, despite the best efforts of President Lukashenko who put an end to Dziady's status as a public holiday.

The ancient Slavic peoples left no chronicles of their mythologies and pagan beliefs: our knowledge of them comes largely from later Christian texts. But in parts of Belarus there's a sense of connection to the ancient folklore that's never quite died away. It can be found in many place names, and in the stories and legends associated with these places, passed on over many generations, even if the core meaning behind these stories has often been lost in the mists of time.

Today ancient folklore is a source of inspiration and material to many bands. There is a spectrum, from pagan metal, to folk metal and folk rock, to more traditional folk. To the extent that all this music taps into a mythic past, one which Belarusians can (however loosely) call their own, it has the makings of a distinctively Belarusian culture. To my mind the more interesting music is that created using traditional instruments, and based on ancient texts and tales; though strictly speaking they are not recreating anything, they're creating new musical arrangements in a modern band format. Pagan metal bands such as Gods Tower, Znich and Apraxia, who all emerged in the 1990s, refract ancient folklore through the lens of male-oriented fantasy novel imagery: for them it's not a matter of chasing some elusive authenticity, they have a formula that packs an emotive punch, and unlike Slavic metal bands in other parts of Europe, they sing at least some of the time in Belarusian.

Stary Olsa are the best known of the new folk bands. Here's how they describe their agenda:

> "The purpose is to completely reconstruct (whenever possible) musical traditions of the Grand Duchy of Lithuania where Belarus was the main cultural and geopolitical part in the 13th–18th centuries, and where there was a unique combination of Belarusian folk and aulic music with European musical achievements of that time… The band's members mix the sound of early Belarusian instruments with all-European mediaeval instruments." [1]

Looking at the range of old instruments that they use, it is certainly impressive; my only quibble would be that the impact of some of them is diminished in the big sound of the band's folk rock arrangements. Stary Olsa have released a dozen albums since 2000, with material ranging from martial music to folk dance to religious songs.

The duda (bagpipe) is a prime example of a dead musical instrument that Belarusian folk enthusiasts have managed to revive. The bag is made from the skin of a goat, and according to Todor Kashkurevich, it would have had special spiritual significance to their pagan ancestors: "the goat is very often used in rituals of sacrifice", symbolising rebirth. [2] Duda tradition is commemorated every year in the Dudarski Fest in Minsk, which was initiated by Kashkurevich in 2006. Headlining the festival in 2015 were Stary Olsa.

Guda are a female singing group who've built up their repertoire through field expeditions and communications with tradition bearers. Their 2013 album, Wedding, contains 31 songs fit for a traditional wedding, with Ales Los's band supplying music on some tracks, and help too from village singers.

Rada describe themselves as a 'community' of singers who've not been conservatory trained, but have a deep fascination with the traditional culture of Polesie: the belt of land which follows the Belarus-Ukraine border where the Pripyat river flows. Mountain, an album of unaccompanied male traditional singing, opens with I TUDY GARA: there's an earthiness and a vitality here in the deep-voiced male harmonies which reflects what the group are trying to achieve. The goal, says Ales Zhukovsky, "is, of course, to deliver the song intact. We try to perform the song exactly like the tradition bearers. But… we are fully aware that we will never be able to sing as they sing. Why? For this to happen, you need a child to live their lives in the environment." [3]

Most of their field expeditions have been in the Polesie region. And Zhukovsky explains, behind every song found during the expeditions which they've learned to sing there is, or once was, a person who's shared his or her life with them. "Our conversations with the people didn't only concern the songs – they related to life."

Osimira was conceived as a one-year, one-album project. In fact it carried on for 11 years, from 2002 to 2013. Bandleader Andrus Palauchenia was interested in creating something that was faithful to traditional music and culture while reinterpreting it in a modern context, but he seems to have had no hard and fast rules because the two Osimira albums are quite different in approach, and Palauchenia's other projects include working with the electro-folk group Pragnavit. Druva, the album from which Strala is taken, is a collection of 17 entirely original tracks based on 'ancient melodies and ritual-ceremonial songs'. [4] Some serious work has gone into this. Several of the instruments used, which include our friend the duda, are authentic medieval instruments. The singers were recorded live in an effort to achieve a natural quality. And during the time of the album's release Palauchenia would come on stage garbed in animal skins and with hand-stitched leather boots: "this clothing reflects our approach to music. We want to dig deep into antiquity, to feel the movement of our ancient land." [5]

The natural sounds which start and end the track **STRALA** take this a little too far for my liking. The song doesn't need any extra ornamentation. It's got a wonderful arrangement, the contrast between the power-drama of the female vocal line and the drone sound of the male voices, and the way in which they cut abruptly in and out in tandem.

While music points the way to a cultural revival, national consciousness remains weak when compared to Belarus's neighbours. Many of the population can't even understand songs sung in the Belarusian language, and this won't be changing soon: the state is resistant to change although language policy remains a hot topic, the number of schoolkids being taught the language is declining, and there is no Belarusian-language university.

NOTES

1. http://staryolsa.com/en/band/bio.html
2. https://vk.com/topic-17266843_26063980
3. http://violex.info/bel/mastactva/253-interviju-z-folk-hurtom-rada.html4.
4. https://folkers.ru/album/Druva
5. https://rg.ru/2012/06/21/smakota.html

BELGIUM

Is there such a thing as Belgian music?

Some would say not. They'd say that people are either Flemish or Walloon. So if you're from the Flanders region in the north, you speak Dutch and consider your culture to be Flemish, while if you're from Wallonia in the south, you speak French and your culture is Walloon. (There is actually a third region – the Brussels-Capital region – but why complicate things.)

Clearly it's important, and many people do regard themselves this way and take pride in their regional culture, and there is a serious possibility that Belgium will be partitioned one day. But there's a lot more than this going on. If anything, music is bringing people together. If you go to a music festival of any description in Belgium you expect to see musicians from different cultures and traditions getting up on the same stage and then often mixing genres when they perform. In both north and south of the country the folk revival has followed a similar course: musicians have had to reinterpret traditional song and dance, almost to the point of reinventing it, such has been the disconnect with the old oral culture.

The story of the modern folk revival starts in Flanders with two men: Hubert Boone and Herman Dewit. Hubert Boone was

DE GOEI WEEK	Water & Wijn & Wannes Van De Velde
WARME GARNARS	Laïs
ONE MORE NIGHT ON THE TRAIN	Fabian Beghin & Didier Laloy

born in 1940 in the village of Nederokkerzeel a few miles east of Brussels. His early training was by teachers who played in village brass bands. Then in his late teens and early 20s he studied music at the Royal Conservatory of Brussels. Up to then his career had followed a conventional path, but this young man had developed a consuming interest in the fast-disappearing folk music of Flanders' rural heartlands. Motivated by the desire to preserve some record of what he found, he began making field recordings:

> *"Folk music in Belgium was a blank page in the 1960s…*
> *due to a couple of people like Hubert they have saved some*
> *of our traditional heritage of folk tunes… Elewijt and*
> *Eppegem are the villages where Hubert found people where*
> *he got the tunes. He named the tunes after the place where*
> *he found them. Polkas and waltzes were common dances at*
> *bals; in that time these bals were like discos today. Bals were*
> *regularly organised; the entire village came out to have fun*
> *on Saturday nights." [1]*

The account is by his son Andries, of whom more later. Boone got a job at the Musical Instrument Museum in Brussels, he's published a number of articles about folk instruments, and as you might expect he played a few himself: his first group (De Vlier) was formed in the late 1960s.

Herman Dewit (born 1946) was another pioneering fieldworker, but that was just the start of it. By his mid-20s he'd formed a folk group ('t Kliekske) and he'd become a professional painter. 'T Kliekske didn't take themselves quite as seriously as De Vlier: they shared the same interest in the old songs, but they also saw themselves as performers and entertainers. This brought its rewards: they reached and inspired a lot of people. A particular passion of 't Kliekske was manufacturing old instruments, and a great deal of time and research went into this. Herman and his wife, Rosita, are equally passionate about training the young and passing on their knowledge. Since 1978, they've been running an annual music school in Gooik where people are schooled in folk music and instrument making; and the success of this gave rise to the setting up of a Folk Music Guild to serve the local area.

Of the artists who emerged in the early days of the folk revival, no one was to make a stronger impression than Wannes Van de Velde (1937–2008). He grew up in working class parts of Antwerp where he says there was a kind of singing culture – "somewhere there was always a window open through which an aria or a folk song would blow." [2] In the same interview, he confesses that his real infatuation as a kid was with flamenco music. At the age of 16 he enrolled at the Royal Academy of Fine Arts in Antwerp where he studied painting while also grabbing at a chance of some private lessons in flamenco. By the early 1960s though, he was listening to folk music and starting to write his own lyrics. He adopted the stage name Wannes and released an album sung entirely in Antwerp dialect. He had his critics who objected to him singing in dialect. But it allowed him to express himself naturally, and it was suitable to the subject matter – working class life, social injustice, urbanisation and his opposition to plans to demolish some of Antwerp's old historic buildings.

Many more albums were to follow. In Antwerp he was much loved; people saw him as their poet, someone who identified with the city and spoke up for it and wasn't afraid to raise his voice in anger. But he didn't confine himself to the Flemish folk tradition. He wrote music for the stage, he collaborated with other artists such as blues singer Roland Van Campenhout, he even returned to his first love by writing a treatise on flamenco music.

Recorded in his later years, Water & Wijn is a collection of 20 'traditional songs from the Low Countries'. Most songs are a cappella, some feature accordion, guitar and violin. The Water & Wijn choir who feature here take the name of a travelling puppet theatre which had been another of Wannes' projects. The singing is simple, honest and direct. On the feature song DE GOEI WEEK each verse corresponds to a day of the week as we catch a lighthearted glimpse of the singer's life.

Ghent singer Walter De Buck (1934–2014) took as his main inspiration the songs of the 19th-century Flemish folk singer Karel Waeri, whom he describes thus: "His lyrics are about the lives of the workers, about working in the factories and mills. With words that were at times mischievous and peppery he managed to get his message across to the common people." [3] In 1969, he was involved in the relaunch of the Gentse Feesten, a music and theatre festival now an essential part of the Ghent calendar every year. He also revived an old song in Ghent dialect, the words to which are believed to have been written by Waeri, 't Vliegerke, and made it into a Ghent anthem which has been adopted by supporters of the local football team.

The revival continued through to the mid-70s with three successful albums by the group Rum. But after Rum split up at the height of their popularity (though they were to reform a few years later with a new lineup) and Flemish folk faded from the public eye. Meanwhile, away from the spotlight, good work continued to be done which would help to lay the ground for a second wave of Belgian folk, and the festivals continued in Ghent, Dranouter and elsewhere. It was in Ghent where a number of folk groups emerged in the late 1990s: Ambrozijn, Fluxus, Olla Vogala. The violinist Wouter Vandenabeele and accordion player Wim Claeys have played in both Ambrozijn and Olla Vogala. "After thirty years of pioneering work," reflects Wim, "the scene is now populated by young musicians." [4] Perhaps the most interesting of the new folk groups was one which had cut its musical teeth at the annual music school in Gooik run by Herman and Rosita Dewit: the group Laïs with its three female vocalists.

Laïs' Jorunn Bauweraerts was the daughter of a folk musician. From when she was a small kid her parents would take her along every year to the Dewit school. Then at the age of 15 she brought her friend Annelies along with her. "On the last evening, everyone started singing with each other; and we started singing and everyone was quiet and listening. That was the start. Among the listeners were some members of Kadril, and they said we had to go on and rehearse." [5] The girls were still in their teens when they released their debut album, with instrumental backing by the group Kadril. The album went gold and folk music was back on the map.

In a way the success had almost been too easy. As Herman Dewit later reflected, "We had to wait 20 years for good instruments. We had to make them ourselves, based on images in paintings and prints... The same is true of the music. We and groups like Rum or Hubert Boone's Brabant Folk Orchestra had to thumb through yellowing manuscripts, and go with a tape recorder to people's homes and ask them to sing a few melodies. The current generation of musicians and singers don't need to search for new material, they can use what's already there. The Laïs song WARME GARNARS is a case in point. They've used the version of the song that we recorded. The final verse wasn't part of the song originally: I wrote that myself." [6] The song itself which is from the debut album is a light traditional number about a young girl who wants to get married and won't listen to her mother's good advice. Laïs confide that the song "should be sung much faster, but this version has evolved from a mishap during rehearsals."

Not having anchored themselves down to a set of traditions, Laïs and other young groups felt no need to define themselves or set boundaries. They were performers: it wasn't a matter of life and death where the songs came from, or even what languages they sang in. They told fRoots magazine that "We started off playing with musicians from a folk background, but soon realised we were suffering from an overdose of folk, so we turned to musicians from the jazz and rock world." [7] They left Wild Boar, the young folk-oriented Belgian label, and signed with Virgin Records. However, they still kept a degree of artistic control, and despite the changes to instrumentation and production their hallmark harmony singing remained at the core of every album.

Today Belgium has a flourishing folk and roots scene. There's a great range of festivals on offer and a couple of excellent record labels, homerecords.be and Wild Boar, each release quantities of strong new material every year. A considerable number of world music artists are based in Belgium, lending their own character and colour to the country's music. Curiously, though, at a time when nationalist sentiments are being stoked ever more strongly, musicians aren't doing much to reinforce people's sense of their own identity: at times it even seems that they're more likely to be interested in Celtic music than in traditional Flemish or Walloon songs.

I realise that this chapter is in danger of becoming about Flemish music. That wasn't the initial intention, so let me redress the balance slightly. Luc Pilartz is a violinist from the Verviers region. Over a few decades he's worked with a wide variety of musicians. Meanwhile he'd also been doing some digging into old Walloon tunes. This led eventually to the album Meslanges – Violon Populaire en Wallonie which draws heavily on an early 19th-century manuscript written by François-Joseph Jamin. Other songs are taken from an anonymous 18th-century manuscript. A number of the songs are from Scandinavia and other countries, which reflects the reality of the time: before the industrial revolution took off, many Walloons would go to places like Sweden in search of work, and this of course influenced the music. The ensemble on the album features three violins, guitar and the accordion of Didier Laloy.

Earlier on I mentioned Andries Boone. In 2011 he formed a mandolin quartet, MANdolinMAN, and their first album, Old Tunes, Dusted Down, was a musical tribute to the fieldwork of Andries' father, Hubert Boone. Even Andries had to admit though that his father, while he enjoyed the album, would have preferred to hear the traditional Flemish melodies performed in the traditional way. [8]

Accordion playing has been a part of Belgian culture since the 19th century. The first workshop to manufacture the diatonic accordion was opened mid-century in Brussels by François Verhasselt. By the end of the century there were numerous accordion makers operating, and with the development of the more versatile chromatic accordion the popularity of the instrument was growing like wildfire. Accordion tournaments were held in halls which the public paid to enter; these could last several hours.

For many years the accordion was on the wane. Music schools weren't interested in teaching it, and it became associated with a style of music whose time had passed. This is now changing and interest is growing once again in the humble accordion. Since 1992, the Wallonian town of Tournai has staged an annual accordion festival. Musicians from Wallonia, Flanders, northern France and further afield descend on the town – every form of accordion one can imagine – and music is free in the streets and the cafés.

My final song then is by two Belgians: Fabian Beghin on the chromatic accordion and Didier Laloy on the diatonic. It was a shortlived but rewarding collaboration: two superb musicians having some fun and exploring what they could achieve by combining their two instruments. ONE MORE NIGHT ON THE TRAIN is an instrumental track which starts off mimicking the metronomic chug-chug of a train before turning into a freewheeling dance number.

NOTES

1. http://www.folkworld.de/50/e/mandolin.html
2. http://www.humo.be/humo-dossiers/21796/wannes-van-de-velde-65-over-zijn-gevecht-tegen-de-leukemie
3. http://focus.knack.be/entertainment/muziek/walter-de-buck-het-laatste-knack-interview-ik-ben-een-goestingdoener-ik-heb-van-niets-spijt/article-normal-520135.html
4. http://poppunt.be/article/folk-in-vlaanderen/
5. http://www.folkworld.de/14/e/lais.html
6. https://laisfans.wordpress.com/2000/05/30/lais-of-het-verhal-van-jonge-blaadjes-aan-een-vlaamse-folkboom/ (loose translation from the Dutch)
7. fRoots 262 (April 2005)
8. http://www.folkworld.de/50/e/mandolin.html

BOSNIA AND HERZEGOVINA

I n these pages we've seen again and again how an exploration of music and culture can help lead people to redefine and reassert their own identity – and how this can be a very positive thing. But the fate of Bosnia and Herzegovina in the first two decades of its troubled existence stands as a grim counter-example, a warning that nationalist movements can destroy cultural diversity instead of creating it.

Prior to the 1990s the city of Sarajevo was renowned for its multiculturalism. Pope Francis who visited the city in 2015 joined many before him in paying tribute to its history:

> "Sarajevo and Bosnia and Herzegovina have a special significance for Europe and for the whole world. For centuries in these lands, communities were present who professed different religions, who belonged to distinct ethnic and cultural groups, each endowed with its own rich characteristics; each fostered its own traditions, without these differences having impeded for any length of time the establishment of mutually fraternal and cordial relationships.
>
> The very architecture and layout of Sarajevo reveals visible and substantial characteristics of these different

DJUL ZULEJHA   Safet Isović

JUTROS MI JE RUŽA PROCVJETALA   Amira

KOLIKO JE ŠIROM SVIJETA   Damir
                                         Imamović

communities, each a short distance from the other –
synagogues, churches and mosques – so much so that
Sarajevo has been called 'The Jerusalem of Europe'.
Indeed it represents a crossroads of cultures, nations and
religions..." [1]

By all accounts, Orthodox Serbs, Bosnian Muslims and Catholic
Croats lived side by side: relations were friendly and intermarriages
were commonplace.

This multiculturalism was embodied in the music. This
chapter will be focusing on sevdalinka music and its development.
But for much of the 20th century sevdalinka singers wouldn't have
thought to define themselves as Bosnian or Muslim or Turkic.
Sevdalinka was a music of the region, a music without borders, a
music which drew on a bewildering array of cultural influences.

The word sevdah refers to feelings of amorous longing. Many
sevdalinka songs are about thwarted love or hopeless love. They're
sung slowly, with sensitivity and emotion. You may hear echoes
of Turkish music, of Spanish (in particular Sephardic) music, of
Roma music. But there is a universality of human experience in
the lyrics which has led some to call it the Balkan blues. One of the

greatest sevdalinkas, Emina, was based on a poem by a Bosnian Serb, Aleksa Šantic, describing his forbidden love for a Muslim girl. Although sevdalinka was mainly associated with Bosnian Muslims, in the wider region there were non-Muslim singers who identified with the music and performed it in their own way.

It was a Christian gypsy woman from Bosnia, Sofka Nikolic, who in the 1920s became the first presenter of sevdalinka on Radio Belgrade. The big gamechanger though was to be the arrival of Radio Sarajevo in 1945. All the leading sevdalinka artists of the day practised and polished their singing voices and vied with one another to get contracts with Radio Sarajevo. The stars of the radio age were not only popular and famous, they were admired by critics too: Zaim Imamović, Himzo Polovina, Safet Isović, Beba Selimović, Emina Zečaj, Serb singer Nada Mamula, and many more. Before the war, sevdalinka performances were usually accompanied by the long-necked saz (cousin of the Turkish baglama). But when Zaim Imamović (1920–94) began singing on Radio Sarajevo in 1945 he had with him a young accordionist. Traditionalists weren't happy, but they would soon have a lot more to find issue with. By the 1960s, Radio Sarajevo employed a narodni orkestar with electric guitar, accordion and drums, and a tamburitza ensemble. Artists responded by devising new musical arrangements and singing styles.

The younger Safet Isović (1936–2007) came to know Imamović well and was a great admirer of his tenor voice, his technique, his control. Imamović didn't only set an example, he opened doors through which younger singers would later pass. So it was that Safet Isović was able to perform at the biggest venues, not just in Sarajevo, but in all corners of Tito's Yugoslavia: the Trade Union House in Belgrade, the Šalata Sports & Recreational Centre in Zagreb, the Hala Tivoli in Ljubljana. It was merited: he was outshining everyone, even Imamović. His voice was exceptional, capable of great power and softness too; and there's a bounce and a joy in his voice that tells you how much he loved the act of singing. **DJUL ZULEJHA** can be found on the Croatia Records' invaluable six-volume compilation, Antologija Bosanskog Sevdaha. It's just a short poem with repeating verses, but he fills it with drama and occasion, makes it uplifting.

In 1992, the war came to Sarajevo. That summer Safet Isović was injured by an exploding grenade and spent 90 days in hospital. Safet Isović was a parliamentary deputy and a supporter of President Alija Izetbegović, but he strongly distanced himself from the Dayton Agreement which Izetbegović signed in 1995 – "I would rather have jumped out of the window," he later claimed, "than recognise the Republika Srpska."[2]. His objections were partly moral: the partitioning of Bosnia effectively rewarded the Bosnian Serb aggressors by giving them the autonomy they wanted. The partitioning also struck a grievous blow against Bosnia's multicultural identity which had already been ripped apart by three years of war, hatred and ethnic cleansing.

No balance sheet can adequately record the effect of a civil war on the social fabric. The most famous symbol of the destruction of Bosnia's social fabric was the bridge in Mostar, Stari Most. An architectural treasure which had stood since the 16th century, the photogenic Ottoman bridge collapsed in 1993 under a barrage of Croatian shells, underscoring the gulf that now separated the Croat population on the west of the river and the Bosnians on the east. After the war the bridge was rebuilt amid hopes that this could become a symbol of reconciliation. Reconciliation, however, remains a distant dream. Racism and hatred, so easily kindled, are much harder to extinguish. There is much fear and distrust. Today the two communities live apart, their identity no longer part of a multicultural city but now defined by their postcode and their religion.

In Sarajevo, a similar story. Cultural landmarks were deliberately targeted during the siege of the city. The National Library which held priceless documentation on Bosnia's history was hit and went up in flames. Two million books were burned to ashes as firemen who tried to rescue the building were shot at. It took 22 years – to 2014 – before the library could reopen. Recovering Sarajevo's multicultural identity will take much longer: it's now a predominantly Muslim city.

Out of the ruins of war sevdalinka music made a reappearance, taking on new forms, gaining popularity among Bosnians of all ages and reigniting hope. This was all the more unexpected because before the war sevdalinka had been in decline, struggling against competition from turbo-folk (techno-pop with an ethnic flavour). What changed was that all music and culture became politically charged. Serb and Croat nationalists insisted that their language was different from Serbo-Croat, they embraced religion as the cornerstone of their chosen identity, they sang patriotic songs, and they rejected anything that they associated with Muslim culture. Bosnian Muslims, for their part, held on to what strengthened their own sense of identity.

Dragi Šestić claims that "the greatest poets of sevdah were born in Mostar". [3] It's possible that he's a little biased, but that's beside the point: he did something which no one else had done, and set out to prove it. In 1993, at the height of the war, he saw the veteran singer Ilijaz Delić (1936–2013) singing sevdalinkas in a small candlelit concert and was so impressed that he brought Delić to perform on his radio programme and recorded an audiotape with him. The dream was one day to bring Delić's music to the world. After the war ended Šestić put together a band and in 1999 Mostar Sevdah Reunion (MSR) released their first album. As well as Delić, the album featured the vocals of Roma singer Ljiljana Buttler (1944–2010) on a couple of tracks. Buttler had given up music in sadness and despair when the war started, and it took Šestić many months to persuade her to sing again. In the early 1980s, MSR recorded two albums with Buttler and two with another Roma singer, Šaban Bajramović. Both were born in what is now Serbia, as was the great Roma trumpet player Boban Marković who played with Buttler on The Mother of Gypsy Soul.

MSR are still active today. They've had numerous lineup changes, but this doesn't seem to have done them any harm: yes their aim is to instil a love of traditional Bosnian music, but new blood and new ideas can help the band to renew itself and reach new audiences. They've certainly had a lot of success in putting sevdalinka back on the international map. In 2013, MSR completed a project dear to their hearts. Tales From a Forgotten City is a tribute to Mostar: a collection of sevdalinkas written by Mostar poets, including one that I mentioned earlier on, Emina by Aleksa Šantić. Some sounds and noises of the city have also been sampled for inclusion on the album.

Born in Sarajevo in 1972, Amira Medunjanin remembers a time when sevdalinka music was part of the city's DNA:

"Almost every house, in the street, in the summertime especially, they would have their doors open so you could hear the radio music coming from their houses. At the time when I was born it was the most popular music really, the most appreciated music." [4]

She never planned on being a singer. She was at college, studying economics and accounting, when the war broke out. During the siege she took what work she could find as a translator. She describes how music provided solace:

"Everything around you is very intense, your emotions become very open and you cannot hide them in certain situations. Sometimes you have nothing to do, you spend your time with your friends and family in a basement, covering yourself from shells. Complete dark, with some candles if you can find them, if you have them. Just to cheer ourselves up a bit I was singing with friends. One of my friends had a guitar and we would gather together for little concert performances."

One of those involved in the underground music movement was her future husband Bekim Medunjanin. Years later when she was starting out on her professional career he would be there to support her.

When Amira sings, it's as though her voice carries within it all the suffering and heartache of the people of Sarajevo. JUTROS MI JE RUŽA PROCVJETALA is an incredibly tender lament for lost love, performed to a minimal musical accompaniment. The song appears on her debut solo album Rosa, on which she's backed by musicians from MSR (Mustafa Šantić puts in shifts on clarinet, accordion and piano). "From the beginning," she says, "I focused on the promotion of our musical tradition outside our area... we were going to try as much as possible to repair the image of the world about us through music." [5] She allowed herself a lot of freedom to reinterpret this musical tradition. With each album came a new musical statement. On Zumra, she worked with accordionist Merima Ključo, making tunes with complex arrangements. On Amulette, her collaborators included Serbian jazz pianist Bojan Z. Bojan Z again appears on Silk and Stone, but now Middle Eastern instruments are added (oud and kanun).

Some traditionalists were uncomfortable with the direction in which artists like Amira seemed to be travelling, openly wondering whether her work could still be termed sevdalinka music. However, as Damir Imamović points out, there's never been a time when sevdalinka has been fixed and immutable:

"What people today consider 'authentic' was a product of work of their and older generations. Sevdah of today is Sevdah codified by Ismet Alajbegović Šerbo, Zaim Imamović, Emina Zecaj, Jozo Penava, Jovica Petković, Safet Isović, Nada Mamula, etc. My teachers were Spaso Berak, my father Nedžad, Emina Zečaj, Hašim Muharemović, etc. All these people were always aware of the need to change and adopt new things." [6]

Damir's grandfather was the legendary Zaim Imamović, but his grandfather never taught him to sing. He went to college to study philosophy. A decade after Zaim's death, now in his mid-20s he got offered the chance to work on an academic treatise about his grandfather; and moved by what he'd learned about Zaim's achievements decided to do his bit to carry forward the legacy. At the same time as learning his trade, he's continued his research, and acquired a lot of knowledge about sevdah and its history. With his first group, the Damir Imamović Trio, he established himself as a moderniser: the combination of guitar, violin and double bass was definitely non-traditional. His current group, Damir Imamović Sevdah Takht, makes fusion music – they're exploring oriental rhythms and how these can work within sevdah.

Like Amira, Damir is interested in what lies at the music's boundaries and what this tells us about its identity. "There are a lot of prejudices about this music that people share," in his view, "even if they are progressive." Past attempts to pigeonhole sevdalinka music are a case in point:

"First it was the music of Turks, then it was the music of Muslims, then music of Slavs versus Turks, then at some point it was the music of Serbs, at one point of Bosnians. Today they are trying to make this entire Bosniak identity, which is like a Muslim-Bosnian identity, and ascribe sevdah only to them. So in terms of ethnic categories it's really stupid. For example, one of the most important authors in sevdah in the 20th century was Jozo Penava from Kiseljak; he was a Croat. Another one was Jovica Petković. He's a Serbian accordionist who lived in Sarajevo his whole life – and made some of the most beautiful songs." [7]

Today it's not unusual for artists like Amira and Damir to perform in the Serbian capital, Belgrade, which tells us that there are plenty of Serbs who don't regard it as an exclusively Muslim/Bosnian music. But I still say that an essential part of the music's character is rooted in Bosnian experience and Bosnian psyche. The song I've chosen from Damir is **KOLIKO JE ŠIROM SVIJETA** which is from his self-titled solo album. It's an old number which his grandfather once sang; it's a heartrending poem sung slowly, lingering on every word; and it feels almost like an elegy for Sarajevo.

NOTES

1. https://w2.vatican.va/content/francesco/en/speeches/2015/june/
documents/papa-francesco_20150606_sarajevo-autorita.html
2. http://www.orbus.be/aktua/2007/aktua1816.html retrieved October, 2015
3. http://www.snailrecords.nl/artist/msr/phone/a-secret-gate.html
4. http://balkanist.net/story-of-sevdalinke-part-iii-the-music-today/
5. http://www.muzika.hr/clanak/49777/interview/amira-medunjanin-
totalno-je-suludo-usporedivati-bilo-koga-s-billie-holiday.aspx
6. http://sevdalinkas.com/damir-imamovic/
7. http://berlin-goes-balkan.blogspot.co.uk/2012/11/berlin-goes-sevdah-
interview-with-damir.html

BULGARIA

Sometime in the late 1980s I bought myself a copy of Le Mystère des Voix Bulgares. The music was quite unlike anything in my record collection at the time, but I listened to it entranced. I hadn't realised that a cappella singing could sound so magical. Now I wonder why I didn't follow it up and try to learn more. It's time for me to put that right.

Luckily, Ivo Watts-Russell was more inquisitive than me. He heard one song which affected him so much that he asked questions and tracked down a copy of the album from which it was taken. He was lucky to find a copy: the album had been released back in the 1970s on his own label by Marcel Cellier, the Swiss ethnomusicologist who had collected and produced the songs. Well, Watts-Russell had his own new wave record label in the UK – 4AD – and he just thought, "if it moves me it'll move other people. So I tracked down Marcel Cellier in Switzerland and arranged to license it from him." [1] The rerelease of Le Mystère des Voix Bulgares by 4AD in 1986 is now regarded as one of the seminal moments in the 'world music' story. (How the album actually fits into the world music genre is a question that we'll return to later.) As word about the album slowly spread, it gained admirers in many unexpected quarters, and a follow-up

PLANINO, STARA PLANINO	*Hristina Lyutova*
IBISH	*Aga Eva Quartet*
FAIRGROUND	*Ivo Papasov*
TZURNI OCHI	*Oratnitza feat Kipri*

album Le Mystère des Voix Bulgares, Volume 2 won a Grammy award for Best Traditional Folk Recording.

But then these weren't your usual type of folk recordings. These were elaborately designed arrangements of traditional folk songs. The Bulgarian State Radio & Television Female Vocal Choir who performed on several songs were at the time a large state-supported ensemble who, under the leadership of classical composer Filip Kutev, had pioneered this style which draws on the rich traditions of choral singing of the Bulgarian Orthodox Church.

Since the 1980s, several Bulgarian women's choirs have tried to capitalise on this success story. (While the majority of traditional singers are women, Bulgarian instrumentalists are overwhelmingly male, due to social stigmas against women musicians which have not been entirely eradicated to this day.) Marcel Cellier provided some order by granting The Bulgarian State Radio & Television Female Vocal Choir sole rights to the name Le Mystère des Voix Bulgares. Since 1988, the ensemble has been directed by Dora Hristova. It's a choir of village folk: women who grew up speaking the regional accents and singing songs that their parents taught them. Over many years working with one another they've become a very closely knit unit: "we never miss the opportunity to be together. Our lives become the life of the choir." [2]

I now know that the woman who sang Prïtourïtze Planinata and Mir Stanke le, two of the most beautiful songs on Le Mystère, was Stefka Sabotinova (1930–2010). Stefka Sabotinova grew up in a village in a Thracian valley. Filip Kutev plucked her from obscurity from hundreds of applicants to include her in his ensemble. There is now a star in the Alriga constellation named after her. But to show that she hadn't got above her station, she pointed an interviewer to a pair of leather shoes hanging on her wall – "I keep these peasant shoes in front of my eyes to always remind me of where I come from." [3] Valya Balkanska has an even more impressive celestial claim to fame: her singing voice is on a disc of music, together with works by Mozart and Beethoven, which was sent into space with the Voyager spacecraft in 1977 as a representation of human culture. Born in 1942 in a tiny village in the Rhodope Mountains, Valya's one of Bulgaria's most celebrated folk singers. She now lives in the ski resort of Smolyan close to her birthplace. And she too has clearly not forgotten where she came from:

> "I believe that the message sent from our Earth will be heard, somewhere there on other planets and among other stars. If there are really any other forms of life or other worlds, they might be better than our own world. I am not proud that I have sung all these beautiful songs or that my voice was recorded on the golden disc with Music from the Earth. What I am proud of is the fact that the remarkable Bulgarian song found its place in the Universe." [4]

You might suppose that world music record labels would have been sending scouts into Bulgarian villages charged with tracking down the next Stefka Sabotinova or Valya Balkanska. But you'd be wrong. In the last couple of decades there has been no particular interest from the international media in new Bulgarian folk music. Which is a shame, because there's plenty of it and it's not lacking in quality. To name just two websites, Balkanfolk and Shop Bulgaria both offer a large selection of folk CDs. For the more adventurous, every five years the small town of Koprivshtitsa hosts one of the largest folk festivals in Europe, with thousands of singers, musicians, dancers, storytellers and lovers of folk culture taking part.

Hristina Lyutova is another singer from an older generation, but she'll serve as an example of the undiscovered gold which is there to be found in the country, and in the Rhodope Mountain region in particular. Born in Smolyan in 1940, she lost her mother at an early age, but her grandparents were there to help bring her up and they taught her many songs. Although she joined the Filip Kutev ensemble in 1976, she only remained with them for a year before returning to her upland home. For some years she was a soloist with The Great Voices of Bulgaria choir – a highlight of her career was performing with them in the Sorbonne in Paris. Over the years she's also performed with various other groups. **PLANINO, STARA PLANINO** is from a solo album that she recorded of songs from Rhodope. It's a wonderful hymn to the mountains that she loves so well. "I do not like folk songs that have been translated into literary Bulgarian," she explains. "The dialect in the Rhodope Mountains is interesting, people there sing as they speak. This specific feature has left its imprint on everything and we are obliged to preserve it as best as we can." [5]

Eva Quartet have, since 2000, released three albums on three Bulgaria-based labels. The four women who make up the group were all plucked from the famous Le Mystère choir. Listening to them is like listening to the human voice at its purest – choral-style harmonies with no artifice and no overdubs. On the album, Harmonies, the songs are drawn from various regions of Bulgaria, with some of the songs being given new arrangements. Most are sung a cappella, but on the popular folk song **IBISH AGA** the group's conductor, Milen Ivanov, provides unobtrusive backing on the gaida (bagpipe).

While the state in Communist Bulgaria was willing to fund ensembles like that of Filip Kutev, which could add prestige to Bulgarian folk music, other musical genres fared less well. Wedding music was disparaged, and excluded from radio and television. It was accused of being "impure" because it contained elements of western music, Roma music and Turkish music. Without doubt, this was a hybrid music. But it was a Bulgarian hybrid, it was highly popular, and in hindsight the actions of the state in trying to suppress it seem foolhardy.

The clarinet wizard Ivo Papasov was born in the Thracian town of Kurdzhali in 1952. His father and grandfather were musicians before him, and legend has it that his mother cut the umbilical cord with a string taken from his father's zurna. He took up the clarinet when he was nine, and by the age of ten he was performing regularly at a restaurant while the official orchestra took their break. His family sent him to music school to study under the clarinetist Peter Filipov, but his real schooling came from doing big wedding concerts with his father, where he mastered his virtuoso technique.

By his 20s, Papasov was doing the wedding circuit with his own band, Trakia.

"We started to create a new style into which we mixed Romani elements. Even though it was forbidden, we put it in. And for that reason we were not recognized for so many years. We mixed styles and we saw that it enriched Bulgarian folklore... The people loved [it], but the government officials in charge of culture started to follow us around, to harass us, to prohibit us from playing. This was the reason they didn't let us appear on radio, even though

we really wanted to record our pieces. They chased us; they fined us." [6]

But it was impossible for the authorities to exercise any real control over what took place in the private world of weddings. In this setting Trakia could play the music that they were born to perform. And what music it was. Papasov once said, "I can eat the same dish twenty times, but I can't play the same thing the same way twice." [7] He loved to startle you with exotic melodies and he loved to improvise. And he had the stamina to keep playing for hours on end. Often people who hadn't been invited to weddings would still show up, sometimes travelling long distances for the chance of listening to this incredible musician. He became the most celebrated wedding musician in Bulgaria. Everybody wanted to hire him. His waiting list grew so long that some people got hitched in midweek rather than the usual Sunday so that they could grab a slot in Trakia's busy schedule.

In the late 1980s, American producer Joe Boyd heard Papasov and knew instantly that this was music which he had to record. The time was propitious: the old Communist regime was crumbling, and new opportunities for artists were opening up. Papasov made two albums with Joe Boyd,, which launched his international career, a career which would see him performing around the world and working with a wide range of stars from the global music scene. The fiery, exuberant instrumental track FAIRGROUND is from an album of the same name which, in 2005, won him the BBC Radio 3 World Music Audience Award.

Today Bulgarian folk music is taking new forms which few could even have dreamed of back in the 1980s. The young band Oratnitza play the Australian didgeridoo, the Peruvian cajon (percussion instrument with more than a passing resemblance to a wooden box) and the kaval (Thracian shepherd's flute). They say that "many young people do not understand folk music," [8] – so to make it more accessible to a younger generation they've tried combining it with drum and bass, dubstep and hip hop. The band's frontman, Ivan Gospodinov (nicknamed Popa – the priest – because he graduated from the Theological Seminary), has a unique singing style which is part Byzantine chanting. TZURNI OCHI, taken from the band's debut album released in 2012, demonstrates that for all their experimentation, the band have a firm grounding in traditional folk music. The female vocals are by the folklore group, Kipri.

The Oratnitza album was an immediate hit within the world music community, getting rave reviews in fRoots and Songlines magazines, and winning the monthly Battle of the Bands on the World Music Network website. It's certainly a good and interesting album, but I can't help asking myself the question: would Le Mystère des Voix Bulgares have received this level of recognition if it had been released in the 21st century? Somehow I doubt it. Surprisingly few of the CDs reviewed in the world music media can be described without qualification as traditional. Instead, there's a fascination with fusion of genres, with cross-cultural collaborations and with attempts to put a modern face on traditional music. Take Kottarashky, an artist signed to Asphalt Tango, a world music label specialising in Balkan music. His first album on the label Opa Hey! was made entirely digitally – the twist being that he had sampled a number of folk and ethnic recordings. (Kottarashky also did a remix of Oratnitza's Tzurni Ochi.) So, Opa Hey! – essentially an electronic work with an ethnic flavour – became a big world music hit, while artists such as Hristina Lyutova, who have spent their whole careers keeping alive the songs and traditions of their region, are overlooked. This example may explain why I am so careful to distinguish between traditional music and world music.

NOTES

1. http://thequietus.com/articles/07510-ivo-watts-russell-interview-le-myst-re-des-voix-bulgares
2. http://archive.rockpaperscissors.biz/index.cfm/fuseaction/current.press_release/project_id/299
3. http://kseniassen.blogspot.co.uk/2013/04/a-day-in-life-of-folk-singer-singing-is.html
4. http://paper.standartnews.com/en/article.php?d=2007-07-13&article=5619
5. http://bnr.bg/en/post/100114711/folk-singer-hristina-lyutova
6. Carol Silverman – Romani Routes: Cultural Politics and Balkan Music in Diaspora (OUP, USA, 2012) p141
7. Ibid, p136
8. http://www.avtora.com/news/2011/10/19/oratnica_vajno_e_vseki_edin_bulgarin_da_poznava_korenite_si

CROATIA

In 1992, while the siege of Sarajevo gripped the world's attention, Zagreb calmly held its annual International Folklore Festival. Speaking at the opening ceremony was none other than President Franjo Tudjman, and I think it can safely be said that the event meant a lot to him:

> *"This festival is the proof... [of the] beauty of the thousand-year-old Croatian folk culture. It was so also in those days when the Croatian people were under the boot of foreign rule, and is so now, the proof of the existence of Croatian people, the proof that Croatian people stay faithful to their roots..." [1]*

Passions were running high. Months earlier the city of Vukovar had been flattened by shelling. Tudjman was smart enough to know that anger against the Serbs wasn't enough to sustain people, they needed a positive, affirmative narrative which could give them a sense of purpose. His line was that Croats and Serbs are divided by history, religion and culture; that the Roman Catholic Croats look west, to the Mediterranean countries, while Serbs worship at the Orthodox Church and their main influences come from the East.

SJETI ME SE, SJETI
BIŽI, BIŽI MAGLINA

TS Ringišpil

Veja

When making the claim that folklore music was integral to Croatian culture, what Tudjman had in mind was a stringed instrument called the tamburica (or tambura), which was widely revered as a national symbol. This, however, was quite a narrow view to take of Croatian folklore, even at the time. In the liner notes to the 1988 Unesco album Croatia: Traditional Music of Today, Svanibor Pettan writes of Croatian music's "rich variety". The recordings, he says, are intended to present Croatia "as a meeting ground of cultural spheres – the Central European/ Alpine in the West, the Balkan in the East, the Pannonic in the North, the Mediterranean in the South."

Tudjman was not the first Croat politician to see in folklore music a vehicle for national aspirations. Stjepan and Antun Radić were two brothers, co-founders of the Croatian Peasant Party. Antun was an expert in Croatian cultural studies who'd developed his own system for the study of folk culture. Unable to get a professorship for political reasons, he made his living through his writings and translations. Making much of their own rural upbringing, the two brothers advocated an anti-modernist, anti-socialist ideology based on the values and interests of the peasant class. And because folklore's roots were in rural villages, the peasantry were romanticised as the true bearers of Croatian culture. Antun died in 1919, and Stjepan in 1928, after being assassinated in parliament. But before his death Stjepan oversaw the formation of a cultural organisation called Seljačka Sloga (Peasant Unity).

Seljačka Sloga was the start of a very Croatian phenomenon – the preservation of folklore as a popular activity. In the late 1930s, Seljačka Sloga branches, folklore groups and singing societies sprang up everywhere. Much of this bore little relation to traditional peasant song. The songs had been rearranged for choral voices and were usually conducted by choir directors. This changed after a number of politically motivated folklorists and ethnographers took over the newly formed folk associations and set about creating rules. At the smotra (folk festivals), "only unarranged songs were to be performed, and the use of a choir director was forbidden. Along with folk songs, each group should present traditional dances, instrumental music, and customs. The performances were to take place in 'original' folk costume, and the entire program would be subject to prior approval by a panel of experts..." [2] It was all done in the name of authenticity. In hindsight though, the problems leap out: a new culture was being moulded which looked backwards to a romanticised, idealised version of traditional peasant culture, and which was actively prevented from evolving musically.

The idea of a Croat nation, and promotion of traditional Croat culture, sat in volatile opposition to Tito's dream of a united Yugoslavia. And long before nationalists lit the powder keg, Croats continued to connect with past culture through folklore. Some did this through the new state-sanctioned cultural-artistic societies known as KUDs. Some joined tamburica ensembles, playing wherever they could, in coffee houses and taverns, and at weddings. These ensembles would again have been looking back to past eras, trying to preserve old music rather than create something new. By the 1970s though, tamburica ensembles were producing their first genuine recording stars, Vera Svoboda and Antun Nikolic Tuca, leader of the group Slavonski bećari. Those early albums remain to this day as good an introduction to tamburica music as you will find.

In 1989 and 1990, the tamburica group Zlatni Dukati released two albums of patriotic songs from the 19th century. It was a defiant statement of Croatian opposition to a united federalist Yugoslavia, and in 1990, Zlatni Dukati were among the groups hired by Tudjman's HDZ party to appear at their election rallies. The popularity of patriotic song in the early 1990s, argues Naila Ceribašić, filled a genuine need at that time. However:

> "Genres that during wartime occupied a large media space and served as official self-understanding for Croats – tamburitza, klapa, and church music – lost such position after the war... tamburitza bands returned to their north Croatian and Pannonian roots, which include tamburitza musicianship from across state and national borders." [3]

In the 21st century, Croatian folklore music finds itself in a new place: no longer so firmly wedded to the need to serve a particular vision of the past; more open to new ideas, new approaches. Contrary to what one might have expected, KUDs, once associated with Tito's Yugoslavia, have enjoyed something of a revival, only now these are fractured communities who are coming together, and they're more likely to be interested in reviving songs of their hometown and region than in following anyone else's agenda. Meanwhile, new folk groups have emerged, groups who might put modern and traditional instruments together, or play old songs with modern arrangements, or perform newly written folk songs.

TS Ringišpil (the TS just means tambura band) are one of the more talented young tamburica groups on the scene. They're not well known though, and weren't on my radar until I chanced on the song **SJETI ME SE, SJETI**. Much later, when I learned that the group listen a lot to Roma orchestras, it clicked why this song appeals to me so much. It's got that urban gypsy swing to it, that love of showmanship. Bandleader Ivan Šarić may be the son of a successful tamburica player, but what makes this band tick is that they're not stuck in the past, they feel freedom to express themselves. There's a video for this song which demonstrates my point perfectly. It's shot not in some pastoral scene, but in the Old Bridge pub in Osijek. The boys are dressed not in folk costume but in matching suits. And the video shows them hitting it off with a group of young girls in the audience. Perhaps not the most original, but it shows attitude. And the music contains both attitude and ideas.

Veja is centred around two brothers, Goran and Saša Farkaš, and an interest in the musical heritage of the Istrian peninsula.

Istria describes itself as a place where Slavic, Romanic and Germanic cultures touch each other. Once a prestigious Roman colony, for hundreds of years the town of Pula was under Venetian rule. Today it boasts an imposing Roman amphitheatre and the Italian influence is visible everywhere. Istria's unofficial musical ambassador is Dario Marušić, whose research, teaching and many musical projects have opened many eyes to a unique musical culture. He himself pays tribute to all the individuals who've helped keep the culture alive:

> *"The many festivals in Istria are the result of many years of work towards popularization. Systematic broadcasting of Istrian music on Radio Pula (with the work of Renato Pernić) that started in 1960s, and regular folklore festivals held since that period have contributed to a revitalization of Istrian traditional music, so that today there is a growing number of young people playing shawms and bagpipes." [4]*

Renato Pernić was music editor on Radio Pula for over 30 years, during which he oversaw countless recordings of Istrian village music. After his retirement a project was launched (Arhiv Renato Pernić) with the aim of digitising and preserving much of this treasure trove of old recordings. By the end of 2016 they had completed the compilation of 20 CDs with 500 songs. It's an amazing resource, and one from which it's hoped that future generations of musicians will take inspiration.

What will they find there? Two-part singing in the Istrian scale has an unusual sound which employs its own musical scale and which is partly produced by singing through the nose. There are a range of traditional instruments: the sopila (or roženice, a kind of oboe or shawm, always played in pairs); the surla (a double-reed flute with a single mouthpiece); the dvojnica (or diple, a double-reed whistle); and the mih (bagpipe made from the bladder of a young goat).

Veja aren't about preserving past culture: for them traditional music is a springboard from which each artist must make their own journey. Croatian instruments such as the mih and the tamburica take their place alongside folk instruments from other cultures. So although most of the songs on the debut album Dolina Mlinova are traditional, Goran's arrangements are not. The title track, written by Dario Marušić, was inspired by Istria's 'valley of the mills' which is where most of the album was recorded.

BIŽI, BIŽI MAGLINA, the band website informs us, "was a nursery rhyme which was specific for the region around the town where we all are from. It was also often sung to a melody of balun, the most famous dance from Istria." In Veja's hands it's a high-energy accordion-led dance.

In the last few years the Valley of the Mills has been the location of another of Goran Farkaš's projects. He's the main organiser of the TradInEtno festival, which takes place every year in Pazin's impressive medieval castle. The festival includes folklore concerts, singing and dance workshops, and a craft fair.

NOTES

1. As quoted in Caroline Bithell & Juniper Hill (eds) – The Oxford Handbook of Music Revival (OUP, USA, 2014), p327
2. Richard March – Tamburitza Tradition: From the Balkans to the American Midwest (University of Wisconsin Press, 2013), p102
3. The Oxford Handbook of Music Revival, p332
4. http://dariomarusic.com/?page_id=409

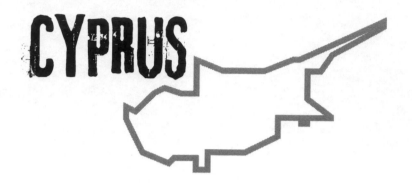

CYPRUS

The physical consequences of partition are all too apparent. 3.5% of the island's land area stretching over 100 miles from coast to coast is a ghost zone, surrounded by barbed wire, patrolled by soldiers whose job it is to keep the communities apart. It's an ugly and brutal sight, but if you look beyond the buffer zone, partition has left other scars which are just as brutal and just as damaging to the lives of both communities.

The culture of the island has been blighted. After so many years of segregation, people quite literally can't understand each other anymore. Young Turkish Cypriots generally can't speak Greek, and the Greeks can't speak Turkish. Schools have been complicit in inculcating loyalty to the 'homeland' – be it Greece or Turkey. This has fostered tribalist attitudes and a narrow, blinkered cultural outlook. July 20th, the anniversary of the Turkish invasion in 1974, is celebrated in the north as a day of liberation, while in the south it's remembered as a day of tragedy.

If I'd been writing this ten years ago I'd probably have been talking here about traditional folk musicians: the heavy-set deep-voiced figure of Michalis Tterlikkas with his leather waistcoats and bushy moustache; or Christos Sikkis or Kyriakou Pelagia. All three are old enough to remember the agony of partition.

VRISI TON PEYIOTISSON *The Amalgamation Choir*

Tterlikkas was still a teenager when he fled his home, the town where he'd been born. Sikkis was born in Aradippou and Pelagia in Paralimni: border towns that swelled in size in 1974 when the refugees came heading south. These singers with their great knowledge of Cypriot music were able to reach out to many people who'd been brought up on a diet of Greek songs and show them that there was such a thing as Cypriot culture which had enough riches to repay a lifetime of study. The thing is though, if you're a traditional Cypriot folk singer there is a lot of pressure on you to be 'authentic', to preserve old songs as they were originally performed. As a consequence Cypriot folk has tended to reinforce a static view of culture rather than treating culture as a living thing that can change as people are subjected to different influences.

Young people in Cyprus are more likely to support the movement for reunification. They're also more likely to be open to music that crosses cultures and boundaries. I'm not saying that there's any causal link here, only that to understand how music can articulate desire for change it's necessary to turn our attention to some musical projects of a more radical nature.

Lefteris Moumtzis is a man with his finger in many pies: founder of Louvana Records, an independent label with a healthy roster of young bands; director of the Fengaros Music Festival, an event that he's revamped by adding on to it a week of music workshops; and alongside these commitments he's been involved in no less than ten bands and musical projects since 2005. Trio Tekke was one of these bands. Lefteris and his friend Antonis Antoniou share a love of old rebetika music: they revisited it, gave it a playful twist of their own, then recruited the English double bassist Colin Somervell to become a trio. There's something about this project that feels right: rebetika came into existence as an urban subculture, it was never meant to be treated too reverentially; at the same time the joy that the trio find in the old rebetika rhythms comes over strongly.

Antonis Antoniou and his bouzouki-like tzouras pop up again in another trio who've been making a name for themselves on the world music circuit: Monsieur Doumani. "At a certain age," says Antonis, "you start listening to other things and underestimating your land's music. Then when you grow and meet all of these other cultures, because we are all interested in world music as well, we became really curious to find out what is happening in our situation in the Cypriot music." [1] The quote is from an interview that the band gave to fRoots magazine in 2014. They go on to identify what they consider to be some of the unique characteristics of Cypriot music: tsiattista, a kind of poetic duelling "which they used to do in weddings or festivals"; pithkiauli, a wooden flute formerly played by shepherds; and the Cypriot Greek dialect – "the musicality of this language is different from Greek."

Monsieur Doumani's interest in Cypriot music is certainly reflected in the debut album Grippy Grappa. Some of the track titles reference folk dances (syrtos, kofto, sousta) which are part of a shared heritage both north and south of the border. And a lengthy Wedding Procession Song concludes the album. Yet it's a stretch to describe this as an album of folk music. It's a whirlwind of musical styles, with a contemporary feel and a desire to have fun. The title of the second album, Sikoses, comes from Greek Cypriot dialect and refers to the last day before Lent, a time of feasting and carnival. Many of the songs are self-written and reflect on current social and political issues. One has to admire the bravery of the reviewer who tries to describe this exuberant music – "For a mere trio, Monsieur Doumani throw in a variety of moods and textures, at times sounding medieval, at times bluesy, jazzy and sometimes like an East Med folk-rock band." [2]

VRISI TON PEYIOTISSON is one of an inspiring set of videos released by Louvana in March 2016 under the name Amalgamation Choir. The Amalgamation Choir is the brainchild of Vasiliki Anastasiou, the daughter of a bouzouki player from Limassol, and recent graduate of the London College of Music. In the videos which are shot in a library we see her conducting this amazing choir of female voices (and a male voice who appears on one of the tracks). The harmonies are well polished, but what makes the videos special is the interaction between Vasiliki and the singers, the freshness of the arrangements and the use that they make of the acoustics of the building. This is a Cypriot song, Vasiliki tells me: "it talks about a fountain in Peyia (a village in Pafos) and how all the girls drinking from that fountain are very beautiful." [3] Most of their material though isn't Cypriot. Vasiliki's interested in exploring the potential of the human voice, and as the project's name suggests, amalgamating together disparate musical elements such as jazz and traditional music, or music from different parts of the Mediterranean region.

As I write this there is real momentum behind the reunification campaign, thanks to the efforts of the leaders of the two communities, Nicos Anastasiades and Mustafa Akinci, though there are still many sceptics who remain to be convinced that this would be a good thing. Critical to any future negotiations will be the stance taken by Turkey, currently in a powerful bargaining position in EU matters as a result of the Syrian refugee crisis.

Regardless of what political changes take place on the island, it would be good to see more cross-cultural projects in the future.

NOTES

1. fRoots 377 (November 2014)
2. fRoots 383 (May 2015)
3. Email 12/3/16

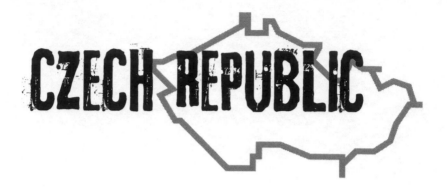

CZECH REPUBLIC

He's known internationally as a composer, but within the Czech Republic the name of Leoš Janáček (1854–1928) is remembered just as much for his contribution to our knowledge of Moravian folklore.

Janáček wasn't the first or the most prolific folk collector from the region. He was greatly indebted to the published work of František Sušil, a Moravian Roman Catholic priest who'd been active decades earlier. Little is known about how his own interest in folklore developed. Although he was born in the Moravian village of Hukvaldy, from the age of 11 he lived in the city of Brno where he trained on piano and organ, and where his exposure to rural folklore would have been limited.

In the 1890s, Moravia was the most fertile source of folk music and dance anywhere in the country, although traditional culture was by then in decline. Within Moravia there was a startling amount of contrast between the different regions and sub-regions: there were local dances, local dialects, different instruments being played, and so on. In the late 1980s when Janáček started out on his field expeditions he travelled to Lašsko, the region where he'd been born. From 1891 onwards, though, he was making regular trips to other regions with strong folk traditions: Valašsko, a

TRENČANSKÝ ZÁMEČEK	Dušan Holý & Musica Folklorica
TA NAŠA LAVEČKA	CM Stanislava Gabriela
OCHTO CHON	Vera Bila & Kale

mountainous region where the hollering of cattle herders had given rise to a unique singing style, and where fast Slovakian dances were popular; and Hanácké Slovácko. With the help of a local teacher and folklorist, Martin Zeman, Janáček made several visits to Velká nad Veličkou, a village in the Slovácko sub-region of Hornácko. Impressed by the dances and the music, he described Horňácko as "the most important center of traditional folk music in Moravian Slovakia" [1] – quite a claim when you consider that Horňácko consists of ten small villages. One wonders whether this was less the scientific observer speaking than the enthusiast. Janáček put his folk studies to practical use, and in the earlier half of his career he wrote various orchestral pieces, choral music and operas directly inspired by the simple folk music that he'd heard in Lašsko, Valašsko and Hanácké Slovácko.

Janáček also wanted to give the cultured folk in Prague and Brno a taste of authentic folk music. In 1895, he organised an Ethnographic Exhibition in Prague which attracted thousands of visitors. Much admired was the exhibition's Moravian Days section, for which Janáček himself had written a special publication about Moravian folklore.

"Moravian Days created a sensation. Czech artists and musicians met at the Hudecek inn, one of the exhibits in the section. Moravian wine and the famous plum brandy, slivovice, flowed; the village band, led by the Velká primas, Pavel Trn, was a triumph." [2]

Janáček must have known a thing or two, because more than a century later the little enclave of Horňácko is still a vital part of Moravian – and Czech – folk music.

A mile or so away from Velká nad Veličkou is Hrubá Vrbka, a tiny village with a history that stretches back to the 14th century. Here two brothers were born: Luboš Holý in 1930 and Dušan in 1933. Folk music was in their blood: their father and grandmother were both excellent singers, who passed down to the brothers hundreds of songs. In 1952, the brothers helped form the Brno Radio Orchestra of Folk Instruments, also known as BROLN, and it seems that they remained part of the ensemble right up to the fall of the Berlin Wall. With BROLN they got the chance to make recordings and to tour the world. The wages weren't great though, so the brothers made separate careers for themselves – Luboš as a teacher at the Veterinary College in Brno, and Dušan as Professor of Ethnomusicology at Brno University.

One of Dušan's research projects was to study the life of Jožka Kubík, a Roma musician from Hrubá Vrbka whose music he'd lived with when growing up. Ninety per cent of the Moravian Roma had lost their lives in concentration camps under the Nazis, but thanks to his musical skills Jožka escaped this fate. Dušan successfully lobbied to have a statue of Jožka erected in Horňácko at the turn of the millennium: it's believed to be the first statue of a Roma person anywhere in the Czech Republic.

As they passed middle age the brothers had the luxury of being able to pick and choose their musical projects. A second cousin of Dušan's, Martin Hrbáč, formed a cimbalom band in Horňácko in 1966, which was still going strong half a century later: Luboš and Dušan jumped when the opportunity came to perform with him again. Luboš died in 2011 and one might have been forgiven for thinking that here the story was about to come to an end.

Released in 2015 on the Czech label Indies Scope, Nejen Zahrádečky is a joint project by Dušan and Musica Folklorica, an ensemble led by the cimbalom player Petr Pavlinec. The delightful artwork on the album cover is by Kornelie Němečková. The ten songs were written by Dušan at different times in his life; they're all ones with a lot of personal meaning for him. TRENČANSKÝ ZÁMEČEK was one that he used to sing as a child, but had forgotten for many years until hearing again. The vocal performance is incredible, enhanced rather than spoiled by the rigours of age. It's natural and not too polished, very rich in tones.

Every year Horňácko celebrates its folk music and culture at Ozveny Horňácka, a small relaxed festival in Velká nad Veličkou. The region's music, claims Dušan, is unique because it has an unbroken tradition, as opposed to other parts of Moravia which have a revived tradition. [3] I would still say, though, check out the music of eastern Moravia generally. There is a real dividing line between authentic Moravian music, which claims to have roots and influences in Eastern European dance music, and the music of the rest of the Czech Republic. The main bearers of musical tradition in Moravia are the cimbalom bands (which I'll refer to as CMs after their Czech name Cimbálová Muzika). The cimbalom is a large hammered dulcimer the size of a writing desk, so the cimbalom player usually takes pretty much centre stage with the string players around him. CMs were a feature of the communist period, having been introduced in Moravia by Jožka Kubík. State support was available to help them get established, but state cultural policies also acted as a brake on creativity and freedom of expression. Since the 1990s, CMs have been slowly but surely evolving and becoming rather more interesting and less predictable. They've looked afresh at what they're about and what they want to achieve. There's been research into the work of Janáček and the cimbalom's 19th-century roots, research into the culture of the town or region where the ensemble is based, and sometimes other regions too.

CM Stanislava Gabriela are from Uherské Hradiště, a town just outside of Horňácko, and the home of one of the oldest and most famous of all the cimbalom bands, Hradištan. Comparisons are inevitable, but Stanislav Gabriel shrugs them off: of course the legacy of Hradištan looms large in their music, but the band have evolved in their own way. This evolution included several years of playing occasionally in wine cellars after the ensemble was formed in 1992. After establishing themselves they've released a series of albums which explore different areas of Moravian heritage. Z Uher do Moravy (Indies Scope 2009) means 'from Hungary to Moravia': a reference to the journey that the musicians embarked on which led to the album, the places whose music they excavated. TA NAŠA LAVEČKA is technically superb, a feast of string playing, but it's the addition of Kláry Plaširybové's vocals that raises it up, adding joy and drama to the music.

In April 2016, the Czech government proposed to allow the country to be called Czechia, as a convenient shorthand for its official title of the Czech Republic. It soon became clear that there was widespread opposition to the change. The most potent argument was that the new name appeared to devalue the country's ethnic diversity. There's a Moravian separatist movement that calls for the right to self-determination and recognition of the Moravian dialect as an official language. Then there's the Silesians and the Roma, two more groups with their own minority language and culture.

If I was doing this by some numerical formula then I might feel compelled to include some Bohemian folk music to represent the country's largest and most populous region. But it's in the country's minority ethnic underbelly, among the ostracised and the marginalised, that some of the most exciting music is being made. Beata Bocek says in her press bio, "I belong to the ethnic minority of Poles living on the Czech side of the border. I do not consider myself being Polish or Czech. I consider myself a Silesian – coming from Silesia. That is 'slónzok'." She plays a variety of different instruments and likes to sing songs that tell stories, often inspired by her own experience. Or take the cellists Dorota Blahutová and Andrea Konstankiewicz. Their bio informs us that, "Blahutová's mother is Polish and one of Konstankiewicz's ancestors was a countess in pre-20th century Poland." They formed a duo, Tara Fuki, who've made some original, haunting music.

A new generation of Roma artists have come to the fore. Their music doesn't conform to common preconceptions of what East European gypsy music should sound like. "Contemporary Gypsy music can surprise people," acknowledges Ida Kelarova, "because it has nothing to do with the old traditional music. I know all the traditional songs and I can play and sing them at a party, but at a concert I want to sing something different, because today we have moved on..." [4] Ida disassociates herself, however, from those who deny their roots. Her father was one such, who married a non-gypsy: "My father denied his roots and all his family denied his roots, because of racism. When he got married to my mother he denied his roots. All his life he pretended not to be a Gypsy." She believes that one can identify both as Czech and as Roma: "I don't really speak Roma, so it's always like that with me. But I must say, I love to sing in the Roma language."

Vera Bila straddles the traditional and the contemporary worlds. She grew up in a small gypsy village among a family of musicians, and learned her trade performing at village festivals and weddings. Then, in the 1990s, she struck up a friendship with the folk singer Zuzana Navarová, they toured together, and Vera recorded her first album, Rom Pop. Navarová produced the album on which, as on all her recordings, she's backed by her own gypsy orchestra, Kale. For this album the band tried to choose songs which they felt were representative of gypsy music, while adding their own contemporary slant.

With the success of the album, the touring began. Vera Bila is a big woman with a big personality, and audiences around the world fell in love with her. The music began to draw more widely on different influences – one of these being Latin music (a passion of Navarová's, who was married to a Cuban). OCHTO CHON is a song from this period, one that I – rightly or wrongly – associate with aching melancholy. The long drawn-out notes give the singer a lot of latitude to express herself, and she does so in a way that feels very authentic.

Navarová was no longer around: she'd died of cancer in 2004, at the age of 45. A few years later, personal issues took her away from music for a while. Vera's husband became sick and passed away, followed soon after by her only son. "Now I'm back," she told the Gypsy Music Network in 2015, "to share my experiences and my suffering with the people through my music and let them take part in it. Do you know something? It is only music now that gives me purpose and keeps me here in this world." [5] In her life, as in her music, she's never abandoned her roots. She once said, "I was born in Rokycany and I want to die here as well." [6]

NOTES

1. Jirí Plocek – Hudba stredovýchodní Evropy – Svetem lidobé hudby a World Music (Torst, 2003), p48
2. Mirka Zemanová – Janáček: A Composer's Life (Northeastern University Press, 2002), p71
3. http://www.mestohudby.cz/publicistika/rozhovory/dusan-holy-jedine-tvurci-postup-je-spravny
4. http://romove.radio.cz/en/clanek/20193
5. http://www.gypsy-music.net/en/interviews/58-interview-with-vera-bila
6. http://romove.radio.cz/en/clanek/18527

DENMARK

Even someone with as fertile an imagination as Hans Christian Andersen needed something to spark his imagination. And he found it in the rich folk culture in the island of Funen in the early 19th century. During his childhood he would listen to old women in the spinning room at the insane asylum where his grandmother worked telling him folk tales, and these had a profound effect on him. What he would later write would be modern fairy tales, not old folk tales, but the folk tales provided him in the earlier part of his career, with vital raw material and ideas.

During Hans Christian Andersen's lifetime two folklorists, working independently, would start carrying out painstaking scientific explorations which, in their scope and ambition, went beyond anything that had gone before. Their names were Svend Grundtvig and Evald Tang Kristensen, and they are rightly regarded as two of the founding fathers of Denmark's folklore industry.

The two men could not have had more different backgrounds. Grundtvig grew up in Copenhagen, the son of a prominent public figure and nationalist philosopher, and he had a very close relationship with his father. When he was just 19 his father took

FLÚGVANDI BIIIL	*Ludvík Justinussen*
MOLV ALS	*Habbadám*
MØNLIREN	*Virelai*
FISKEN OH KUNNE DU	*Habadekuk*

him to Britain so he could visit the great libraries in London, Oxford and Edinburgh, study old ballad manuscripts and make translations. Kristensen's father died when he was a young child. A stepfather moved in, but no love was lost between them. They had a small farm in Jutland in the north of the country, and life afforded few luxuries. Later in life, Kristensen would also develop a very different approach to his source material to that of Grundtvig. Grundtvig's approach was very methodological and text-oriented: he would rigorously scrutinise all the different written versions of a particular ballad. For Kristensen, on the other hand, context was all-important. He always tried to empathise with the working-class people who told him their tales, and he took care not only to capture their regional dialects but also to record what he could about the place and the person telling the tale, even to the extent of getting someone to draw portraits of them. For him, oral culture was not an abstract art form: it was the living culture of Denmark's peoples and communities, and of its working class.

In 1854, Grundtvig wrote an article in Dannebrog, a new magazine, urging readers to go out and collect folklore. In no time people from all over the country were sending him material, much of which was compiled in a three-volume collection of folklore that he published over the following few years. The system of classification used here by Grundtvig would some years later be replicated in Child Ballads, the landmark collection of folk ballads by the American folklorist Francis James Child, who had studied Grundtvig's methods and consulted extensively with him. In his later years Grundtvig himself had made plans for a more elaborate classification system. Though he never realised this in his lifetime, he would have been delighted to see the creation of the Danish Folklore Archive (Dansk Folkemindesamling) in 1904.

By the time the archive was established, oral culture was in decline, and just like everywhere else this process continued through the 20th century. It was to take the efforts of another dedicated folklorist, Ewald Thomsen, to rekindle interest in traditional music and in the contents of the national archive.

In the 1930s, Thomsen began making cycle trips from his home in northern Denmark, travelling to villages and seeking out people who knew some of the old songs, ballads and folk tales. In between the hard grind of making a living he managed to accumulate a great store of songs. He helped found a society to preserve the folklore of Himmerland, and in 1951 they saw the opening of the Rebild museum. Rebild gave folk musicians a gathering place and a sense of belonging to a common project. The museum burned down in 1963 with everything in it, but fortunately Thomsen had kept copies of all his own notes and writings. In 1971, thanks to the intervention of Thorkild Knudsen at the Folklore Archive, Thomsen was appointed as a consultant at Folkemusikhuset, a new folklore centre on the west of Jutland run by Anelise and Thorkild Knudsen. Now finally Thomsen was able to give up his day job as a boilerman. As the folk revival gathered pace in the 1970s, Thomsen became a prominent figure, appearing on TV and radio and hailed as an icon of the movement.

The Faroe Islands are a good deal nearer to Scotland than to any other part of Denmark, and their glorious barren landscapes could easily be mistaken for one of the treeless Scottish isles. The 47,000 Faroese, like the Scots, have flirted with the idea of independence, but up to now have settled for a form of self-government. One of Denmark's finest folk bands, Spælimenninir, is based in the Faroes. Somewhat disappointingly, it turns out that only one of the six musicians is actually Faroese, but there's probably not much about Faroese music that the band, who were formed back in the 1970s, can't tell you, and their music is very accessible.

The Faroese language is quite different from Danish – it's descended from Old Norse. The Faroes have also retained much traditional culture. Faroese folk music is mostly vocal. The place to go to listen to Faroese music (of all genres) is the Faroe-based Tutl record label. Tutl have released several compilations of unaccompanied Faroese singing: Alfagurt ljóðar mín tunga (1995), Flúgvandi biðil (1997) and Traditional Music in the Faroe Islands 1950–99 (2003). The title track of **FLÚGVANDI BIIL**, so they tell us, is a ballad, "about a young man who, with advice from his stepmother, makes himself some silver wings so that he can fly to a young maiden he is smitten with."

Another far-flung corner of Denmark is the island of Bornholm (population 40,000) which sits in the Baltic Sea, much closer to Sweden than it is to Denmark. It doesn't look very Danish: it's heavily forested and rests on granite rock. The Bornholmsk dialect has features in common with Swedish. And it's no surprise to learn that for centuries Sweden and Denmark have vied for control of this strategically positioned lump of rock.

In the interest of candour, I would still be ignorant of the rock's existence today were it not for the music of the young trio, Habbadám. The group was formed by violinist Ditte Fromseier Mortensen, a Bornholm native and a graduate of the Carl Nielsen Academy in Odense and of the Irish World Music Centre in Limerick. She is joined by two other highly talented musicians:

folk guitarist Sigurd Hocking, and saxophonist Hanna Wiskari, who's Swedish. Morten Alfred Høirup tells us that most of the tracks Habbadám have recorded to date are drawn "from a treasure trove of a score of Bornholm music manuscripts Ditte Fromseier has ferreted out in various museums and collections. Many of them had lain untouched for years, and it was not until Ditte started playing through this vast collection of material that she realised just how special the music actually is." [1]

Indeed, it seems to have been a voyage of discovery as much for Ditte as for her audiences:

> "The music we have dug up is primarily dance music, and has been used at parties and other celebrations through the years. Today, not many people play the music but there is a Bornholm Fiddlers' Convention who play the music for their dance evenings. In Habbadám we work together on the tunes, trying to let the arrangements grow naturally out of playing them rather than structuring and designing them... There is a fantastically rich collection of dialect songs, love songs, humorous songs, lullabies and so on." [2]

Wiskari's saxophone is the lead instrument on MOLVALS, a graceful, beautifully arranged waltz.

The music of the Faroes and Bornholm tells us something interesting: that Denmark's culture is much richer and more varied than one might expect for a relatively small nation. In part this is because of the country's maritime heritage which has continually brought it into contact with other cultures. But it also reflects the fact that Denmark itself with its many islands has long been a patchwork of different communities with distinct cultural traditions.

Danish folk music is well served by national institutions such as the Folklore Archive and the Danish Folk Council. But in my view just as vital to its continued good health are regional organisations and their ability to bring people together. To take an example: one of Denmark's largest and most successful folk festivals takes place in geographically the most unlikely of locations – Skagen, Denmark's most northerly town (excluding the Faroes and Greenland), on the extreme tip of the Jutland peninsula. No doubt tourism is a factor: people are attracted to the remote location. But the fact that Skagen is Denmark's oldest folk festival having run continuously since 1971 points to something else: a living regional culture. The Nordjylland region is home to the Fiddler's Museum (Spillemandsmuseet), which has replaced the museum that burned down in 1963. The Rebild musicians' guild is still active and organises regular events at the museum. Nearby you can learn to play folk instruments at the Himmerlands People's Music School. All these are small-scale enterprises, but that's the point. Around Denmark there are other folk music houses, people running classes, small festivals of folk music and dance. All these enable the formation of networks which connect musicians to one another, and through this to their own local culture.

Danish folk music has moved on from the 1970s. It's not lost its character: the fiddle and the accordion still dominate, the old ballads are still loved. But it's more established, more secure than it was 30 or 40 years ago. Young people are studying traditional music and coming in numbers to the big festivals at Tønder and Skagen. The record label GO Danish Folk Music releases quantities of CDs every year, which together tell a story of a genre that's not simply rooted in the past, but is being reshaped all the time as artists develop new interesting ideas.

As I was writing this, I stumbled across a series of interviews on YouTube with industry figures at the 2014 Tønder festival, who all have much the same perspective. The German journalist Uwe Golz says that he's "never been to any other festival where I've had this wide experience of music". He praises Dreamer's Circus, who "play Bach and mix it with traditional roots music, this," he says, "is typical of the new Danish folk groups; they've found their way of keeping roots traditional music alive and don't make it into a kind of museum art. It's a living art, and that's what I think a lot of people forget, that the folk music is the heartbeat of a nation as well. It's not rock music. Rock music's some international business." [3] Irish promoter Tom Sherlock believes that Danish folk music has come a long way since the 1970s and is "on an upward trend":

> "I think [Danish folk music] is in a position to go out and share stages with music from anywhere in the world, because with bands like Habadekuk, Big Basco, Dreamer's Circus who played an astonishing gig here last night, and there are many more, bands and individuals… I know from marketing and selling Irish music and Celtic music that that kind of brand – well, they had a 30-year start on you guys, so maybe it's time for music from the Nordic countries to catch up." [4]

Søren Hammerlund belongs to a new breed of Danish folk musician. He grew up ignorant of his native folk culture. Then one day he was at a gathering of musicians in Ireland where everyone had to sing an old song from their own country. He was stumped. Afterwards he did a bit of digging and discovered this rich heritage of old songs and ballads. He wanted to bring some of this heritage to modern audiences, and to do it in a way that resonated with his own character and beliefs. So he traded his electric guitar for a mandolin, and taught himself to play an old drone instrument, the hurdy-gurdy; then in 1999 he formed the band Virelai, who play their own take on medieval music and folk music. Virelai are the kind of group who like to put themselves at the same level as the audience: they wouldn't dream of charging $50 for a concert ticket. They perform regularly at medieval markets – a form of mini-festival that seems to be quite popular in Denmark. They also perform in schools. They encourage audience participation: chanting, clapping, dancing. They're passionate about popularising traditional instruments.

It may not be a project for strict traditionalists, but what it does do is to build interest around traditional instruments and ancient melodies. On MØNLREN, Søren's hurdy-gurdy and Martin Seeberg's flute combine with some vigorous drumming to make a big stage beat – medieval music has never sounded so good.

Fiddler Kristian Bugge says that: "We started Habadekuk a few years back, because we thought Denmark needed a big, new, party band. The original idea was to blow some wild folk music into people's heads." [5] After leaving school, Kristian spent five months at Raduga Art College in Moscow where he was taught by Mikhail Tsinman, the first violinist of the Bolshoi Theatre. He then spent a few months studying in Sweden before starting his degree in folk music at the Carl Nielsen Academy of Music in Odense. In 2005, his debut album netted him two awards: Danish Debut of the Year and Danish Folk Instrumentalist of the Year. He performed with several other folk bands before forming Habadekuk.

In Habadekuk, Kristian's fiddle is joined by accordion, trombone, trumpet, sax, double bass, piano and drums. Their music, as Kristian explains, is based on old traditional tunes: "We collect material and use the most exciting stuff. Inspiration for our arrangements often comes from other types of music. We try to play with enough energy to reach out over the footlights and start a party." [6] The album titles – Hopsadaddy, Kaffepunch, Mollevit – tell us from the off that they want to be known as a band who like to have fun. Kaffepunch is named after a drink with coffee and schnapps thought to have originated on the small Danish island of Fanø. It's said to put hair on the chest of men and hair on the teeth of women. Habadekuk describe it as "the 1800s version of Red Bull".

FISKEN - OH KUNNE DU is from Mollevit. This, the band tell us, is made up of two traditional tunes from the island of Fanø, learned from the playing of fiddler Peter Uhrbrand. The rearranged version is still string-led, though the rest of the band chime in to produce a big stage sound. Elsewhere on the album the horns are much stronger as the band put hair on the teeth of traditional folk music.

NOTES

1. http://media.wix.com/ugd/22631a_c6d1446d38443358ea7d0f5c0d4c749e.pdf
2. Ibid
3. https://www.youtube.com/watch?v=4VqwlWJx9bA
4. https://www.youtube.com/watch?v=Okw62TNHOg4
5. http://www.folkworld.de/45/e/habad.html
6. Ibid

ESTONIA

Rune singing spread across Estonia and its northern neighbour Finland in the late Middle Ages. The basic meaning is singing poems. Estonian rune song is called regilaul. It has a standard (poetic) metre, and the songs have many functions: some are associated with religious rituals, some are dance tunes, some work songs.

Over hundreds of years regilaul music flourished in Estonia, passed on through oral tradition. But by the mid-19th century it had become a dying culture. Fortunately it was also a time when there was a growing national consciousness in Estonia, and one consequence of this was a big campaign to collect folk songs and record the lyrics.

The Estonian Literary Museum in Tartu became home to this national folklore archive. It was to be a long time before anyone was to take much of an interest in resurrecting the old folk culture, but when they did they knew where to look. Herbert Tampere worked in the archive between 1928 and 1945: his five-volume anthology of Estonian folk songs, published between 1956 and 1965, drew attention to this intriguing musical heritage. There were a few others researching old folk songs in the 1960s and '70s, but they faced all sorts of difficulties, as this wasn't a discipline

PROLOOG (TÜTARDE SAATUS)
(THE DAUGHTERS' FATE) *Veljo Tormis*
SULA *Mari Kalkun*
TULETANTS (FIRE DANCE) *Duo Malva & Priks*
LABAJALG *Maarja Nuut*

that the Soviets were keen to encourage, and until 1978 none of the universities had their own folk music department.

The man who's done most to revive regilaul is not a musicologist or a folk musician. His name is Veljo Tormis (born 1930), he's Estonia's most eminent choral composer, and his interest in old folk music began quite unexpectedly. He'd already been interested for some time in the use of folk song as a basis for a national music when in 1959 he led an expedition to the island of Kihnu, a place where oral tradition still survived, and there they attended a traditional wedding with old Estonian folk songs and dances. Tormis made a study of Kihnu wedding music and wrote a song cycle based on what he'd learned. After this he often worked with old folk song material, adapting it for choral singing. "We should know who we are and where our roots lie," he once said. [1] He befriended folklorist and regilaul expert Ülo Tedre, and together they brought out a regilaul songbook – not as an academic exercise, but as a means of encouraging people to sing.

In 1980, the Olympic Games was held in Moscow, and Tallinn hosted the sailing regatta. Tormis was commissioned to write a new work for the Estonia Theatre for the occasion. For him this was an opportunity to create something new, weaving together regilaul, singing and dance in an orchestral setting. His wife, Lea, takes up the story:

> "The choice of narrative songs that form the basis of the whole work was made collectively. The final selection consisted of six ballad-style songs, of which, thanks to Ülo Tedre, the most suitable authentic versions are now used. For the purposes of a theatre production, however, the different ballads could not simply be presented one after the other – there had to be a story to unite them all. I was entrusted with the task of creating the whole..." [2]

The dark themes of the ballads didn't sit well either with classical ballet or with folk dance. So some non-traditional dance routines were devised to go with the work, which they called a ballet-cantata. Eesti Ballaadid (Estonian Ballads) premiered in 1980 and PROLOOG (Tütarde saatus) is the opening number on the soundtrack album. It's the kind of experiment that often makes me cringe, but not this time: they're treating the source material with real respect, trying to bring out the dark drama of the poem by way of the slow-paced vocals and understated orchestral arrangement.

The work was composed, says Lea, at a time when hopes of a new dawn for Estonian language and culture were fading, and opponents of nationalism were on the offensive. "However, precisely because of the political pressure coming from above, people started looking to their roots as a means to understand who we are and where we come from, and what is truly ours that we can rely on."

A few short years later, the mood had changed again. Laulupidu means song festival: it's a national tradition that dates back to the first national song festival in Tartu in 1869. The first festival in an independent Estonia took place in Tallinn in 1923 when a giant stage was built to hold a joint choir of thousands of people. From then on the festival has been held every five years whenever possible. 1988 wasn't supposed to be a festival year. But the Soviet Union was beginning to crumble and Estonia was simmering with unrest. After a rock concert was stopped by the authorities, crowds walked three miles to the Tallinn song festival site. Here, for six nights in a row, people gathered in their tens of thousands, brought out their banners and sang patriotic songs. The spirit of the people had been woken, and from this moment independence became inevitable. The independence movement became fondly known as the Singing Revolution.

Despite this, when Estonia regained its independence the nearest thing to an authentic folk tradition were the song and dance ensembles approved by the Soviet authorities. Even the concept of researching folk tradition and exploring one's roots was new and unfamiliar. When a young student, Igor Tõnurist, formed the group Leegajus in 1970 to explore regilaul singing, he was "summoned to the Ministry of Culture and told that his work was 'nationalist', not conforming to Soviet culture." [3] Leegajus agreed to expand their repertoire to include material from other cultures, but refused to modify their research-based approach. The band remained active up to independence but without inspiring many imitators. So when a Culture College started up in Viljandi in 1989, the students had few models that they could look to. By studying archive recordings they learned about their musical heritage and traditional instruments. But it was only when they visited a folk camp in Sweden that they began to see how folk culture could be revived:

"In Falun we encountered a quite different approach. We saw living tradition. We saw young people who were playing old tunes for their own pleasure, who were looking for a place after the studies during the day in order to play for their own enjoyment, or jam with friends just for the fun of it. They were still playing those old and very old tunes, yet adding this modern feeling and connection to them…

We realized that folk music is not merely something ancient that does not stand changes, instead it can belong to the everyday life of people even today." [4]

These are the words of Ando Kiviberg and they're part of his fascinating account of how he came to set up Estonia's largest and most important folk festival in this small but historic town. And it was all the work of the students, who first set up a Young Musicians Society with the aim of promoting traditional folk music, then set about raising finance so they could hold a festival. An audience of just a couple of hundred turned up to the inaugural event in 1993, but the 1994 festival was already much bigger and more ambitious, with several international bands performing, and workshops as well as concerts.

Since the turn of the millennium the Viljandi Folk Festival has been the beating hub of a folk music revival that is starting to grow pace. Musicians love to play there, and each has their own fond Viljandi memories. It's become a very social event, Mari Kalkun tells me – "it's the place where you meet friends and can have awesome jam sessions." [5]

Krista Sildoja (born 1973) joined Leegajus as a fiddle player when still in her teens, leaving the group after a couple of years to continue her musical education at the Viljandi Culture College. Here she met other young musicians eager to introduce people to some of the old traditional instruments. Soon after graduating she'd joined a couple of folk groups, Vägilased and Wirbel. Two friends from the college, vocalist Meelika Hainsoo and Kristjan Priks, also played in both groups. In Wirbel, Krista and Meelika both play the jouhikko (bowed lyre): an old Baltic instrument which had become virtually extinct until being recently revived by Finnish folk groups. Kristjan plays the chrotta which I assume he must have made himself or had made for him, as this is a small medieval harp. A fourth member, Elo Kalda, plays the chromatic kannel. The kannel (zither) is Estonia's most emblematic instrument: similar instruments but with different names exist in the other Baltic states. In the 19th century it was said that "almost every Estonian makes oneself a kannel and can play with it". [6] Some people tried adding extra strings to improve the sound. Then in 1952 Väinö Maala constructed a chromatic kannel with strings laid out like on a keyboard. This increased the instrument's range and versatility, and nowadays all Estonian kannel players use the chromatic kannel.

Mari Kalkun was born in 1986 in the woodlands of southeastern Estonia – "our house there is on top of a hill, the woods are all around and cars rarely pass." [7]. Her home region is the only remaining enclave of speakers of the Võro language. Inspired by the music she was hearing at the new folk festivals, she went to the Viljandi Culture College: "there I also dived into the traditional instruments world and started to play (by taking some lessons and teaching myself) small kannel and accordion. I continued making new songs on these new instruments and meeting some really talented musicians with whom we later formed a band."

The richest, most essential side of Estonian music, Mari Kalkun believes, is its runo-song tradition: the poetry of these songs, she told me, has its own logic and a meditative quality, which can't be found in modern music and poetry. She writes most of her own songs, inspired by Estonia's forests and frozen landscapes, and by old poetry. When I interviewed her she was embarking on her Runorun project, which culminated in the release, in 2015, of the album Tii Ilo (The Beauty of the Road). The band include an Australian and two Finns, and their songs are like little journeys in sound, employing two female voices with kanteles supported by double bass and percussions. The heart of the album is Mari's desire to capture the themes and feelings that she feels when hearing rune songs. She has adapted old songs from her home region, sung in the Võro language. She also sings in Estonian, Seto, Votic and Livonian. It's a nice fusion of the old and the new; an album that stretches boundaries yet is respectful both of traditional song and of the natural world.

On Ilmamõtsan (2017) she reverts to the Mari Kalkun of her earlier solo albums: most of the sounds that you'll hear are her own, as she accompanies herself on kannel, piano, accordion and guitar. Ilmamõtsan translates as 'In the Wood of the World', and the sense of an ancient spiritual link between the vast forests and the people who live there runs right through the album. The beautifully arranged slow number SULA celebrates the first signs of new life at the end of a long winter.

This very youthful folk movement balances its interest in traditional Estonian instruments with a sense of musical adventure. The Estonian-Ukrainian band Svjata Vatra (Estonian bagpipes, Ukrainian trombone, accordion, wooden horn) call their music fire-folk – a reference to the band's name which means 'holy fire'. Ro:Toro played folk rock bagpipe music: one of their number, Sandra Sillamaa, was a founder member of Trad. Attack! who since 2014 have been putting Estonian folk rock on the world music stage.

Duo Malva & Priks is a collaboration between two Viljandi musicians: accordionist Kulno Malva (formerly of Svjata Vatra) and percussionist Kristjan Priks (formerly Wirbel). "We're really a trio," says Priks, "if you also include the sound technician". [9] Sonic experimentation is the duo's raison d'être. Priks loves to surprise his audience – "I don't think that folk music should sound the same way as it was a hundred years ago." So they take Pulmalaul, a choral wedding song, and turn it into a bass-heavy rock number. TULETANTS is a Priks composition: this is power folk, folk-based music that's been revved up and that sets out to assault the senses; and what the duo have achieved here with their unfashionable instruments is little short of a triumph.

Fiddler and singer Maarja Nuut is one of the boldest and most interesting musicians in Estonia today. Past projects have included the international music collective Ethno in Transit: a group of young musicians from various European countries (and one from Chile) whose music is truly trans-national. The group, of which Sandra Sillamaa is a past member, emerged from Ethno music camps in Europe in 2009. Maarja's currently collaborating with Alhousseini Anivolla, a Tuareg musician from Niger and member of the band Etran Finatawa. They played a number of concerts in 2015: visually it makes for a striking contrast, but Maarja's fiddle and Alhousseini's electric guitar are a winning combination.

LABAJALG is from Maarja's one solo album to date, appropriately entitled Soolo. The fiddle playing on it is wonderful. But you'll hear something else going on: electronic sounds looping in the background. Like all the tracks on the album, it's beautifully produced. For want of a better word, what she's created are a set of soundscapes, building on old village songs and fiddle tunes, and creating an ambience around them that evokes the rhythms of life of a distant past.

MARI KALKUN'S RECOMMENDATIONS FOR FURTHER LISTENING:

- *Kärt Johanson CD 'Unidstadt' (2007, ARM Music)*
- *Riho Sibul CD 'Jahe sinine' (2003, Vagabund)*
- *Celia Roose/Tuule Kann/Robert Jürjendal/Arvo Urb – CD 'Suurõ Pilvõ' (2010)*
- *Anne Maasik CD 'Rännak Lauluvainule' (1980/rerelease 2012 Terra Records)*

NOTES

1. http://estonianfolksong.weebly.com/veljo-tormis.html
2. http://www.estinst.ee/publications/estonianculture/I_MMV/tormis.html, retrieved September 2015
3. Guntis Smidchens – The Power of Song: Nonviolent National Culture in the Baltic Singing Revolution (University of Washington Press, 2013) p290

4. http://www.folk.ee/festival2015/en/home/the-beginning
5. Email 6/9/13
6. http://www.kandlekoda.ee/history.htm
7. http://www.marikalkun.com/biography/autobio/
8. Email 6/9/13
9. http://kes-kus.ee/matsiv-massiv-ja-massiv/

FINLAND

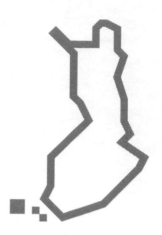

Finland is a land of mystery. Its northern province, Lapland, extends deep into the Arctic Circle: here there are weeks during the summer when the sun never sets. But in the far north of the province the sun stays below the horizon for the whole of December and the period of gloom does not end until 16th January. Winter days are brightened a little by the crisp white snow which reflects any light. Winter is also peak time for seeing the Aurora Borealis. According to an ancient legend of the indigenous Sami people, the Northern Lights are caused by a fox sweeping its tail over the snow and sending sparks up into the sky.

Finland is the most forested country in Europe, with vast forests covering most of its land surface. As well as foxes, the forests are home to brown bears, wolves, elk, reindeer, lynx, beavers and red squirrels. In the autumn they turn into a riot of red and gold before the dark impenetrable winter sets in. These forests have been the setting for many Finnish myths and legends.

For centuries the poems, songs and legends of the region had been passed on by oral tradition. By the early 19th century there was a growing interest in documenting some of this folk culture. One of those interested was a young physician called Elias Lönnrot. He was aware that oral culture was still strong

KIIRIMINNA	*Värttinä*
EIPÁ MIKÁÁN LINTU	
(NO BIRD FLIES SO HIGH)	*Sanna Kurki-Suonio &* *Riitta Huttunen*
JUHON POLKKA - POLKKA	*Juuri & Juuri*
TULE TÁNNE UNIUKKO	*Pekka Käppi & Petra Käppi*

in the Viena district of East Karelia where villages were dotted around in the dense forests. (East Karelia today is part of Russia, but in the 19th century it was in the Grand Duchy of Finland, an autonomous region of the Russian Empire.) In the early 1830s, Lönnrot embarked on a series of field expeditions where he would collect vast quantities of poetry, most of it from the Viena district. In the course of doing this he had the idea of compiling it all to form one continuous epic narrative. He named his work the Kalevala.

The Kalevala was first published in 1835, then after further field expeditions Lönnrot produced a considerably expanded version in 1849. It's a classic of world literature, a collection of epic song/poems consisting of 23,795 verses, edited and tidied up by Lönnrot to form a logical sequence. The Kalevala is populated with gods and heroes; it's full of tales of quests and great deeds and tragedies, of love and war; its songs reveal a vast imaginative world where magic is very potent.

The Kalevala went into print at a time of rising national consciousness, and over time it was to have a profound impact on national sentiment and people's sense of their national identity. The poems had a specifically Karelian origin, which would have been reflected in the very distinctive Karelian dialects of the runo singers. Lönnrot, though he was fully aware of the oral character of his source material, standardised the language, partly to remove what he considered to be impure elements and also to create the impression of a unified work spoken by a single voice. In so doing he gave the Finnish language a voice of its own, even a new vocabulary, and in later years he himself became a leading authority on the Finnish language.

As Finnish people grew in confidence and asserted their right to self-determination, the cultural heritage contained in the Kalevala was held up as emblematic of a specifically Finnish identity. February 28th, the date when Lönnrot signed the foreword to the Kalevala, was already being celebrated by the end of the 19th century. In 1910 the poet Eino Leino wrote:

"The Kalevala and its celebration are only a symbol of the right of the Finnish people to defend their own existence as a nation and as a civilized people. A nation which has created the Kalevala has not been born into the world without reason." [1]

Since gaining independence in 1917, Finland has continued to mark February 28th as Kalevala day and a day to celebrate Finnish culture.

When we come to consider the influence of the Kalevala on Finnish folk music, it has to be said that for most of the 20th century that influence was limited, especially in the west of the country. The dominant form of folk music was instrumental folk dance music in the form of traditional dances like polkas and schottisches, where the lead instrument would normally be a fiddle or an accordion. Representative of the style were the Kaustinen band Purppuripelimannit, formed in 1946. In more recent decades as the Kaustinen Folk Music Festival has grown in size and significance, the music of the region has changed along with it. Kaustinen bands such as JPP and Troka continue to make dance music, but the instrumentation is less traditional, and the music has a vigorous modern feel to it.

The moment that Finnish folk music got its mojo back was when Värttinä arrived on the scene.

Värttinä was started by two sisters, Mari and Sari Kaasinen. They grew up in the east of the country. Their mother introduced them to old Karelian poems, and they would recite, sing and play kantele together. "At first it was just a fun hobby," says Mari –

"music was in our blood. But when we discovered that there was such incredible interest in what we were doing, it began to take up much of our time and became more important to us. We soon realized how special and endangered Karelian culture was, and the hobby became more of a mission to keep the musical tradition alive, from the old songs, poems, and runos to the old women's stories and songs... Not long after we got going, we also realized that we could not just perform these songs in the same way as the old women, but we had to make them more contemporary, to inject ourselves and the modern world into the songs and styles. That is the real birth of Värttinä, and our goal ever since." [2]

The young band began to make a name for itself on the folk circuit, but in 1989 several members left the group, putting its future in doubt. A decision was made to continue with the band and to give it the best possible new start. The Kaasinen sisters enrolled at the Sibelius Academy Folk Music Department. Talented musicians were recruited who'd had experience with other bands. The group expanded their repertoire of traditional music and worked on developing their own style. All this came together in the album Oi Dai, released in 1991. The album was a huge success, achieving sales almost unheard of for a folk group, and put Finnish folk music on the international map.

At this time there were ten people in Värttinä. The five female vocalists stood in front, with the five instrumentalists behind them. The confident powerful vocals on songs such as KIRIMINNA set the band apart from the fiddle-led dance music that could be heard wherever folk music was played. But the content of the songs was important too. This is from an interview with Kari Reiman, who was the sole fiddle player on Oi Dai:

> "The word runo is Finnish and its original meaning was 'singer' or 'wizard'... Before western influences, runos were the most common songs in Finland along with laments, which are even older. Runo songs are sung with a certain poetic style which we nowadays call 'Kalevala style', since Kalevala was compiled from ancient runos and uses this poetic Finnish language of runos. This style has certain rules, like 8 syllables per line, and instead of rhymes at the end of the line, this style has rhyming syllables in the beginning of each word on a line, etc.
>
> On Oi Dai we used both runos and a more modern traditional style, called 'reki songs'... Later on our style has moved closer and closer to runo style, and on the last albums we have had no reki songs at all." [3]

Sari left the band in the 1990s, but at the time of writing Mari is still a member and Värttinä are still very much active. Since the mid-90s their recordings have all been of original material as opposed to traditional songs, remaining true to their Karelian roots while taking the music in new directions.

The Sibelius Academy in Helsinki deserves special mention, if only because almost every Finnish folk musician of note seems to have studied there or taught there. In 2008 its Folk Music Department won the WOMEX Award for Professional Excellence in the Service of World Music. Here's part of the citation for the award:

"*The department acts as a missing link between past and present in the chain of tradition. In the early days, old masters were frequently used as teachers and some of them are still available for that purpose. However, since the living tradition of many of the folk instruments and traditions has already been almost forgotten, the teachers and students have had to dig deep into the vast archives of traditional music and poetry in Finland.*

The history of the department has been full of experiments and adventures, as well as challenging and dissolving musical and other barriers. Its musical base is in the Finnish and global folk music traditions, but another key focus is to create new music, also in interaction with other fields of music and the arts in general. As a result, traditional music in Finland has become more alive than what was imaginable. The educational structure has also had an effect throughout Europe, encouraging other institutes to establish similar departments dedicated to traditional/world music.

As well as making new music, research of the historical tradition is of equal importance at the department. Many of the ancient, almost forgotten instruments have been brought back to life because of the work done by the students and teachers of the department. Good examples would be the revival of bowed lyre (jouhikko), jew's harp, overtone flute and the various types and historical styles of kantele music." [4]

Sanna Kurki-Suonio is a former teacher at the Sibelius Academy, and Riitta Huttunen a former student. For several years Sanna sang and toured the world with the Sweden-based folk rock band Hedningarna. On the album Kainuu she set out to explore her Karelian roots. It's an album of traditional songs and hymns from the eastern Kainuu region, sung by Sanna to the simple accompaniment of Riitta's kantele. The graceful acoustic sound of tracks such as EIPÄ MIKÄÄN LINTU is something characteristically Finnish: in land filled with so much natural wilderness, its people have learned to appreciate the beauty of quiet sounds. (Loud sounds, it seems, are also popular: Finland boasts the most heavy metal bands per capita of any country in the world.)

Emilia Lajunen currently teaches at the Sibelius Academy, but how she finds the time for her teaching as well as all her bands and musical projects is a mystery. She's a virtuoso player of the five-string violin and the nyckelharpa (keyed fiddle). With three other bandmates on accordion, harmonium and bass she was a member of the ensemble Spontaani Vire, named Group of the Year at the 1995 Kaustinen Folk Festival, and who released their third album in 2008. By this time two of the band, Emilia and harmonium player Eero Grundström, had started their own side project Juuri & Juuri. Since 2004, Emilia has also been a member of the trio Suo who've released four CDs to date despite all having other projects on the go. In 2012 she released a solo album, Turkoosi polkupyörä (turquoise bicycle). Then in 2013 a double album was released by Juuri & Juuri, and it's this that I want to focus on.

The double CD Pelimannit/Hiljainen Haltioituminen showcases two sides of traditional music. A pelimanni is a traditional folk musician (spelman, for those who know their Swedish). It's often translated as fiddler though it can also refer to someone who plays a different instrument. Pelimannit is a collection of dances and melodies played in similar style to how they would have been performed by pelimanni decades ago. JUHON POLKKA is a delightfully elegant polka; by contrast, Imattran Rannalla, on which Emilia sings to harmonium accompaniment, is about a girl sitting on the riverbank and planning to jump into the water and end her life. The tracks on the second CD are longer and more melodically complex. They're old songs, originally performed on a single instrument. Emilia and Eero breathe new life into the tracks with the natural-sounding flow between their respective instruments.

The jouhikko is a bowed lyre made with horsehair strings, played held between the knees while seated. It produces a drone-like sound. By the early 20th century the art of jouhikko playing had been more or less completely forgotten. The Finnish ethnomusicologist A. O. Väisänen managed to collect recordings from among the last few surviving players. But to all intents and purposes the jouhikko was a dead instrument, and so it remained until, in 1978, music researcher Rauno Nieminen built his own jouhikko. Working together with the musicologist Heikki Laitinen, Nieminen taught people how to make ancient instruments like the jouhikko and how to play them. The two men also formed a band, Primo, to showcase the ancient instruments.

Soon the numbers of jouhikkos and jouhikko players began to increase. Among of the more interesting new bands was Jouhiorkesteri (The Horse Hair Orchestra) made up of four jouhikko players, one of whom was Pekko Käppi.

"After finishing high school and trying to figure out what to do," says Pekko Käppi, "I found myself reading an article about the history of Finnish folk music and there was a few lines written about this strange instrument I had never heard of. Then I started furiously to search more about it and I am still kind of on that road." [5] Pekko has also studied the Finnish runo-singing tradition. While at university he met Petra, and they became a couple and began to make music together.

Pekko and Petra were among the founders of the Tampere-based Uulu Culture Cooperative which aims to promote Finnish folk music alongside other cultures from around the world. Its members handcraft traditional instruments, do workshops and supply education services. In 2009, Uulu started its own record label and the first release was an album of Finnish lullabies performed by Pekko and Petra. I asked Petra to tell me a little about the track I've taken from it, **TULE TÁNNE UNIUKKO**: "The lyrics describe dream land for children. A recurring idea in Finnish traditional lullabies is that you travel to the magical dream land when you sleep. Dream land is described as a beautiful, calm and very soft place. Uniukko is the 'sleepman' who brings the sleep on his back when he comes to see children in the evenings." [6]

When asked to comment on how the Kalevala had influenced her, Petra unexpectedly said that she'd found other primary sources that were just as rewarding: "I love searching text from folk archives. No one's manipulated these texts. Kalevala is largely a vision of Elias Lönnrot. In the archives there are many more different voices and visions."

Finnish folk music today looks very different to when Värttinä were starting out. There's a greater knowledge and appreciation of the roots of the music, and the Kalevala and runo songs have been restored to a more central place in the culture. Some old instruments have made a comeback. At the same time, there has been an embracing of modern ideas. Both these trends can be seen in the music of Pekko Käppi. He draws heavily on his studies, his knowledge of the tradition; but he's also a very creative musician who's not afraid to collaborate with musicians from other genres and to take traditional music to new places.

NOTES

1. Quoted in Urpo Vento – The Role of the Kalevala in Finnish Culture and Politics (1992) http://www.njas.helsinki.fi/pdf-files/vol1num2/vento.pdf
2. https://vk.com/topic-53351064_28030936
3. http://www.pentatone.fi/runot.html
4. http://www.womex.com/realwomex/award.html, retrieved October, 2014
5. http://www.3ammagazine.com/3am/maintenant-62-pekko-kappi/
6. Email 29/4/14

FRANCE

I've lately come to realise something about myself: when I think of French music and culture, I naturally think of Paris. That shouldn't be the cause of any wonder. Generation after generation have grown up knowing Paris as a cultural hub. Even if we confine ourselves to the last hundred years and the modern music era, the excitement and magic of Paris has been celebrated in poems, songs, paintings and films; and as fashions and musical styles have moved on, the ever-young city has moved on with them.

The 1920s were the années folles, a period of decadence and excess. While America struggled with Prohibition, Paris was the go-to city to drink and dance and have a good time. Artists, writers, poets, musicians and intellectuals also flocked to the city, attracted by the café culture which was concentrated on the Left Bank of the Seine. "We all went to Paris," Gertrude Stein is reported to have said. "It was where we had to be." It was a golden age of Parisian music and dance: the Folies Bergère and Moulin Rouge were at the height of their popularity, and in these houses many stars were born or made – Maurice Chevalier, Josephine Baker, Mistinguett and Jeanne Aubert to name but a few. In the postwar period Paris-born Édith Piaf became France's most popular singer: she seemed to articulate the spirit of the city

MARV PONTKALLEG	Alan Stivell
TRINKAMP MARC'HADOUR	Annie Ebrel, Nolwen Le Buhe & Marthe Vassallo
LA COCHINCHINE	Baron Anneix
LINELIS	Plantec
SCOTTISH DE WALTEM/TROIS DEMOISELLES	Amuséon
SAN PLATO	Lindigo
VOLTASION	Dédé Saint-Prix

like no one else before or since. Another singer, Juliette Gréco, became a muse of the still thriving Left Bank scene in these years: "You should have seen us all after a dinner, roaring with laughter in St Tropez's deserted streets at night. We were very naughty." [1]

When we look at Paris today we see a multicultural city. In the Île-de-France region, which includes Paris, almost two million people were born outside France, including many from North Africa: over 10% of the region's population are believed to be Muslim. France is the world's second largest market for hip hop, and it's in the multiracial banlieues of cities like Paris and Marseilles that many hip hop artists started out on their journey. Paris is also a hub of the world music scene. There are no data on this, but from the hundreds of biographies of African musicians that I've read while researching this book I'm quite sure that more emigrate to

Paris than to any other European city. To service the diverse music of these new immigrants a whole infrastructure has developed of world music record labels, agents, festivals, and so on.

If we are to get to the roots of French music though and appreciate it more fully, we must leave Paris behind and explore the music of the regions. This is a vast and rewarding subject, and those whose curiosity may be piqued by this chapter are encouraged to do their own explorations. France's 27 regions include five overseas territories: Guadeloupe and Martinique in the Caribbean, French Guiana in South America, and Mayotte and Réunion in the Indian Ocean; these, as you would expect, have quite separate musical traditions, and I've devoted some space to them as they're not covered elsewhere in the book.

From ancient megaliths to medieval kings, Brittany (Bretagne in French, and Breizh in Breton) has history in abundance. The development of Breton language and culture is believed to date back to tribes of ancient Celts who came to French shores from Britain during the first millennium AD. It wasn't always valued like it is today. When compulsory universal education was introduced in France in the 1880s, French was the only language that could be taught in schools or even spoken in the schoolyard. Breton language was stigmatised as being rural and backward. Signs were posted in public places which said: "No spitting on the ground or speaking in Breton." If possible, its reputation sank even lower after World War II, during which a small minority of Breton militants had actively collaborated with the Nazis. Many Bretons accepted the inevitable, speaking French in their homes, taking up French instruments like the accordion rather than traditional instruments of the region, and so on. To these and others, the language and culture seemed destined to be consigned to history.

But Breton activists never gave up their struggle, and of much importance that struggle has been the modern reinvention of Breton culture by politically minded musicians.

Loeiz Roparz (1921–2007) organised his first Fest Noz on 26th December 1954. The idea hadn't just come out of the blue. As a child he'd seen dances to celebrate the harvest and music played at Breton weddings. While teaching at university he'd also studied Breton music. In 1949 he formed a pipe band, Bagad Kemper; he was also an accomplished singer in the kan ha diskan singing style. The fest-noz was a conscious effort to revive interest in this culture: a typical event would include both traditional singing and lively dance music performed by a couple de sonneurs – bombarde (oboe) and binioù (bagpipe) – and would be both inclusive and participatory. Here's one account:

> "One of the best nights of music and dance that I've experienced was at a fest-noz in the little town of Huelgoat in central Brittany. An area of Brittany that still retains much of what is left of traditional rural life, this is also the land of the gavotte. People here are very enamored of this dance.
>
> The little dance hall was set up with a small stage for the musicians and singers, a well-worn wooden floor for the dancers, and a small bar dispensing beer, cider, wine and soft drinks. The music for the evening was provided by two pairs of sonneurs, the group Storvan, and two pairs of kan ha diskan singers.
>
> …Gavottes were indeed plentiful, and I was in the midst of a long chain when an older fellow jumped into the centre of the circle. The crowd cheered as he ran across the floor and took the hand of one of the younger singers, Annie Ebrel. He escorted her into the middle of the floor, and they executed some fancy steps together, his red face beaming. They finished with four little kisses on the cheeks, and the man stepped back into the crowd.
>
> I discovered with a mixture of pleasure and horror that my hand was being taken by the singer, and I was being led

*into the circle to execute (or rather, massacre) some fancy
steps that I had never quite picked up in my years of contra-
dancing. I managed to hop about in a reasonable imitation
of what she was doing, and I remembered the kisses. She
smiled and stepped back into the line. I smiled and stepped
back into the line, too, which elicited howls of laughter and
protest. Back I went into the circle to choose a partner for
another series of funny little hops and funny little kisses,
before I was finally allowed to melt back into the group of
dancers."* [2]

Note the importance of the locality. There are four distinct
Breton dialects which are spoken in different parts of Brittany,
and it turns out that quite a number of things are also strongly
associated with certain areas of the peninsula. For instance the
hurdy-gurdy is mainly played in northeastern Brittany, whereas
the veuze bagpipe comes from the south.

As festoù-noz began to appear across Brittany in the late
1950s, one of the first vocal groups to emerge was Les Soeurs
Goadec: three sisters who were part of a large family who had
all learned the techniques of a capella call and response singing
(kan ha diskan) and ballad singing (gwerz) from their parents.
With their repertoire and vocal abilities, Maryvonne, Thasie and
Eugénie set a high standard, and were a big influence on many
who were joining the movement.

Among these was a kid whose name was to become
synonymous with the Breton music revival: Alan Stivell (born
1944). Alan's father, Jord Cochevelou, had constructed a Celtic
harp – an instrument that had virtually died out in Breton
tradition – and the young boy was keen to learn how to play it.

*"J'étais fasciné par cet instrument, et quand la première
corde a été posée, c'est moi qui ai demandé. Je voulais tout de
suite en jouer... C'était un amour fou... J'avais l'impression*

d'entrer dans la légende, dans la mythologie, dans l'au-delà." [I was fascinated by this instrument, and when the first string was plucked I was on the case. I wanted to play right away. It was a crazy love... I felt like I was entering into legend, into mythology, into the afterlife.] [3]

He joined a scout group which doubled as a pipe band, so now he was also learning to play the Scottish bagpipe. Later, after the boys decided that they'd rather be musicians than boy scouts, they won several competitions. During this time Alan recorded a couple of harp albums, one of which featured on vocals Andrea Ar Gouilh, a pioneer of Breton singing.

In the late 1960s, Alan began putting together a band. He had a couple of revolutionary ideas: they should sing in Breton and they should fuse Celtic music with rock music. A series of landmark releases followed: Reflets (1970), Renaissance de la Harpe Celtique (1971) and À l'Olympia (1972). **MARV PONTKALLEG** from the Renaissance album is a reinterpretation of a traditional gwerz about the romantic figure of the Marquis de Pontcallec who was beheaded in 1720 for his part in a Breton uprising. Surprisingly Alan Stivell dispenses with the words, leaving us with a touching and beautiful piece of harp music. If Renaissance was a critical success, Olympia was a popular triumph which confirmed that Breton music had 'arrived'. Recorded live before a rapturous Paris audience, while also being broadcast live on French national radio, the fusion of Celtic rhythms with modern instruments proved to have genuine crossover appeal, and the album sold a million and a half copies.

As activists tried to join the dots between the new music, the Celtic heritage and the language issue, there was a flurry of initiatives. In 1971, the city of Lorient held its first Celtic music festival: the Festival Interceltique de Lorient is now one of France's best-loved festivals, and a potent annual reminder of Brittany's claim to its own ancient Celtic heritage. Every year musicians come from every Celtic-speaking region of the globe to take part in the festival. Then there is Dastum: founded in 1972, Dastum has worked ever since to preserve Brittany's oral heritage, creating a vast library of songs, manuscripts, photographs and audio recordings, and making this accessible to communities who are committed to renewing old traditions. Breton language speaking was in steep decline, but the first in a network of Diwan schools was opened in 1977, while a few young politically committed adults started to learn a language that their parents had forgotten. In all this, the festoù-noz continued to play a vital part, bringing people together in a spirit of egalitarianism and participation, and giving them a sense of common cause.

Forty years on, Breton language is still in crisis, still denied official recognition, but some small victories have been won. There are now Breton language road signs and radio stations that broadcast in Breton. And respect for Brittany's unique identity is now widespread, if not universal: "I think half of the people in France are now open to Breton culture," reckons Alan Stivell. "They consider that Breton culture is part of the wealth and the richness of the French Republic. And the other half are thinking we must go on to destroy, to reject, because it's a risk to France; they think the next step is Breton independence." [4] But the best guarantee of its survival lies in the strength of Brittany's reinvented traditions: the bagad bands, the Celtic circle associations, the huge numbers of festoù-noz and folklore festivals that take place in Brittany every year, and in the many bands who've emerged from this scene in recent years. Christian Anneix reckons that two thirds of all professional traditional musicians in France are based in Brittany, which is an astonishing claim. [5]

Inevitably there has been much diversification, but many traditional groups are still modelled on the a capella singers and the bombarde and biniou dance bands from the early days of the fest-noz. Annie Ebrel, Nolùen Le Buhé and Marthe Vassallo are all champions of Breton singing and three close friends whose paths have often crossed over the years. On Teir they perform as a trio: though grounded in the singing traditions with which they're familiar the album's notable for its sometimes startling vocal experimentation. **TRINKAMP MARC'HABOUR** is a typically complex composition, with a nice transition from individual voices to polyphonic singing a couple of minutes into the song.

Jean Baron (born 1951 in St Malo) and Christian Anneix (born 1950 in Rennes) first met in 1973 in the town of Saint Grégoire while attending Le Cercle d'Outre Ille. This is one of the Celtic circles – Breton cultural associations. The circles offer dance classes and organise dances, which unlike those at a fest-noz are well rehearsed and performed in traditional costumes. It's hard to imagine Baron or Anneix in formal costumes: theirs is the wild folk image, shoulder-length hair and bushy beards and casual clothes. When the two met, Anneix was already part of a singing duo, but he felt that his artistic freedom was limited as long as he was part of the circle, and one presumes that he saw in Baron a like-minded spirit.

And so a partnership began – Baron on bombarde and Anneix on binioù kozh – which was to last through numerous albums across the decades, and a series of awards. **LA COCHINCHINE** is a lovely introduction to their work. Playing over a quiet drone, the sound of the pipe is playful and light-hearted: an open-hearted Breton welcome, inviting you to the dance.

Anneix tells us that the duo are most strongly drawn to Vannetais music. The Vannes region has its own character: the gwenedeg dialect which is spoken there can be hard even for other Breton speakers to understand. Baron's early mentors were both Vannetais specialists: Jean-Yves Blanchard and Jakez Philouze. Mostly, though, it's a matter of personal preference: "les mélodies vannetaises sont vraiment extraordinaires, et ce sont celles que nous ressentons le plus." [6] Of course, their great achievement is to show that couples de sonneurs can be credible musicians in a modern context, and part of what has kept them fresh and kept audiences entertained through so many concerts and festivals and albums has been their versatility and openness to different agendas – they've certainly teamed up in a few different ensembles.

Plantec began life as a guitar/bombarde duo. They were two brothers, Yannick and Odran Plantec, whose parents used to take them to festoù-noz when they were children; and the water in which they swam was Brittany's fest-noz scene. As the band grew in size and reputation they performed in a good many European countries. In every interview they reiterated that their roots lay in fest-noz, that this was the tradition they represented; yet at the same time they were redefining that tradition. Theirs was fest-noz music amplified and electrified for the techno generation.

Around 2012, a change of direction: Yannick and Odran transformed Plantec from a seven-member to a three-member band, the third person being Gabriel N'Dombi D'Otala (alias DjiBriL) on keyboards. The synergy which these three possessed – fortified by three years of touring – gave the band a more natural balance, a sharper definition. **LINELIS** features Laurita Peleniute on guest vocals: it's high-energy good time music by a band who love performing live, rooted in Brittany's Celtic folk tradition. It's taken from the 2015 album, Kontakt, and a version of the song also appears on their 2018 CD/DVD release, Live au Festival Interceltique de Lorient.

In northeastern France traditional music had nothing like such deep roots. When Ghislaine Desmaris listened to bagpipes and decided that she had to have one of her own, she was told "you won't find any of them in the music shops". So she looked further afield:

"La première que j'ai choisie était une cornemuse à soufflet, d'Angleterre, fabriquée par Jonathan Swayne, un Border pipe. J'aimais beaucoup le son très doux et riche en harmoniques qu'elle produisait. Au bout d'un moment, j'ai commencé à me poser des questions sur ici, en Picardie: quel

répertoire traditionnel? Quels anciens le jouaient? Y a t'il une
cornemuse locale? On n'entendait parler de rien de tout cela!"
[The first one I chose was a bellows bagpipe from England,
made by Jonathan Swayne, a Border pipe. I loved the sound
it made, very soft and rich in harmonics. After a while I
began to ask around about Picardy: what's the traditional
repertoire? Which are the old musicians? Is there a regional
bagpipe? No one had heard anything about any of this!] [7]

In fact there was a Picardy bagpipe, the pipasso, and although
it had fallen into disuse, a Belgian instrument maker, Rémy
Dubois, had recently begun making them again. Undaunted by
all this, Ghislaine acquired her pipasso and taught herself how
to play it. But she couldn't stop there – she felt a responsibility
to help ensure that this wonderful instrument would have some
kind of future. She began giving lessons. And she formed a
band: Amuséon.

Amuséon combine elements of the traditional and the
modern: on Picarokeur the instruments played are pipasso,
accordion, fiddle and drums. The pipasso doesn't limit or define
their music: the aim is a listening experience that's varied and not
over-predictable. Which is more or less what we get on SCOTTISH DE
WALTEM/TROIS DEMOISELLES, where a jaunty Scottish dance leads us in
to the light-hearted song. Amuséon are more than your regular
band; they're involved in a number of projects, about which the
band keep people informed through their website. They organise
a Festival Pipasso in Flixecourt, of which Ghislaine is the artistic
director. They've released a compilation album, Cornemuse
Picarde, with a number of live recordings from the festival, plus a
studio album and a 150-page booklet featuring the small handful
of players who are keeping pipasso playing alive, including both
Ghislaine Desmaris and Rémy Dubois. They've even set up their
own research company to carry out research into the traditional
music of Picardy.

Like Breton, Occitan is a language in decline. In 1999 there were over 600,000 Occitan speakers, but they were dispersed widely, from Catalonia to the Italian Alps, and the lack of stronger geographical concentrations hasn't helped their cause. Again, as with Breton, there was a cultural revival peaking in the 1970s in which musicians played a leading role. The names were as unfamiliar to me as the language: Claude Marti, Patric, Mans de Breish, Marie Rouanet. The music though felt more familiar. This was politically committed folk song reminiscent of the type of folk music that was coming out of South America in the same period. They were singing of love and politics, and sometimes putting Occitan poetry to music. By far their most radical act was something that no other singers had done for years: to sing publicly in the Occitan language.

A record label was formed: Ventadorn, named after a 12th-century troubadour (some of the new singers modelled themselves after the troubadour tradition). Then when things began to take off, 20 artists and activists got together to form a non-profit group, also called Ventadorn. Dozens of albums were released on Ventadorn over a 15-year period, and the association was able to plough back the proceeds into new cultural initiatives.

The movement declined, activists became disillusioned, record sales fell. In 1985, the Ventadorn company decided to disband. What they've left behind is something intangible: a pride in this minority language. Today, it no longer seems strange to find bands who sing Occitan. They're not part of any movement: each has their own influences, their own ideas. One such group is La Mal Coiffée, five female singers from Languedoc who combine harmonies and polyphonies with supreme skill. As their singing is inspired by ancient choral methods, it's only fitting, they say, that they should sing in the language spoken by their parents and grandparents. It's also a language that they love, according to Myriam Boisserie: "Nous chantons en Occitan parce que cette langue est magnifique." [8]

Before considering issues of cultural identity in France's overseas territories, it's pertinent to ask how these territories acquired their current status. The short answer is this: in March 1946, the people of Martinique, Guadeloupe, French Guiana and La Réunion all voted in favour of becoming a department of France. (Mayotte followed suit in March 2009.) Most of those casting their votes were the descendants of slaves whose ancestors had been forcibly taken from their homelands by the French. They were voting to belong to a country where French is the only official language and Creole is no more recognised than is Breton or Occitan. So what are we to make of this?

The timing of the referenda may have played a part in their outcome. Martinique's white minority, for example, had been supporters of Vichy France; and the rise to power of Charles de Gaulle in the wake of the Nazis' defeat was taken by many as an assurance that France would always protect democracy and freedom. Metropolitan France was seen as more enlightened than the local white elite. More fundamentally, the way people voted reflected a genuine aspiration of a large section of the population to be French. In the French Caribbean, mixed race people tended to have more education and higher social status than those of darker skin: for many of them assimilation into French society meant an opportunity to get on in life.

The attitude of the French authorities can be summed up as paternalistic: the assumption was that they were dealing with more backward cultures, and that consequently more assimilation would be a good thing. It was attitudes such as this which led to the tragedy of Les Enfants de la Creuse. The French minister, Michel Debré, had set up a department called Bumidom to facilitate the migration of people from the overseas departments to mainland France. Under its auspices, between 1963 and 1982, 1,630 children from Réunion – including many with living relatives who had not been properly consulted – were sent thousands of miles away to new homes in France. Only when the scandal broke decades later was there any kind of reckoning of the trauma caused by these enforced exiles.

It's only fair to add that government attitudes have changed since then. A positive sign was the appointment in 2012 of a black woman from French Guiana, Christiane Taubira, as France's Minister of Justice. On 10th May 2001, when she was just a deputy, she got the French Senate to adopt a bill declaring slavery a 'crime against humanity.' May 10th is now recognised by the French government as a memorial day to honour the victims of slavery and its abolition. Taubira resigned in 2016, after criticising government plans to strip French nationality from dual citizens who are convicted of terrorism.

The importance of Chirac declaring slavery to be a crime can't be understated. It was a step along the road to acceptance of the fact that France's ethnic minorities had their own history, heritage and culture, but that this didn't make them any the less French. And while the question of independence will continue to be debated, for many people in the overseas territories this is as far as they want to go. They have multiple identities: Afro-Caribbean, Creole, French, and so forth. And when they assert their black heritage that's different from being an advocate for independence.

Maloya is seen today as an integral part of the culture of La Réunion, rivalled only by sega music in importance. Yet for years it was banned by a French government who feared that it could incite nationalist sentiment – a ban which remained until as recently as 1981, when François Mitterrand became the French president. Maloya music and dance come from Creole culture, and songs are normally sung in Creole. It has roots in spiritual ritual, but it's also come to represent the cry of the slaves, the cry of an oppressed people. It sounds African: there's a lot of drumming and chanting, and of course it's meant to be danced to.

Danyel Waro grew up with Creole culture and left wing politics. His father was a supporter of the Communist Party, and it was when attending a Communist Party festival at the age of

18 that Waro first heard maloya. The singer who made such an impression on him that day was Firmin Viry. Soon Waro was Viry's student, occasionally performing in his band before starting out on his own. His lyrics were angry and socially conscious, following the example of Firmin Viry and of another singer, Granmoun Lélé. At the age of 20 he was thrown into jail for two years for refusing to do military service: he used the time to work on his songwriting and to write a novel. After maloya became legit in the 1980s his career took off in earnest. He remembers the time fondly: "The renaissance of maloya gave back a worth to all that African part of ourselves that had been devalued and hidden for centuries. We won back a piece of ourselves." [9]

Olivier Araste and his band Lindigo are part of maloya's new generation. Their motto is "Quand tu sais d'où tu viens, tu sais où tu vas" – when you know where you come from, you know where you're going. Araste is proud of his ancestral Madagascan heritage, but he's not shackled by this. Just as the blood of many races flows in Réunion people, so the music of Lindigo is open and accepting of many cultural influences: "I was born Maloya, I breathe Maloya, I sweat Maloya, I die Maloya. But it must be open to the world, just like spices giving even more flavour to my music. I like Western music, I love Fela Kuti, I love Bob Marley." [10]

Lindigo's hallmark is their infectious energy, and to help them capture this they recorded their 2014 release, Milé Sèk Milé, which was recorded in just three days. SAN PLATO is the opening track on the album. It's about an artist searching for his roots, and I've chosen it for its unadorned directness: the call and response singing and the percussive beats. The album as a whole is free ranging and unpredictable. Parisian accordionist, Fixi, guests on many of the tracks, Jimmy Itema's keyboard and Guillaume Perret's sax make appearances, and various African instruments like the balafon, ngoni and the djembe drum are used. What brings it together is the powerful and engaging personality of Olivier Araste, who's finding his voice, singing about themes that to him are fundamental: the island, its history, its traditions, and the troubles and joys of island life.

In Martinique, as in many of its Caribbean neighbours, carnival is the centre of cultural life. The island's musicians turn out in force to provide the soundtrack to four days of colourful parades, each with its own theme rooted in local myth and tradition. The end of carnival on Ash Wednesday is marked by the ritual burning of the carnival king (Vaval). If there's one band who know all there is to know about carnival music, it has to be the Guadeloupean band Kassav. Zouk is the name given to the high tempo dance music, played with brass, keyboards and drums, which they've done so much to popularise.

Dédé Saint-Prix (born 1953) could have been a big zouk star – but he had different ideas. Hearing musicians from Guadeloupe who'd taken up traditional instruments so they could explore percussive gwo ka music inspired him to go back to his own musical roots in Martinique. He remembered from when he was a kid the chouval bwa that used to be played in fairgrounds. Chouval bwa is Creole for wooden horse (from the French cheval bois), and each fairground worth its salt would have wooden horse rides. At the centre of the carousel a small orchestra played rhythmic music, and this music also came to be called chouval bwa.

That was back in the day when the rides had to be pushed by hand. After they became mechanised the orchestras disappeared. In the early 1980s, Dédé Saint-Prix began trying to revive chouval bwa music. He took its basic elements: the tibwa (a length of bamboo beaten with small sticks), chacha (rattle), bel-air and tanbour (large drums), a bamboo flute or an accordion; and he added modern instruments. During this period he played in various bands, making use of the musicians' creativity. Meanwhile he carried on his career as a music teacher until, in 1991, he finally gave it up so that he could concentrate on playing.

VOLTASION is from a later album and we can see from it

that Dédé's musical philosophy hasn't changed. Traditional instruments – bamboo flute, tibwa, chacha, tanbour – form the base of the music, giving it a lovely lilting rhythm. Dédé sings in Creole which he loves for its stories and its images. "This heritage still inspires me," he says. "This is a very rich music and, even though it doesn't make money go round, it has much wisdom and spirituality." [11]

Since this chapter was written there have been a series of disturbing events which remind us that France's multicultural heritage can't be taken for granted. I refer to the Charlie Hebdo attack in 2015, and to the fivefold increase in attacks on French Muslims which followed it. I refer to the carnage caused by militant Islamists in Paris in November 2015, and to the success of the Front National in France's regional elections the following month. Tensions were further stoked when Mohamed Lahouaiej-Bouhlel drove a 19 tonne truck into crowds celebrating Bastille Day in Nice in 2016. Nice is part of the Provence-Alpes-Côte d'Azur region which has long been a stronghold of the Front National. And in another part of the region, Bouches-du-Rhône, the authorities in Marseille have, since 2015, been cutting subsidies to cultural associations in the name of fiscal discipline. The contemporary dance festival Dansem has had its funding slashed, as has AFLAM, organisers of the film festival Les Rencontres internationales des cinémas arabes. Then, in December 2017, a shocking announcement: the annual world music and jazz expo in Marseille, Babel Med, was forced to cancel its conference at three months notice due to an 80% cut in its funding from the local region. Organisers are determined to make sure that the event returns in 2019. And they are clear as to why: Babel Med is not just a vital resource for world music professionals; it's a part of the lifeblood that sustains the health and vitality of the region's rich culture.

NOTES

1. http://www.theguardian.com/music/2014/feb/17/juliette-greco-miles-davis-orson-welles-sartre
2. David Surette – Traditional Breton Dance Tunes Fest Breizh (Mel Bay Publications, 2010), p10
3. https://hommesmigrations.revues.org/537?lang=en
4. http://www.stevewinick.com/stivell
5. https://ethnomusicologie.revues.org/1216
6. Ibid
7. http://www.amiens-ouest-tourisme.fr/pipasso-musique-picarde,fr,8,131.cfm
8. http://www.lamontagne.fr/auvergne/actualite/departement/allier/vichy/2014/09/26/la-mal-coiffee-nous-chantons-en-occitan-parce-que-cette-langue-est-magnifique_11159094.html
9. http://www.andymorganwrites.com/danyel-waro-say-it-loud-mongrel-and-proud/
10. http://www.outremersbeyou.com/lindigo-je-suis-ne-maloya-je-respire-maloya-je-transpire-maloya-je-mourrai-maloya/
11. http://www.africultures.com/php/?nav=article&no=375

GEORGIA

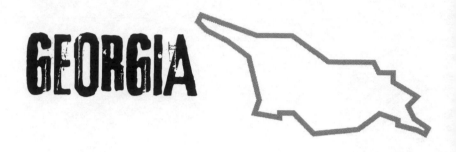

'll put my cards on the table: just a few months ago I didn't own any Georgian music and couldn't have introduced you to any. Now I have an expanding collection, I'm passionate about the music and have a sneaking fascination for this ancient culture.

The Caucasus Mountains (the highest mountains in Europe) stretch between the Black Sea and the Caspian Sea, forming a barrier between the Russian Federation and the states of Georgia and Azerbaijan. Just to the south lies the small state of Armenia. The location of these three countries makes them a natural buffer between the three giants Russia, Turkey and Iran. And many wars have been fought in the past on Georgian soil as neighbouring powers have vied for supremacy over the region.

One legacy of Georgia's history is cultural diversity. As well as those Russians, Armenians and other communities who've come and settled, the majority Georgian population is itself a composite of many communities each with their own traditions, different dialects, and in some cases their own ancient languages, preserved over the centuries.

Another legacy, equally important, is a strong distinctive national culture. The Georgian language has ancient roots, it's very different from that of its neighbours and has its own writing

ELE-MELE KISMETI	Tutarchela
DAIMOHK	Aznach Ensemble
RA LAMAZIA TUSHETI	Lela Tataraidze & Kesane
MTIELTA TAMASHOBA	Les Soeurs Gogochurebi

system: Georgian script, one of only 14 alphabets in the world today. The Georgian Orthodox Church is one of the earliest Christian churches in the world: Christianity was adopted as the state religion of what was then the Iberian kingdom in 337 AD. By the fifth century the Bible had been translated in Georgian, which was crucial in consolidating the language. There are churches and monasteries in towns and on top of hills all over the country, many of them centuries old.

Georgian nationalists have always allied themselves closely with the language and the Church. In the run up to independence in 1991 dissidents such as Zviad Gamsakhurdia spoke about how the suppression of the language and Church under the Soviets was inextricably linked to the suppression of the people. (Ironically the man who bears most responsibility for this, Joseph Stalin, was born in Gori in central Georgia.) Today a large majority of Georgians identify themselves with the Orthodox Church, and a significant minority attend services and rituals. For many of them the Church provides a connection with traditional culture. This connection is key to understanding why Georgian polyphonic singing has such strong and enduring appeal.

Polyphonic singing is an important part of many cultures,

notably in Eastern Europe and Russia, but it's in Georgia that it's left its strongest legacy. The word polyphony just means multiple voices, but in polyphonic singing there are not just multiple voices but also multiple melodic lines which come together to create a harmonically unified whole. This could be two sets of voices, or three, or four, or even more. Within Georgia there are all kinds of different forms of polyphonic singing, with different styles associated with different regions. The most common form though is three-part singing. You'll hear three voices, or sets of voices, chanting, perhaps one and a half octaves apart. One or possibly two voices will 'take the lead', effectively turning the chant into a song.

If you've encountered Georgian singing before, you probably heard the Ensemble Rustavi who announced themselves to the world with their Georgian Voices album in 1989, on the Nonesuch label. Or it may have been Table Songs of Georgia by the Tsinandali Choir, released in Georgia in 1988 and distributed internationally through Peter Gabriel's Real World label five years later. The booming male voices make a powerful impression. While some of the songs are devotional, many are secular.

The small town of Rustavi is dwarfed by a massive Soviet-era metallurgical plant, a reminder of its chequered past. Although a village with the same name had stood on the Mtkvari River since long before the birth of Christ, the town was razed to the ground by invading Mongols in the 13th century, leaving nothing behind. The modern town was built with the aid of labour from German POWs to help meet the needs of Soviet heavy industry during World War II and beyond. As a centre for traditional music, it didn't seem a very promising location. But even in a place such as this, that sense of spiritual connection to one's ancestors, and to a shared history, had survived. The Ensemble Rustavi (founded 1968) paved the way for others to follow. In 2004, Tamar Buadze formed the all-female choir Tutarchela. An all-female choir was nothing new – Tamar Buadze had led one or two of them herself –

but Tutarchela was notable for its range of registers which enabled it to cover tracks traditionally sung by men. The choir is largely made up of graduates of the Tbilisi State Conservatoire, and most of them play Georgian folk instruments such as the panduri, chonguri and doli. Equipped with this and with the considerable vocal talents of lead singer Nana Shanidze they're able to take on a very broad repertoire. On **ELE-MELE KISMETI**, though, we find them singing unaccompanied, it's delivered with a perfect control matched only by the purity of the women's voices.

Now four stunning new compilations of Georgian and Caucasian music have opened the lid on a treasure trove of sounds previously inaccessible to western ears. First we have Songs of Survival: Traditional Music of Georgia, and Songs of Defiance: Music of Chechnya and the North Caucasus (both released by Topic in 2007), then The Sounds of Georgia on Vincent Moon's Petites Planètes and Mountains of Tongues: Musical Dialects of the Caucasus (L.M. Dupli-cation), both released in late 2013.

The Topic CDs were compiled by Michael Church, an experienced British world music journalist, and together they really give you a sense of the multitude of ethnic groups and folk styles in this small area of the world. Writing later about his adventures, Church recalled with particular fondness his encounter with the Aznach Ensemble:

"My most memorable Chechen encounter comes in Georgia, where the tribe from which the Aznach Ensemble is drawn have lived since their ancestors were deported in the nineteenth century. And what Aznach purveys is Chechen music in its purest, most electrifying form. The group consists of four women, including a mother and two daughters, with a balalaika for colour, and an accordion – the Chechens' favourite instrument – for ballast and momentum. But when mild-mannered 20-year-old Tamta Khangoshvili opens her mouth to sing, she's as though

possessed: her naturally soft timbre hardens to a guttural shout...

They drive an impressively hard-nosed bargain before departing for their eyrie in the mountains, but since they've given me one of the least expected musical thrills of my life, I'm more than happy to stump up. What made my encounter with Aznach particularly poignant was that it had taken place in the Georgian capital, Tbilisi: the driven austerity of their music was in stark contrast to the confident ease of performers on these southern slopes of the Caucasus." [1]

With voices like these you don't want a lot of instrumentation, but the accordion provides a perfect complement on **DAIMOHK**.

If I can be permitted to include one more accordion-led song, it will have to be this one by Lela Tataraidze and her Kasane Quartet. Lela is from Tusheti, a mountainous region on Georgia's northeastern border, and she has become the voice of Tusheti, her haunting songs its soundtrack. **RA LAMAZIA TUSHETI**, I understand, means 'How beautiful is Tusheti'.

The Sayat Nova project is a non-profit initiative by two Americans and one Gibraltarian who set out to document the musical dialects of the Caucasus. Some of the results can be heard on Mountains of Tongues. It's an eclectic and interesting mix. Many languages are represented, including a couple that have rarely ever been recorded (Lezgi and Batsbi); and a wide variety of folk instruments are on show. Stefan Williamson-Fa believes that we have a tendency to label and pigeonhole music that we associate with particular countries, and this is something that he wanted to get away from:

"Obviously in the post-Soviet period there's lots of nation building and nationalism, and that's affected everything that goes on there in many ways. But even outside [the region], if you go to any record shop, if they have a CD

on anything to do with the Caucasus, it'll be Georgian polyphony music, or Azerbaijani mugam, or Armenian duduk. That's always the way the world music industry works, it's always in terms of countries and fixed and bounded groups, and the more we engaged with musicians in the region, the more we realised that's not the way it works. [That model] hardly works anywhere – it's not like that most places in the world – but especially in that part of the world, which is so ethnically diverse and has a history of extreme multiculturalism and contact between people and religions and ethnic groups and languages. So that triggered us to try and think of ways of dealing with this music that didn't just repeat these ideas.

Originally we were thinking about stuff like working with ethnic minorities in Georgia, but then we realised that even by focusing on minorities or ethnic groups as bounded groups as well, you're still promoting that idea of distinct cultures. So obviously what we've done so far isn't perfect, but the idea is to get to the point where we're promoting discussion, and an idea of interaction as opposed to separation." [2]

I don't go along with this entirely. I think it's fair to say that there are distinct cultures which may be associated with particular regions or ethnic groups, and to seek to preserve aspects of these cultures where oral tradition is seen to be dead or dying. Understanding these cultures can inform and enrich dialogues about nationalism. Sayat Nova are right however to point to the fact that every culture is a complex amalgam of influences and is ever-changing in its fluidity.

The Vincent Moon compilation is a digital album, downloadable from Bandcamp on a 'name your price' basis. There are 50 songs on it, which seems a lot, but I can honestly say there's little on there that I'm not happy to keep. The collection seems well representative of different regions and different traditional genres. One band in particular drew my attention: the Gogochurebi Sisters (Debi Gogochurebi). They are four young sisters from Khevsureti, a mountainous region adjacent to Tusheti but even more remote. Shatili – an eighth-century village on the Chechen border remarkable for its fortified stone towers – is inaccessible six months of the year, and reachable in the summer months only after a long hair-raising drive. The Khevsurs were once a warrior people and their history is preserved in songs and ballads. The sisters come from a large musical family – they say on their Facebook page that their grandmother helped them to recover old folklore.

MTIELTA TAMASHOBA (Mountain Song) isn't among the half dozen sisters' songs recorded by Vincent Moon. It's on a CD not available outside the region. But I have to include it here because the song's lodged itself inside my heart. The sisters play their three-stringed panduris as though their lives depend on it, and the pace gets gradually faster. For this isn't music to sit and admire – it's music to dance to.

NOTES

1. https://freemuse.org/news/chechnya-recording-songs-of-defiance-and-survival/
2. http://thequietus.com/articles/14268-caucasus-music-interview-mountains-of-tongues

GERMANY

The Deutsches Volksliedarchiv, Germany's national folk song archive, marked its centenary in 2014 by changing its name. It's now called the Centre for Popular Culture and Music. Director Michael Fischer is unapologetic. "We're not an archive," he says, "we're a research institute, and we study different forms of popular music." Later in the same interview he makes a more unguarded comment. "An institute," he says, "must address socially relevant issues, and traditional folk music simply doesn't form part of the national conversation." [1]

John Meier, who founded the Archive, must have turned in his grave. Meier was a folklorist who dedicated his life to preserving the German and Swiss folk heritage. He understood that a culture's value is not a transitory quality, and that research, recording and preservation work becomes more, not less, important when the culture that you're studying is threatened or dying.

What is indisputable is that Germany's centuries-old tradition of volkslieder (folk songs) is not looking too healthy right now. There's a lot of history to this, but the root problem can be stated very succinctly: at different times folk music has been utilised by German nationalists to promote particular ideas about German national identity.

MÖNCH UND NONNE	*Zupfgeigenhansel*
IN A FREMBER SCHTOT	*Jontef*
WANDRERS NACHTLIED, EIN GLEICHES	*Hüsch!*
TURLHOFER	*Zwirbeldirn*

In the 19th century supporters of German unification were divided as to what it was that they wanted: a federal approach that respected cultural differences and different tongues, or the promotion of the national idea through getting people to speak one language and bonding them to a common culture. Folk song collectors like Ludwig Erk and Franz Magnus Böhme purported to be revealing a shared national heritage. They would certainly have been aware of the song collections published a century earlier by Johann Gottfried Herder, who saw the importance of popular culture, hence his use of the term 'volkslieder', songs of the people. But despite his strong belief in language as the basis of nationhood, Herder didn't try to isolate German songs.

By all accounts Erk and Böhme were pretty scrupulous: they wanted everything they published to be authentic, and they weren't averse, either, to including non-German material. But their system of song classification overlooked one obvious issue: in the field, these songs were almost all performed in regional dialect and bore the hallmarks of the local region. So when anthologies of published folk songs started to come out this regional specificity was glossed over by the editors. These collections were all in High German, with songs selected to conform to a nostalgic view of rural life.

It was no accident that the Archive was founded in 1914. The link had now been made between folk music and the idea of a strong, united Germany; and the nationalist pot was being vigorously stirred. In the 1920s, Meier's organisation embarked on a highly ambitious project, documenting folk songs from every region of Germany and publishing them in a multi-volume series. Although each region received separate treatment the whole idea was of a national project which would reaffirm German identity.

Hitler and the Nazis borrowed various nationalist stereotypes and ideas that were in common currency and wove them into their ideology. In so far as volkslieder didn't conflict with the Nazi idea of das volk – their racist conception of the German people – they found that folk song had its uses. Workers' songs were not tolerated, even songs in regional dialect were frowned upon, but some old songs were given the Nazi treatment and sung at Hitler Youth rallies. The extent to which John Meier was personally compromised by all this is a matter for debate, but he remained as director of the Archive throughout the Nazi years.

In the postwar decades, German folk music fell into disrepute. It carried too much baggage with it from the Nazi era: even terms like 'volk' and 'volksmusik' had become toxic. In time volksmusik came to denote something different: a brand name of convenience for the folk-pop hybrid also known as volkstümliche musik; derided by many music lovers for its crude commercialism, its sentimentality and its plonk-plonk rhythms. These groups have given us some volkslied, but shorn of its historical context: barely a trace remains of the original singing styles and dialects.

The 1970s did see a folk revival in Germany, but from the start it was much weaker than in a number of other western countries. Groups identified with the revival included Zupfgeigenhansel, Elster Silberflug, Fiedel Michel and Liederjan, the twin brothers Hein & Oss, and the singers Hannes Wader and (from the East) Wolf Biermann.

Zupfgeigenhansel and Liederjan both released a series of albums in which they tried to reclaim the term volkslied. The Zupfgeigenhansel albums are a joy to explore: it's like a light going on as you realise that there are all these sides to German folk music which have been quietly forgotten about in the course of the 20th century. There's anger in these songs, and passion too; there's a sense of history and time and place; and there's wit and scabrous humour. From Volkslieder I, **MÖNCH UND NONNE** is a 17th-century song about a monk and a nun who have intimate relations in a church. The lyrics are packed with double meanings, but the band don't ram this down your throat – the singing is elegant and melodic.

Erich Schmeckenbecher believes that "there is no future without a past". [2] The need to access our cultural roots is deep within us. When Erich and Thomas Friz formed Zupfgeigenhansel they named the group after an old songbook by Hans Breuer which had inspired them. In so doing they advertised their link to the German youth movement of the early 20th century with its romantic ideals. Their achievement was to show that romanticism is not the same thing as sentimentality and is not lacking in intellectual depth.

The hope ignited by these albums was shortlived: the stigma affecting German folk music wasn't so easily banished. I'd be interested in hearing from any current German folk singers whose repertoire includes folk songs retrieved from Erk and Böhme or from the Volksliedarchiv, or who've organised any volkslied festivals for traditional song enthusiasts – but given how little I've found, I'm not holding out much hope of this.

Does this invalidate Erich Schmeckenbecher's belief that people have a need to connect with their cultural roots? Not at all. There's no absence of desire in Germany to feel rooted. The 21st century has seen a dramatic increase in women wearing dirndl and men wearing lederhosen at Oktoberfest, especially in Bavaria. Then there's the extraordinary popularity of Irish music in Germany. There's more here than the pull of an exotic foreign culture. What makes Irish music special for so many people is its authenticity, its rootedness in tradition. And Germans have embraced this in a big way. Irish folk groups are everywhere in Germany – not only that, but they seem to be maturing and well on the way to developing their own styles. Here's Marcus Metz, guitarist with the Irish traditional outfit An Tor:

"In the 1990s Pogues-like folk rock bands were very popular. It seems this is out of fashion. After an enduring time of languish, there are newly arrived groups playing traditional Irish music. The number of people showing up at folk concerts and the number of people attending folk music workshops is not too bad. There are a lot of beginners that want to play the tin whistle, the fiddle or the bodhrán, and there are many fresh faces. This is fine, even if young people are missing somehow. The youngest of the established players are beyond thirty, and the new students are no teenagers either, but forty or fifty years of age when discovering Irish music. However, our own offspring… is growing up with Irish music. Maybe this is the next generation." [3]

Where there is a disconnect it's with the German national idea, which is coming under sustained assault. Popular support for EU membership, and all the obligations which go with it, is at very high levels. Like its European neighbours, Germany is changing: in 2017 it was calculated that 22.5% of the population were first- or second-generation immigrants with at least one parent born without German citizenship. One and a half million Turkish citizens live in Germany, and there are probably as many again German citizens of Turkish origin (such as the footballer Mesut Özil). They have a big stake in German society, but of course they have their own music and culture.

A recent compilation album, Songs of Gastarbeiter –

Vol. 1, documented some of the early history of this wave of immigration. West Germany began recruiting men from Turkey as extra labour for its booming economy back in the early 1960s. The term gastarbeiter was coined to describe this reserve army of labour, and for the first couple of decades the term seemed to fit: they were guest workers, most of whom planned to return home at the end of their contracts. Life for them was no bed of roses – working in menial, low-paid jobs, living in dormitories or barracks half a continent away from their families, and often the target of racism. The opening track by Ozan Ata Canani, rerecorded for this album, is a homage to these men: the cleaners, the welders, the railway workers.

Most of the songs are in Turkish. As the album's co-compiler Imran Ayata puts it, "whether I'm singing in Turkish or in my Zazaki mother tongue, it's part of German culture." [4] It's unlikely that many people would have made such a strong assertion back then. Yüksel Özkasap was known as the nightingale of Cologne, but her name was little known outside the Turkish community. Her songs are laden with homesickness and nostalgia. Other artists who appear on the compilation reflect the German experience in different ways. So while in general it may have been true that the community listened to Turkish music by Turkish artists, the seeds of a new culture were already starting to germinate.

By the 1980s, the new communities were setting down their roots. Migrant organisations sprang up, and many of them organised folk dance or baglama courses, while at night people would go and dance to the music in Turkish clubs. [5] Kurds and other ethnic groups would each have their own entertainment. There was quite a range of music, but the common factor was the baglama (or saz), the long-necked lute which is Turkey's national instrument.

In the 1990s, second-generation immigrants gave the German-Turkish experience a new voice through hip hop. Hip hop likes to style itself as a ghetto music, and German hip hop it seems is no exception, but what these sons and daughters of immigrants were doing was more akin to breaking down the walls of the ghetto. Their records sold well both in Turkey and in Germany. Fluent in Americanised 'gangsta' cliches, they were becoming part of Germany's urban youth culture, just as deserving of attention and respect as their peers. Even Kreuzberg, the Berlin suburb known as Little Istanbul because of its ghettoised Turkish community, "was transforming," we're told, "into a popular district thriving on cultural differences and alternative lifestyles. Even in the more marginal areas… immigrant youth are readily able to experience the cosmopolitan cultural life of Berlin." [6]

The pace of integration has quickened in the 21st century. A new generation of German Turks is growing up with greater language skills, greater identification with Germany. Intermarriage is becoming more common, and there is more cultural exchange between Turkish and native communities. Thanks to Turkish radio stations and Turkish weddings, it's no longer a rarity for ethnic Germans to become exposed to Turkish music and culture. Second- and third-generation Turks meanwhile are just as likely to be into pop, rock or electronic music as they are to the sound of the baglama. The signs are though that the baglama is there to stay. In February 2013, the Landesmusikrat Berlin named the baglama its instrument of the year. Over the year a number of concerts, workshops and masterclasses were organised to showcase the instrument, and in September 2013, Berlin hosted an international baglama symposium. But just as significant as any of this was the recognition that the baglama was a part of German culture, deserving of protection and support.

Music is a powerful force in the drive to integrate Germany's large immigrant communities. We see some of this in the amount of fusion music that's being made: artists flipping between genres, using unfamiliar instruments, performing with musicians from other cultures and other countries. It's led to a rich and vibrant world music scene in Germany, with bold, innovative bands – such as 17 Hippies – who play music from around the world on a crazy array of instruments, including at various times banjo, ukulele, double bass, guitar, violin, cello, accordion, clarinet, trumpet and trombone; or Willy Schwarz's Bremer Stadtimmigranten Orchester, an exciting combination of 11 musicians from nine countries all stretching their musical boundaries; or Bavaria's LaBrassBanda, a full-throttle brass band whose influences include Balkan gypsy music, ska, reggae, funk and techno.

Angela Merkel said at a meeting in 2010 that the idea of people from different cultural backgrounds living side by side didn't work, and that multiculturalism had failed in Germany. She should reflect on the fact that Jewish klezmer music is enjoying a revival – thanks largely to the interest of Germany's gentile population. The great Israeli klezmer clarinetist Giora Feidman, who performed on the soundtrack of the film Schindler's List, was invited to perform at a theatrical production in Berlin in 1984. One thing led to another, and he ended up returning to Germany many times. He speaks very affectionately of the country:

> "Fortunately, I speak the language of music, and the entire planet is my home. However, my homeland, Israel, has something unique, both in its human qualities, and in its history. The second place that fascinates me is Germany. I'm at home here, because I am a Jew. And I love the relationship between Germans and Jews, which has nothing to do with the past, but is in the here and now. Of course, both nations respect the past and teach their children the history. But we all want to live in peace. I love it in Germany, as the people pay attention to my music when I'm on stage." [7]

According to a New York Times article about the klezmer revival, there are more than 100 klezmer bands in Germany – "This summer in Berlin one could hear the music performed every night of the week. Record sales are strong, and festivals and workshops have multiplied… Among the Jewish-music events this summer was Klezmer Wochen Weimar (Weimar Klezmer Weeks), a month-long festival and workshop in its fourth season. More than 160 participants, mostly German musicians in their 20s and 30s, came to study Yiddish song, Yiddish language, instrumental music and traditional dance from a mostly American-Jewish faculty." [8] Yes, that's right: those now learning Yiddish include a significant number of non-Jews. What's their motivation? Yiddish is a language very close to German, reflecting the deep European roots of the Ashkenazi Jews. So it's possible that Yiddish may help some Germans to connect with their own history. It's also possible that the beautiful klezmer music has touched their soul…

You'd need a heart of stone not to be touched by Jontef's instrumental number **IN A FREMDER SCHTOT**. Hans Joachim Günther plays a haunting melody on his clarinet before the music speeds up and we're invited to dance. The band are from the southern town of Tübingen (which has its crosses to bear: the Tübingen synagogue was burned in Kristallnacht in 1938). Singer Michael Chaim Langer is an Israeli immigrant. His father had grown up in the Krakow ghetto and, while still a teenager, miraculously survived five Nazi concentration camps. The experience was so harrowing that he couldn't talk about it, even to his family, until the age of 40. On stage Jontef regale their audiences with Yiddish anecdotes and humour, but they also play their part in ensuring that the history of the Holocaust is never forgotten.

But what of indigenous German folk music – is there such a thing, and can its credibility and popularity ever be rebuilt?

Hüsch! are three men and a woman who would tell you that it can. The idea for the band came about, we're told, during the Thüringer Waldzither Symposium in 2013. A waldzither, in case you're wondering, is a stringed instrument native to the Thüringer region, which had been in serious danger of dying out until Martina Rosenberger took it on herself to research the instrument and then to start organising these symposiums.

Hüsch! want to reclaim folk music from commercialism and patriotism. Why? Because they see it as part of their identity. Hüsch! are one band who take their research seriously, using "songs in dialect (Hennebergisch and Vogtländisch), which have either found their way into the repertoire by oral tradition or have been unearthed in archives (thanks to the Volkskundliche Beratungs- und Informationsstelle für Thüringen)." [9] That said, the band do give the material a modern makeover, rearranging the songs to make full use of the wide range of instruments at their disposal.

WANDRERS NACHTLIED is a famous poem by Goethe first set to music by Franz Schubert. In the context of the album it arrives like a moment of stillness and reflection: the spotlight focuses on the figure of Hanna Flock, singing and playing piano, with only minimal support from the rest of the band. Hanna tells me that Ilmenau, where the group are based, was a place to which Goethe often used to come for work and recreation. Today Goethe heritage is a big deal in Ilmenau, and that's how the group came to be commissioned to set the poem again to music.

Goethe became especially attached to the Kickelhahn, the highest mountain in the area. For him this was a place of peace, an escape from the noise and confusion of the city. A small hunting cabin was erected in a place with spectacular views close to the summit of the mountain, and it was in this place, on the night of 6th/7th September 1780, that he wrote the words to the poem. The cabin was burned down in 1870 but faithfully rebuilt four years later.

"So we went there," recalls Hanna, "as we had done many times before, but with a very special attention to the poem's words – 'The silence above the hilltops, not even a waft or whiff of anything, the birds stay silent; wait – soon you'll also rest.'" The reference to resting is ambiguous – is this a state of being, or death? Hanna believes he was talking about inner peace. A few years earlier, on the slopes of Ettersberg near the town of Weimar,

Goethe has written another poem with the same title in which he expressed his craving for peace. The group combined the two poems, noting the emotional shift that took place between them. "Playing the song live I first have to concentrate on this inner peace to play soft and slow, calm and peaceful." [10]

Bavaria is particularly proud of its traditions, so what better place to look than the Bavarian capital, Munich. Here I came across a troubling article in Das Spiegel about the last folk music degree course in Germany. [11] The course has been offered since 1963 by the arts university Hochschule für Musik und Theater München. Students can learn to play the dulcimer and zither, and research Bavarian dancing and yodelling. Lecturer Josef Hornsteiner bemoans the fact that the genre's reputation as a serious discipline for study has been ruined by the commercialised volksmusik that's played on the radio and TV. For him, folk music means something very different: music made and sung by ordinary people using their own resources. The article, which was written in 2012, struck a pessimistic tone: at that time the course had just six students and its future seemed uncertain.

Since the article was written, though, Hornsteiner has retired and his position's been taken by Simone Lautenschlager. An accomplished clarinetist, she's a member of Niederbayerische Musikantenstammtisch, a loose-knit group, based in Munich, of young musicians who play lively tavern music on brass and accordions, taking their repertoire from old Lower Bavarian folk tunes. She's also a member of the quartet Die Singermaschin which I mention because, also in this group, is Evi Keglmaier of the band Zwirbeldirn.

Zwirbeldirn was formed by three women: Evi Keglmaier, Maria Hafner and Beatrix Klöckner, who all sing and play violin and viola. They teamed up with a man: bassist Simon Ackermann (who we're told doesn't sing!). Klöckner later left the band to be replaced by the equally talented Sophie Meier-Rastl. Like Niederbayerische Musikantenstammtisch, they're young, they're Munich based, and they're trying to make Bavarian folk music fresh and exciting. Keglmaier acknowledges that the term volksmusik is problematic because it's used to refer to different things, but she doesn't shy away from it: "We describe what we do as folk music. Only we're the good guys." [12]

TÜRLHOFER is from the group's second album, Jabitte, released in 2014. The strings are kept on a tight leash: this is punchy tavern music with a chorus that's meant to be sung along to. The album which was recorded live in the studio is surprisingly diverse, including yodels and songs taken from old manuscripts, songs from Europe and South America, and even a blues number. They're a band that follow their musical instincts without being constrained by tradition, and this is part of their attraction: the idea that folk music doesn't have to be a reverential thing following certain rules and performed in dirndls and traditional dress. Right now Zwirbeldirn are just one more little-known band in a crowded marketplace vying to be noticed. But there are people going to their concerts who've grown up in the years since reunification, for whom folk music has never been a part of their lives, and now it means something to them; and it's in this that we can glimpse the possibility that German folk music can have a future as well as a past.

NOTES

1. http://www.badische-zeitung.de/kultur-sonstige/wir-sind-kein-museum-fuer-volkslieder--86872724.html
2. http://www.erich-schmeckenbecher.de/erich/
3. http://www.folkworld.eu/34/e/girish.html
4. http://www.tagesspiegel.de/kultur/neues-album-songs-of-gastarbeiter-melodien-der-malocher/8981930.html
5. Martin Greve – Migration of Music from Turkey to Germany https://heimatkunde.boell.de/2011/11/18/migration-von-musik-aus-der-tuerkei-nach-deutschland
6. Serhat Güney, Cem Pekman & Bülent Kabas – Diasporic Music in Transition: Turkish Immigrant Performers on the Stage of "Multikulti"

Berlin (2012) http://www.tandfonline.com/doi/abs/10.1080/03007766.201
2.736288# subscription required

7. http://www.mainpost.de/regional/schweinfurt/Interview-Giora-Feidman-
   Der-ganze-Planet-ist-mein-Zuhause;art742,7768484
8. http://www.nytimes.com/2004/08/29/arts/music-klezmer-s-final-frontier.
   html
9. http://www.songs-of-heimat.de/index.php/die-band/
10. Email from Hanna Flock 22/10/17
11. http://www.spiegel.de/unispiegel/studium/die-uni-muenchen-hat-
    deutschlands-einzigen-studiengang-volksmusik-a-822362.html
12. http://www.deutschlandradiokultur.de/portraet-zwirbeldirn-die-
    avantgarde-der-volksmusik.2177.de.html?dram%3Aarticle_id=301142

GREECE

I wasn't planning to mention the culture of the Ancient Greeks. It was only when I started to research Greek folk dancing that I really began to appreciate its relevance. There are thousands of Greek folk dances that have been documented in modern times; these folk dances are very much a product of Greece's long history, and without the folk dancing a lot of folk music simply wouldn't exist. Just as importantly, there are musicians and artists in the 21st century who feel strongly that the ancient culture is part of their identity, and who in some cases are keen to learn more about it and to lay claim to it.

There is a schism that runs through Ancient Greek culture between the Apollonian and the Dionysian. In Greek mythology, Apollo and Dionysus were both sons of Zeus. Whereas Apollo was seen as representing the power of reason and order, Dionysus stood for the supremacy of emotion and was associated with the wild and the orgiastic. When the Ancient Greeks were creating masterpieces of art and literature they looked to their gods to show them the way. There was the wild physicality of Dionysian ritual dance, there were also circle dances whose order and precision was thought to mirror the harmony of the celestial order. Dance was integral to Greek drama, its rising status

ANAMESA NISSIROU	Kristi Stassinopoulou & Stathis Kalyviotis
MIKRO MOU KASTELORIZO	Euaggelia Xenopoulou
DEN PAIZO PETRA SE DENTRO	Psarantonis
PENTOZALI	Kostis Mouzourakis
ARAPÍNA MOU SKERTSÓZA	Kompania

reinforced by scholarly articles by the critic-philosophers Plato and Aristotle who viewed it as an essential part of education. The chorus in Greek drama didn't just comment on the action: the players would dance and sing their lines. Music, poetry and dancing were all closely interlinked, valued and respected, and to all intents and purposes had become high culture.

The contribution of the Ancient Greeks to music alone was immense. They gave us a lot of the musical terminology that we use today. Their ideas and writings on music were profoundly influential and still have a resonance today: the entire discipline of music therapy has its origins in the theories of the Ancient Greeks about the healing power of music. Byzantine music, whose influence stretched across the Eastern Mediterranean region for hundreds of years, was founded on principles established by the Ancient Greeks.

Greek ethnomusicologists used to believe that there was such a thing as a 'pure' Greek folk music descended from ancient and Byzantine traditions. It's nonsense, of course: music is continually changing as it adapts to new influences, and in over two millennia there have been a lot of changes. But all the same there is something special and unique about Greek folk music. I have to make a distinction here: in Greece there's a big gulf between urban and rural music. It's in the rural areas where the older song and dance traditions can be found – the dimotika songs of the countryside and the nisiotika music of the islands. I'll be discussing these first, before taking a look at the comparatively modern urban-based tradition of rebetika.

What's fascinating about the rural folk music isn't its uniformity but quite the opposite: it encompasses numerous regional and local traditions. Every region, and to a large extent every island, has its own traditional dances, and the character of the music changes with the dances, the instruments used, the singing techniques, and so on. This tells us something important, something that's hard to grasp on to at a time when boatloads of desperate refugees are arriving on the shores of Greek islands on a daily basis: for centuries these have been very settled, rooted communities which, despite being part of a maritime culture, mostly had little or no experience of mass immigration and retained their community traditions and ways of life well into the 20th century.

There are an abundance of good-quality recordings of Greek folk music. All of these series – though not every individual album – are available on iTunes: the Guardians of Hellenism series, some 14 CDs surveying the different regions; Ta Nisiotika, two CDs of folk songs; The Greek Folk Instruments, 12 CDs of instrumental music; Bagpipes of Greece, five CDs – not to be confused with the album on Topic which is also called Bagpipes of Greece. Exploring them was a fun task, but as I did so I began to ask myself some questions. Where were the CD reviews? Where were the record company blurbs copied from site to site? And who were the artists, none of whom seemed to have any kind of internet footprint?

It was as though the artists and their music were invisible. Clearly, what I was listening to weren't commercial recordings aimed at a mass market: they were recordings made by musicologists or possibly folk enthusiasts, with the aim of making a permanent record of regional styles which were in long-term decline, and at the same time to make the best of these recordings available to interested parties. Although there's still – at least until quite recently – enough good music around to fill all of these albums, it's a music that's marginalised and unfashionable. There's no money to be made from traditional music, hence the absence of record labels and of professional musicians.

Each CD would have required an investment of time and money to bring it into being. It's not music that's landed on someone's desk: soneone would have had to believe in the music in the first place, enough to go and seek it out. Domna Samiou (1928–2012) was a great believer. Her parents introduced her to folk music from a young age, and in her mid-20s she was lucky enough to land a job working in radio in Athens where she would often see folk musicians coming into the studios to record. Most would have been content to learn about folk music this way, but not Domna: she began travelling to rural areas, recording traditional song for her own personal archive. After a few years of this she gave up the radio station job so she could spend more time singing and carrying on with her fieldwork. Kristi Stassinopoulou remembers her fondly as a performer: "A woman with great passion in all her activities and goals and with a very good taste in music. All the albums she left us are treasures." But even more precious is her extensive archive of recordings: "the songs she was revealing from the past, and recording are real diamonds." [1]

Unlike Domna, Kristi Stassinopoulou and Stathis Kalyviotis were latecomers to folk music. Both were city kids who started out playing rock music. "Stathis was one of the first punks in Athens," Kristi laughingly remembers. They were in different bands when their paths crossed and they decided to make music together. According to Stathis, the idea of performing traditional songs didn't take root until some years later:

"Speaking for myself it was never 'back to' anything. I grew up with the music of the city, with rock, with funk. For me 'traditional' was something that I discovered in my 20s. Nobody in my circle knew about it. It was something new... I have an uncle who is from Pontus and we went to his house and he put on music from Pontus. It had a very strong beat. I heard it and I said, 'Oh my god, this is punk rock!' So for me it was new." [2]

Kristi on the other hand had been into traditional music before she met Stathis. However, as she told Ian Anderson:

"That was the time of the Greek junta, and unfortunately Greek traditional music had been used as a means of nationalist propaganda, and this made a large amount of people, mainly the people of the left, against traditional music. So I was afraid to even admit that I loved traditional music, because they would say 'you're nationalistic'." [3]

They both began to listen to a lot of folk songs and Byzantine music. The work and recordings of Domna Samiou proved a fertile source, but they also found that even though there was no folk music industry to speak of, there was still a living tradition in many rural areas which could be experienced by attending local feast days (panigiria). They made a series of albums which did very well in the world music charts, blending traditional and contemporary sounds using modern production techniques. Greekadelia (2012) was of most interest to me, because the production was less intrusive and there was more focus on capturing the essence of traditional songs. ANAMESA NISSIROU, a traditional song from the Dodecanese islands about sailors praying to their patron saint Archangel Michael Panormitis to save them from sinking in the Aegean waves, has acquired a new eerie relevance as a result of the 2015 refugee crisis.

I asked Kristi for her thoughts on folk dance. In her reply it was apparent just how much it had meant to her to attend panigiria and to experience the music in its traditional context:

> "Most of these demotika dances are in circles. So they are totally communal dances. We hold each other by the hands, or we embrace the shoulders of each other and then, we all step the dance round and round, following the same music, the same rhythm and speed, the same breathing. It's like a whole community breathing together. Our vibes of joy, of pain, of passion, resonate in such a way, that the circle becomes like one being. This unification feeling that arises cannot be observed from the outside, but can only be felt and experienced once you try it yourself." [4]

She also told me that traditional song is no longer seen as a taboo subject, that increasing numbers of younger and older musicians are becoming interested in it. But Kristi and Stathis have decided to move on: at the time of writing they're working on an album of songs written by Kristi.

The second featured song is also from the Dodecanese islands. In 2015, thousands of (mainly Syrian) refugees made the short journey from Turkey to the main Dodecanese islands en route to what they hoped was a safe haven somewhere in Europe. International TV crews who'd come to the islands by safer means recorded their arrival. Europeans who looked closely at the maps must have scratched their heads: how did these islands just off the Turkish coast come to be a part of Europe? It turns out that these islands situated at the gateway between continents have seen their share of refugees before. In 1922, thousands fled from Asia Minor after the city of Smyrna (now Izmir) was destroyed by fire. Those who stayed in the

Dodecanese helped to change the islands' culture: Asia Minor songs were added to the traditional canon, and the violin was adopted by musicians in several islands, in preference to the traditional lyra. [5]

We can hear the violin – and the Middle Eastern nuances – on **MIKRO MOU KASTELORIZO**. Kastelorizo is the smallest of the Dodecanese with a population of just 492 in 2011, and Euaggelia Xenopoulou has for many years been at the forefront of preserving the island's music and dance traditions and, by the sound of it, is something of an unofficial cultural ambassador.

Greece's largest island, Crete, also has long developed music traditions, although its roots and influences are not dissimilar to the rest of Greece. Crete was once home to the Minoan civilisation, and the Ancient Greeks certainly knew of and respected these people who had used written language and used song and dance in acts of worship over 1,000 years earlier. Today the emblem of Cretan music is the lyra, but various other instruments are played, of which the most important is the laouto (long-necked lute). Crete can also boast several categories of dances (both fast and slow) and several different song forms.

When I said that traditional music is marginalised and unfashionable, Crete is the exception. The Aerakis store in Heraklion is a great source of Cretan music old and new, and it even has its own record label. In recent decades the music and dance scene has remained active and dynamic, and young musicians have stepped up as older ones have dropped out. And there is no better demonstration of the enduring strength of Cretan music than the Xylouris family.

Nikos 'Psaronikos' Xylouris (1936–80) rose to fame not just in Crete but across Greece in the late 1960s. He was a talented musician and singer who could sing many types of folk song. As his popularity rose, his songs became strongly identified with resistance to the Greek junta. To his younger brother, Antonis 'Psarantonis' Xylouris (born 1942), he was an idol: "He was the best one of all of us… He was complete with his appearance, his bravado, his pride – he had it all. That man had charisma." [6]

After the untimely death of his brother, Psarantonis kept making albums and growing as an artist, with his immediately identifiable voice and style establishing himself as the face of Cretan music. "Tradition is the root," he told anyone who would listen. "Without roots we can't have leaves, or fruit." [7] His genius though was to breathe life into tradition. Every time he picked up the lyra and sang, he brought the energy of that moment: "I never play a song exactly in the same way. If I play it again one time, it will not be the same. I decorate it, different each time." [8] He would sing with his eyes closed to help him connect with his inner emotions. He believed passionately that music had to come from within, it couldn't be taught in a school – "Don't listen to them who draw dots on a paper."

DEN PAIZO PETRA SE DENTRO is a beautiful song: there's so much tenderness and humanity in Psarantonis's deep husky voice, and the melody is beguiling too. Psarantonis still travels around the world to perform, very proud to represent Greek and Cretan music. And when he's eventually laid in his grave with his lyra, his legacy will still be strong. There's a third brother, Yiannis 'Psaroyiannis' Xylouris, who plays the lute. Both Antonis and Yiannis have children who are accomplished musicians: Antonis's son Giorgos (or 'Psarogiorgis') is internationally known for his lute playing, and two of his sons are regular members in his band.

Santorini appears on the map as another dot in the Aegean Sea south of Athens and north of Crete, part of the Cyclades islands. One of the island's few landmarks, jutting out from the top of a hill, is La Ponta, a 13th-century stone tower which was once part of the Castle of Akrotiri: a fortified settlement built to keep out marauding pirates. For a five year period this tower was to become host to an attraction which receives a startling number of rave reviews from its 40,000 visitors every year: a bagpipe exhibition and workshop.

Yiannis Pantazis had moved to Santorini in 2007 with his Greek-American wife, Argy Kakissis. For a couple of years he'd been researching the playing and the construction of the strange-looking Greek bagpipe, the tsabouna. On Santorini most locals told him that they had little knowledge of the instrument, but he persevered trying to track down old recordings. Then one day Argy rescued a chicken that had been trapped in a fence. As she got talking to the grateful owners she learned that there was a tsabouna player in the family. Before long Yiannis was giving lessons to the man's son. They built tsabounas together, making the best of the limited space they had. Then one day the young man brought Yiannis and Argy to the abandoned tower: this belonged to his family, he told them, why not use this for your workshop?

Of course Yiannis and Argy were entranced, and slowly a vision took shape – "We aimed to create a workshop, exhibition and performance space to showcase our beloved instrument – the Greek bagpipe – the tsabouna." [9] Investing their own money they remodelled the tower's interior. Visitors who came to the little island could now listen to Yiannis's stories about the history of the bagpipe, see for themselves how tsabounas are constructed and attend the regular concerts. "Last year, at the height of our success, we received the news that our lease in the tower was not going to be renewed. We soon seized on an opportunity to purchase new premises in the village of Megalochori, a 605 square meter turn-of-the-century winery that had lain empty for fifty years. And so, in 2018, we begin a new era..."

Tsabounas are traditionally made, not by specialised instrument makers, but by the players themselves. The bag is the skin of a whole goat, and the two other essential parts are a mouthpiece and a chanter with fingerholes. I'm not sure what a bagpipe expert would make of this, but it seems to me that this whole process gives the pipes of the Greek islands a special character and personality that is rooted in the soil. But judge for yourself. Kostis Mouzourakis plays his tsabouna a bit like a fiddle: it's a folk dance, he gives it all he's got, and you can almost see the dust rising as the tune gathers momentum. Kostis is from Crete, and the track PENTOZALI is from a compilation album called Bagpipes of the Aegean Sea, which the record label Aerakis tells us "is the recording of a concert held in Yéryeri, Crete, in August 2006" – hence the applause at the end.

At the start of this chapter I said that rebetika music was a comparatively modern tradition. That may be so, but part of its fascination today is its association with the urban underworld of the early 20th century: a world of hashish dens and whorehouses where fedora-clad men pick up their bouzoukis and sing of lost love and broken dreams. So the 2011 documentary film My Sweet Canary followed three young musicians from Israel, Turkey and Greece as they embarked on musical journeys to the roots of rebetika and learned about the life of one of its most famous icons, Roza Eskenazi.

Roza (mid-1890s–1980) was born in Constantinople to a Sephardic Jewish family. When she was a kid the family relocated to Thessaloniki and her parents took what low-paid work they could find to survive. As Roza grew into her teens a desire grew to become a singer and a dancer, even though her parents were vehemently opposed. At one time they were living in an apartment in Thessaloniki near the city's Grand Hotel Theatre, and they got to know some of the dancers there. Every day Roza would help two of the dancers carry their costumes to the theatre and dream of being on that stage herself. In her late teens she eloped with a wealthy man. He died young, leaving her with a tiny child. Roza persuaded the father's family to adopt the toddler, leaving her free to set out on her musical career.

We don't know much about the early part of her career, but Roza was getting work in theatres, taverns and clubs, she was singing and dancing, and it must have seemed as though much of what she'd dreamed of had come to pass. In fact she'd barely even begun. In 1929 she made her first recordings. Suddenly she was a popular star, one of the first commercially successful rebetika singers. She began performing nightly at the Taygetos nightclub in Athens, earning the kind of money that her parents had never seen in their lives. The recordings came thick and fast: Roza recorded over 500 songs in the 1930s alone, singing in Greek, Turkish, Arabic, Yiddish, Italian, Ladino and Armenian – a remarkable enough accomplishment in itself for a woman who'd never attended school and had only a basic education.

In the 1940s, her life turned on its head once more as Greece fell under Nazi occupation. Undaunted, Roza continued performing and even opened a nightclub with the son she had once abandoned, now reunited with her. For a time she was running incredible risks, concealing her Jewish identity, hiding Resistance fighters in her home and trying to protect those like her own family who were at risk of deportation to Auschwitz. After the war she never regained the level of fame and popularity she had once enjoyed, but she lived to see the birth of a rebetika revival in the 1970s. After her death, her partner Christos had her body buried in an unmarked grave in the village of Stomio. And there it lay until 2008 when the local community raised the money to erect a simple tombstone, with the legend 'Roza Eskenazi, Artist'.

Although rebetika's roots go back to the 19th century, the great wave of immigration from Smyrna and Asia Minor in 1923 clearly had a lot to do with its popularity in the ensuing years. The music itself wasn't imported – it was more like a cultural cocktail, typically performed in café amans where Greeks, Turks, Armenians and gypsies, would gather to eat, drink, take hash and play bouzouki music. While the music drew some of its form from the Turkish maqam, there were also influences from Greek folk music, European music, Byzantine chant, and so on. The social and ethnic makeup of the country was changing, and the culture was changing with it.

Today, love and knowledge of rebetika music is growing in Greece and internationally. Many artists incorporate rebetika songs in their repertoire, while a smaller number dedicate themselves to the old music. Appearing on the soundtrack of My Sweet Canary are Greek singers Maria Koti, Sotiris Papatragiannis and Katerina Tsiridou – Katerina Tsiridou is now the vocalist in the five-piece band Kompania; another new band with a foot in the past are Theodora Athanasiou's Apsilies.

ARAPÍNA MOU SKERTSÓZA is a Roza Eskenazi song, a love song for a dark-eyed girl. The vocals contain pain and hope in equal measure: they're complemented by the song's strong rhythm. On the album this is taken from, Round Trip, Kompania cover songs from other greats of rebetika's golden era such as Vasilis Tsitsanis and Kostas Skarvelis, alongside songs from a couple of lesser-known rebetika artists, and three traditional songs.

What does the future hold for Greek traditional musicians, at a time when state funding for arts and culture has been decimated as a result of the financial crisis? Kristi Stassinopoulou shrugs off the difficulties: "yes," she says, "it was a big gain when funding was secured in the 1990s for the teaching of traditional music in music schools. But that's all. Further than that… any state involvement in music and in culture in general, can only just destroy what is remaining of it. It destroys the joy and the authenticity, and turns everybody into PR, into bargaining for money and for positions." Musicians and artists, she believes, will survive this crisis as they have others in the past.

NOTES

1. Email 11/10/15
2. http://www.krististassinopoulou.com/greekadelia-interview-froots-dec-2012/
3. http://www.krististassinopoulou.com/froots-feature-march-2003/
4. Email 11/10/15
5. http://www.ohfs.org/newsletter/2002_first_quarter.html
6. http://neoskosmos.com/news/en/the-instrument-of-the-gods
7. Ibid
8. https://freegankolektiva.wordpress.com/2011/12/28/featured-artist-psarantonis-epitome-of-deep-rooted-tradition-and-genuine-innovation/
9. http://www.laponta.gr/our-journey/7-our-journey

HUNGARY

The revival of folk music and dance in Hungary got started on 6th May 1972. On this date members of four professional folk dance companies held Budapest's first tánchaz. Tánchaz literally means 'dance house': the word can refer to both the venue and the event, a social dance gathering. As a result of the tánchaz movement, instrumental dance music has become so integral to Hungarian music that it's impossible to imagine one without the other. Béla Bartók would be turning in his grave.

Béla Bartók (1881–1945) and Zoltán Kodály (1882–1967) are the two great folklorists whose names have long been synonymous with Hungarian folk music. The research that they did in the early years of the 20th century, when they recorded many thousands of folk songs using a phonograph, opened people's eyes and ears to the richness of peasant song tradition. They presented authentic village music as being a centuries-old vocal tradition, not to be confused with gypsy bands who played instrumental dance music. Today, of course, we would say that the music of those gypsy bands was just as much a part of tradition and deserving of study.

In Transylvania, the tánchaz or social dance was part of village tradition, though only single men and women were able

FEHÉR GALAMB SZÁLL A HÁZRA MEZŐSÉG	*Muzsikas & Marta Sebetyen*
ZAJDI, ZAJDI	*Söndörgő*
DEM REBN TANTS	*Di Naye Kapelye*
NINCSEN PÉNZEM, SE KÉSEM	*Parno Graszt*
O DILO	*Vojasa*
KEZDETBEN	*Bazseva*

to attend: married folk had to content themselves with dancing at festivals and weddings.

> *"For generations, the táncház was the only form of recreation available to young peasant men and women in Transylvania... The musicians were generally engaged for ten Sundays at a stretch; the house was rented for a year or longer. The young people who frequented the táncház all contributed to paying the rent and the musicians in cash, labor, or produce."* [1]

More often than not, they hired bands of gypsy musicians. The dances would be local to the particular region.

The modern táncház movement has a crucial difference: it's an urban, not a rural phenomenon. The táncház itself will normally be run by musicians, not by a local community, and the dances won't be specific to any one region. People join out of interest – in general, they will have no community tradition of dancing to fall back on. They attend expecting to receive instruction. They're 'reclaiming' a tradition which is not part of their own personal upbringing.

Márta Sebestyén's career spans both traditions. Her mother had studied with Zoltán Kodály at the Budapest Academy, and as she grew up she became fascinated by the different styles and techniques of folk singing. Like her mother, she ended up studying music at the Budapest Academy. Her timing could not have been more fortunate: this was the mid-70s, young people were turning on to folk music, and there was an active táncház group at the Academy. Márta threw herself in: she loved the fact that this was a grassroots movement, not initiated by the Communist authorities, and there was a sense of freedom – it wasn't about following rules, or dressing in 'authentic' costumes.

As a singer, Márta was relentless, studying the styles of village singers and training herself to sing in a way that honoured them. Her abilities did not go unnoticed, and a young band who'd emerged from the student táncház movement, Muzsikás, persuaded her to team up with them. The albums that Muzsikás recorded with Márta Sebestyén in the 1980s and '90s are jewels, not only of Hungarian music but of world folk music. They were all passionate about bringing authentic Hungarian music to a wider audience, and collectively they spent a lot of time making expeditions to remote villages to record songs that were in danger of being lost. The results can be seen in albums like Blues for Transylvania (1990), a collection of Transylvanian song; and Máramaros: The Lost Jewish Music of Transylvania (1993), a collection of melodies from a community that had been destroyed in the Holocaust.

FEHÉR GALAMB SZÁLL A HÁZRA – **MEZŐSÉG** is a slow, elegiac number, and even without Márta's vocals this would be very special thanks to the sheer heartwrenching expression which the musicians produce from their strings; then when Márta sings it transports you to another place and another time.

Another group that Márta performed with in the early days was Vujicsics. Ethnomusicologist Tihamer Vujicsics was a mentor to them in the early days, he was their guide to folk music, folk instruments and dance; and after he died in a plane crash in 1975 they decided to name the group after him. They were also influenced by György Martin, a folklorist whose work had helped to shape the táncház movement. The band's approach was very traditional; their main goal was to revive the music of South Slav peoples from both sides of the Danube river. Perhaps if they'd been starting out 20 years earlier they'd have done more songs and ballads; instead the stars of the show are not the singers but the tamburas and the violin.

Vujicsics gave birth to Söndörgő. That's not intended literally, though Kálmán Eredics of Vujicsics did father the four brothers who went on to form Söndörgő. I mean the musical inheritance: "We grew up with the music of Vujicsics. As children we went to a lot of their concerts and listened to their rehearsals from the other room so it was the traditional way of learning music personally from the 'fathers'. But on the other hand all of us did classical music studies too and the classical composers, especially Béla Bartók, influenced our thoughts so much." [2]

Another influence was Márta Sebestyén, who guested on Söndörgő's 2006 album, Oj Javore: "Márta is a living legend, it was a great pleasure to work with her. She knew us from the times we were kids because she worked with the band Vujicsics. When we made the recordings together one time she said to us: 'I sang with your fathers, now I sing with you and I hope I'll sing with your sons too.'"

ZAJBI, ZAJBI (with the stunning vocals by guest singer Kátya Tompos) is from the 2011 album, Tamburising, Söndörgő's greatest achievement to date. The album title is a tribute to the fretted instrument which they seem to have made it their mission to revive. This is still largely inspired by South Slav traditional music, but it's a distance apart from the music of Vujicsics. Here there is a greater creative freedom. The band isn't afraid to take risks and to set their own stamp on the songs. Pressed on the differences between themselves and their father's band, they acknowledge that "the approach is very similar but the attitude is different".

Since the 1990s, Hungary has – remarkably – seen a revival of klezmer music, and in my view there are few better klezmer bands anywhere than Di Naye Kapelye. The band came together, Bob Cohen tells us, "through a surprising set of circumstances, many of them soaked in pálinka – Hungarian plum brandy". [3] Some of the original members were Hungarian born, others were American born, and the palinka, it seems, is more efficacious even than music in bringing klezmer musicians together.

Cohen's a New Yorker, born to a Hungarian mother and Moldavian father, who was drawn to Hungary firstly through a love of tánchaź and then from a desire to search for his Jewish musical heritage. Di Naye Kapelye play exclusively Yiddish folk music, based mainly on the research that Cohen and other band members have carried out in Hungary and Romania. DEM REBN TANTS (the Rabbi's dance) is a glorious piece of music, a very strong melody and a driving beat, with an infectious slice of wordless chanting thrown in for good measure.

Roma music was boosted by the tánchaź movement, although by and large Roma musicians stuck to their own ethos and ways of making music. The Hungarian Roma bands that are internationally known are nearly all urban groups. That's certainly true of Kalyi Jag, the group who first popularised Roma music in Hungary with their 1987 album on the state Hungaroton label, and of groups such as Romano Drom who played at high voltage and didn't shy away from mixing their music with other genres. (Romano Drom describe themselves as a fusion band – "Antal Kovács (founder and composer of Romano Drom) combines the centuries-old musical culture with Catalan rumba, Arabic, Balkan and even pop rhythms." [4])

Parno Graszt are of particular interest because they're a genuine village ensemble from the village of Paszab. The group are all in some way related, they still live in their home village, they've never moved to the city. They play guitars, double bass, tambura, accordion, spoons and milk jug; they sing in Hungarian and Romani, and the band's retinue includes several dancers.

This is music that comes across as organic and real, because it's rooted in a place and a dialect and because it's not trying to be something different. They're a band who believe in giving people a good time, and their albums are best when the music's raw and unfiltered. Reggelig mulatok (2011) is their fourth album, released on both CD and DVD; it features the great gypsy cimbalom player Kálmán Balogh. I've not seen a lyric sheet for **NINCSEN PÉNZEM, SE KÉSEM** (Got no money, got no knife), but it comes across as a fun song. There's a nice build-up before the beat kicks in; you can hear the band riffing off each other as they play; and it has those moments when everyone can join in.

Vojasa represent urban gypsy music, though I note that Gusztáv Balogh was village born before he moved to Budapest at the age of eight.

Vojasa started playing together in 2011, but several band members already had long CVs, having played in other gypsy outfits such as Kalyi Jag and Romano Drom. They hadn't all grown up though listening to the same music – quite the reverse: some used to imbibe jazz, rock, pop, reggae and hip hop; others were more keyed into gypsy music from Hungary and other countries. This, Gusztáv Balogh explained to me, pointed the way to how the band was to develop: "The majority of Vojasa's songs are not based on the gypsy song heritage, they are original compositions. We find it very important to preserve certain elements of traditional gypsy music in our songs, such as the role of the water can, oral bass and the gypsy language, also some melodies. On the other hand, due to the fact that the members of the band have experience in different musical genres, our music is built up eclectically from many types of musical elements." [5]

Vojasa are all about high-energy, joyous music drawn from different sources. **O DILO**, with its rapidfire guitar sound and ska beats, could be described as a folk punk song. O Dilo means 'the fool', and the song's about a wife's concern over her husband who's been spending too much time out on the lash.

I asked Gusztáv for examples of Vlach gypsy dance.

"I could mention the botoló, which is a combat dance performed with a stick. This dance symbolises the fight of two men for the love of a lady. While the men fight the lady stands between them and tries to put an end to the battle. The men try to overcome each other without hurting the woman, which makes the 'stick fight' even harder. The duel continues until one of them wins or gives up. After that the winner dances with the lady, this time without the stick. Another dance is the csalogató (seducer). This one is performed by a man and a woman. The man tries to win the woman by a certain combination of steps, while the woman tests the man with another set of steps. Both of them try to get behind the other one's back. The man gets the woman if he succeeds. If the woman wins, the man is pronounced not worthy for the lady's heart. It's the game of seduction symbolised in the dance!"

At the time of the interview the neo-Nazi party Jobbik was the third largest party in Hungary. Roma communities have been terrorised by Jobbik supporters, and all too often the police do nothing to bring the perpetrators to account and the government does nothing to protect the victims. Gusztáv Balogh fully shares these concerns, but he tells me:

"The members of the band are not part of any political group or organisation, but they all find it important to fight against racism, antisemitism. The language of music is colourless. It is incompatible with prejudices against faith,

skin color, sex, or sexual orientation. Music is an absolute value which can bring those who have ears for it closer. Fighting against prejudices (exclusion) in our own way is one of our most important principles."

According to one of my sources, there are currently 60 or 70 táncház orchestras in Hungary. The enduring popularity of táncház underpins a flourishing folk music scene. Bazseva are one of a number of younger groups taking up the baton. They have a couple of female singers and four male instrumentalists (cimbalom, violin, viola, bass). They play traditional songs from the Carpathian basin, retrieved from archive recordings; and their style is fresh and lively. KEZDETBEN is a dance number full of life and energy: you'll need strong legs for this one, because the musicians keep going without pausing for breath for a full seven minutes, playing with such brio that you just have to keep your feet moving.

GUSZTÁV BALOGH RECOMMENDS:

- *Lamm Dávid – 1st the 1 (…then the other)*
- *Monamo – Don't Let Me Fall*
- *Azuma Clan – Stealth*
- *East Gipsy Band – Ageless Message*
- *Balogh Kálmán és a Gipsy Cimbalom Band – Aven Shavale*
- *Söndörgő – Tamburising*

NOTES

1. http://folklife.hu/roots-to-revival/living-tradition/tanchaz-method/the-tanchaz-movement/
2. Email 25/9/13
3. http://www.oriente.de/en/di-naye-kapelye-en/23-kataloge/oriente-cds/177-di-naye-kapelye-traditional-klezmer-music-en
4. https://www.womex.com/virtual/vilagveleje/romano_drom
5. Email 16/10/13

ICELAND

Björk's Homogenic for me was more than just a great album – it almost seemed to define Icelandic music. Now, as I came to examine the country's music more critically, I wanted to go back and view again the hour-long programme on the South Bank Show that I'd first seen on BBC TV in 1997, which had compelled me to go out and buy the CD. And through the magic of YouTube, I was able to do this.

After ten successful years, Björk had set out to record her most personal album to date, an album that would celebrate her roots and her Icelandic identity. The interesting thing is, when she tries to define this identity, she doesn't reach for a common culture passed down over the centuries. Instead, she takes as her starting point Iceland's landscape: "Iceland is geographically probably the youngest country in the planet. It's still changing and growing and very raw... so there's a lot of energy here. I wanted the beats to be like this." She wanted to evoke the feelings that she got from the country's beautiful but volatile geography. At times she seemed to acknowledge the difficulty of doing this without having a frame of reference to fall back on – "it's very hard to start from complete scratch with no tradition whatsoever." The way that she resolved this

ÞEGAR VETRAR ÞOKAN GRÁ

Steindór Andersen & Hilmar Örn Hilmarsson

MÓÐIR GUÐS OG MEYJAN SKÆR

Spilmenn Ríkínís

was to employ a string orchestra made up entirely of Icelandic musicians. Though she saw the musicians as a source of creative input, they weren't operating from scratch: they did have frames of reference on which they could rely. One of them talks about the interplay between the two cellos in the track The Hunter which he says use a motif that would have been recognisable to anyone familiar with Icelandic folk songs.

As we shall see, Iceland does indeed have distinctive musical traditions, but Björk was far from alone in her lack of knowledge and/or connection to them. Just four years later though, Icelanders got a reminder of their traditions when Sigur Rós, who'd recently enjoyed their first taste of international success, recorded a limited edition EP of six songs with a fisherman reciting traditional Icelandic poetry. The band's interest in folk music had developed spontaneously after they'd been together for a few years. Sigur Rós frontman, Jónsi Birgisson, spoke at the time about how "something connected inside me" when he heard at first hand Steindór Andersen's deep resonant voice. [1]

As it happened, Steindór Andersen was himself a late arriver on the folk scene:

"I first discovered the old rhymes when I worked as a child in the country. Later, when I was 40, my mother told me that my grandfather chanted for me sitting on his knee when I was two or three years old – something completely lost in my memory. It was not until many years later, after 20 years as a fisherman, that I recovered the rimur tradition and began to study the manuscripts. By then I was a fisherman on a stern-trawler. Three years later I bought a small fishing boat and gave her the name Idunn... The radio on board has always been out of order, which doesn't matter because I chant all the time for myself and the seagulls." [2]

Iðunn was a Norse goddess associated with youth. It's also the name of Iceland's rimur society. When Steindór joined it, the society had become a small unfashionable organisation whose members would meet up once a month to practise rimur chanting. But Steindór transformed the society after becoming its President in 1997 and throwing his full weight behind efforts to revive interest in the genre.

Epic tales of battles, romances and great deeds, rimur are living proof of a national love affair with storytelling which goes back at least to the 14th century. Passed down by oral tradition over centuries, the stories must have changed many times in the telling. The poems followed complex rules and were often very lengthy. Performers used to wander from farm to farm and needed to be able to entertain for many nights while they stayed in one place. Icelanders used to live in turf houses which were dark and cold during the winter months, and they must have loved the chance to listen to these old tales.

Another decade on, another CD of rimur chanting. On Stafnbui, Steindór collaborated once again with Hilmar Örn Hilmarsson, the producer who masterminded the Sigur Rós project. The album also featured some distinguished 'guest' musicians: Páll Guðmundsson on stone harp, Örn Magnússon on langspil, and two string quartets plucked from the Icelandic Symphony Orchestra. For those unfamiliar with rimur tradition, the CD came with an 80-page hardback book. My advice? Just sit back and soak in Steindór's magisterial baritone and Hilmar Örn's evocative string arrangements on **ÞEGAR VETRAR ÞOKAN GRÁ**.

The langspil is a bowed zither that makes a distinctive drone-like sound. Örn Magnússon describes it as "a very lonely, sweet sound". [3] He began playing the instrument in 2006 and one of his first tasks was to make his own langspil. The instruments were traditionally made using driftwood from the beach, and have been made using several different types of wood. He also formed his own band – Spilmenn Ríkínís – who are a family band centred around Örn and his wife, Marta Guðrún Halldórsdóttir. Spilmenn Ríkínís perform music from old Icelandic books and manuscripts using traditional Icelandic instruments. The featured track **MÓÐIR GUÐS OG MEYJAN SKÆR**, stripped of adornment, has a quiet understated feel, but there is a lot of emotion contained in the female vocals.

Despite the growing popularity of Icelandic folk music, the two albums from which my two tracks are taken are admittedly unusual. There are still very few musicians playing traditional instruments such as the langspil and the fiðla (Icelandic fiddle). And believe me, I've searched for others.

What causes a tradition to wither and die? Iceland is no different from any other country in the world in having gone through a sharp decline in oral tradition as a means of preserving culture. But in Iceland's case old traditions were already in decline decades before the arrival of radio and TV. In the 19th century Iceland was under Danish rule. Its small population of under 100,000 were mostly struggling to make ends meet. When the weather was bad, small farms suffered, and there were many such years. Some people emigrated to Canada and the USA. For the fledgling independence movement trying to kindle nationalist passions, it wasn't an easy time.

What a difference a century can make. By the end of the 20th century Iceland had been independent for over half a century and its population (which was about to soar to over 300,000) was as happy and prosperous as anywhere in the world. Naturally there was much national pride. And a few people didn't like the idea that aspects of the country's musical tradition could only be learned by visiting a museum.

The starting point is to get hold of an instrument. There are three fiðlas in the National Museum, the most recent of which was made around 1905 when the folk song collector Reverend Bjarni Þorsteinsson asked the carpenter Stefán Erlendsson to make him a replica from memory of an instrument his uncle had played some 50 years before. The fiðla that Bára Grímsdóttir and Chris Foster own is a modern copy of this one. Once made, they then had to deal with the problem that practically no sound recordings or written material existed to tell them how the instrument used to be played: "there is an almost total lack of musical information regarding tuning (pitch and intervals between the strings), playing technique and repertoire." [4] So the reintroduction of the langspil and the fiðla into Icelandic folk music is dependent on the ability of artists like Bára and Chris to reinvent these traditional skills and create music that will appeal to the sensibilities of a 21st-century audience.

Bára and Chris have been busy spreading the word about the old instruments. As well as the CDs that they've recorded under the name Funi, they have an excellent website, they run workshops and they run a folk music course at the Icelandic Academy of the Arts. As I mentioned earlier, interest in folk music generally is on the rise. The Folk Music Centre opened in 2006 in the fishing village of Siglufjörður, in the house where Reverend Bjarni Þorsteinsson had once lived. It has an exhibition about the life of the Reverend, but the time to visit is in early July, when it hosts an annual folk festival, alongside a Folk Music Academy at which students can learn about singing and dance, and rimur and instrumental tradition.

All the music discussed in this chapter can be purchased from the website icelandicmusic.com. If the site's extensive lists of albums are anything to go by, then traditional folk music is still very much a minority interest within the folk community. But it will be interesting to see if this changes at all over the next few years.

NOTES

1. Quoted in http://spellbindingmusic.com/steindor-andersen-sigur-ros-a-ferd-til-breidafjardar-vorid-1922/
2. Paul Sullivan – Waking Up In Iceland (Sanctuary Publishing, 2003)
3. http://grapevine.is/culture/art/2008/09/12/langspil/
4. http://www.funi-iceland.com/#!research/cqt8

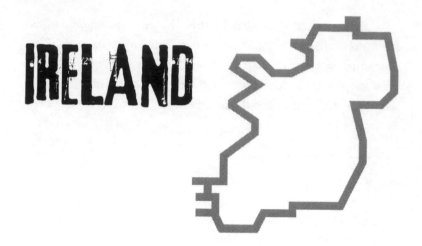

IRELAND

The first myth I want to unpick is the myth of the Irish Rebel Song. The idea of the Irish Rebel Song is sold to us today as a green, white and orange-coloured package which comes with the implication that all the songs included belong to a single cultural and political movement. Which of course is nonsense. Take the well-known song Down by the Glenside. Written by Peadar Kearney, a freedom fighter who took part in the Easter Rising, it's a stirring hymn to Irish Republicanism, and to all the soldiers past and present who've fought for its cause:

"They loved dear old Ireland, to die they were willing
Glory O, Glory O, to the bold Fenian men."

For all its merits it's an uncritical song which doesn't shed light on any real issues. By the time that Peadar died in the 1940s any edge that the song may originally have had was lost. It posed no threat to the institutions of the Irish state, the Catholic Church and the Fianna Fáil government, for whom it had become part of a pantheon of patriotic songs which underscored their legitimacy.

The reality for many Irish people in the 1940s and '50s was very different. The economy was in bad shape, unemployment was

SEAN TREACY	*Dominic Behan*
REEL AND JIG: GORMAN'S	
KITTY'S RAMBLES	*Packie Russell*
REELS: THE TEMPLEHOUSE/	
THE TAILORED JACKET	*Louise Mulcahy*
BEAUTY DEAS AN OILEÁIN	*Sean McKeon*
THE GREEN WOOD LADDIE	*Maighread Ní Domhnaill*
THE TRI-COLOURED HOUSE	*Lynched*

high, and emigration to Britain and America was commonplace. In other countries Irish immigrants weren't celebrated as they are today: they were often mocked and despised, and outside the immigrant communities there was no great appetite for Irish music and culture. From there to the extraordinary position of strength that Irish culture has around the world today has been a very long journey. Along this road, music has played its part again and again, instilling a new-found sense of belief in, and belonging to, a culture that doesn't simply look back to the past, but is also dynamic and forward looking.

In the late 1950s, Dominic Behan, a nephew of Peadar Kearney, penned a powerfully worded repudiation of patriotic songs. He was a republican, but he was also a socialist, and he wasn't prepared to act as cheerleader for an armed struggle which he disagreed with. After The Patriot Game became his most popular tune, Dominic's comrades tell us that he was far from happy to see it co-opted by republicans as a Rebel Song – "He was a strong opponent of Nationalist and Loyalist terrorism and was always incensed that the Provos had stolen his song." [1] He was also incensed that Bob Dylan stole the song and rewrote all the lyrics, but that's another story.

Dominic was a child of the city, who'd grown up in Dublin's Crumlin district where he once quipped that "the only grass we ever saw we were asked to keep off it". He was a wild, big-hearted character who had a way with words and who was political to the core. Songs like McAlpine's Fusiliers and Liverpool Lou brought a rare wit and social realism to the Irish canon. But it's for his many Irish political songs, above all, that he'll be remembered.

SEAN TREACY is a song that seems slightly at odds with Behan's politics if you know who Sean Treacy was. I know who he was because I own a secondhand copy of a book dedicated to him, the remarkable autobiography of his closest friend and comrade, Dan Breen. In January 1919 they were among a group of County Tipperary volunteers who shed the first blood in the civil war. At that time, as Dan Breen records, they had virtually no support for their action even among those who had fought in 1916. Yet because they did go on to gain support, and because this helped to trigger the chain of events that led to Irish independence, they are celebrated as freedom fighters rather than being reviled as terrorists. Dominic Behan's song avoids the more difficult questions; at the same time it's no dumbed down or prettified version of history. Told as a first person account of Treacy's death in 1920 in a bloody gunbattle with British soldiers, it has a vividness and an immediacy to it, yet despite the drama of the tale it's sung with a surprising gentleness and restraint. In this way Behan conveys the message that Treacy was not some reckless outlaw, but a passionate human being, loved by many.

It was thanks in no small part to Dominic Behan that political songwriting would feature in the Irish folk revival and that songwriters would feel empowered to comment on current events. He was an important influence on The Dubliners and helped them to launch their career. In return they helped to secure his legacy by recording many of his songs. Christy Moore also remembers him warmly:

> *"He mesmerized me with an enormous repertoire of songs, reflections and poetry. Himself and his wife Josephine were very kind to me. Like myself back then, he seldom put the cork back into the bottle. The sessions went on 'til the bitter end. I learned so much from Dominic Behan. He took the time and trouble to organize my first recording session. He set up the musicians and created the deal with Mercury Records." [2]*

The 1970s were a fertile period for Irish political song. The IRA's campaign north of the border and the British reaction (internment, Bloody Sunday) created a heightened political atmosphere and an appetite among artists and audiences for political songs. In 1972, a new group called The Barleycorn topped the Irish charts with a song about internment, The Men Behind The Wire. The song was covered months later by another rising political group, the Wolfe Tones. It was one of a number of militant anthems on the Wolfe Tones album, Let the People Sing, which also included their own comment on internment (Long Kesh), a tribute to James Connolly, Dominic Behan's Come Out, Ye Black and Tans, and Frank O'Donovan's On the One Road. Bands on both sides of the Irish Sea were building their repertoire around songs like these; however, the leading folk groups of the day, with the exception of The Dubliners, preferred to focus on more 'traditional' material. Christy Moore was becoming more politically engaged: in 1978 he released an album of political songs recorded by various Irish folk artists simply called H Block; and his 1984 album Ride On included a couple of songs written by the IRA hunger striker Bobby Sands.

As the 1970s turned into the '80s Irish rebel music began to look more and more like a spent force, a pastime for bearded middle-aged men with guitars, overtaken by more exciting developments such as the rise of the big folk group (The Bothy Band, Planxty, De Dannan) and Riverdance. Then something unexpected happened to shake things up once again: a band called The Pogues began playing Irish traditional songs in a manner inspired by punk. I had been following The Pogues since the early days, but it was only when I saw them perform at the Fleadh festival in London's Finsbury Park around 1990 that I realised I wasn't just watching a band, I was witnessing the emergence of a whole new scene. The crowds were swollen by large numbers of youths who'd come along to dance and do their thing to The Pogues, and after the gig you couldn't take a bus down Seven Sisters Road without being serenaded by Pogues songs. By no means all Pogues songs were political, but they left no one in any doubt that they stood in the tradition of the Behan brothers and The Dubliners; and the Celtic folk punk genre which sprang up in their wake has produced hundreds of bands from across Europe, the north American continent and beyond, most of whom play at least a few Irish rebel songs.

Of course The Pogues' influence went way beyond the Celtic folk punk movement. It contributed to a new kind of narrative about what it was to be Irish, a feeling of confidence and of pride in Irish identity. Irish music was in vogue, but it was more diverse than ever before, there were many different scenes that people were into. This all posed a number of questions to traditional musicians who could see crossover artists achieving levels of success and recognition which they could only dream about. It's time that we took a look at how traditional musicians responded to this challenge.

Every year sees the release of literally hundreds of traditional music albums in Ireland alone, generally of very high quality, though many are self-released and have limited distribution. They mainly consist of instrumental dance music: reels, jigs, hornpipes, polkas, slides and so on. As such, they represent a very conscious effort to stay true to how music was performed (and danced to) in Ireland's rural heartland from the days before radio was invented. Which begs the question, how authentic can it be? The recordings are already a stage removed from live performance. Live music has changed: it now mostly takes place in pubs whereas less than a century ago it would have been in private houses or open public places. So if you're playing to a room of people who may not necessarily be into the dancing, who've probably got a broad musical knowledge, and you're competing with people talking among themselves and other distractions, then you have to deal with all of that.

An equally big issue, and one that much engages the fiddle player Caoimhín Ó Raghallaigh, is the way in which music is learned today. It's probably a fair bet that most musicians you see performing publicly will be able to read music, and that many will have studied in one or more of Ireland's music schools. Despite the impressive numbers of people who are trained to play traditional instruments and who have a feeling for traditional music, Caoimhín is convinced that something valuable has been lost:

> "We've attempted to replace an oral tradition with a very poorly evolved education system. If you analyse the steps that a traditional music student goes through, and what they are taught, it's almost non-existent. They get taught tunes, they get a few masterclasses, but they don't get a coherent system of understanding that allows them to freely pluck the nuances of any particular style out and use them. That's not a replacement for an oral tradition. I feel that people are coming out of third-level musical education at the level of understanding that they should have been going in to it." [3]

What he's saying is that all too often musicians today start with a fixed idea of how a tune should be played, which will be much the same whether they're in Cork or Donegal. Regional styles of playing are almost forgotten, and there's not enough encouragement for musicians to express themselves, to look beyond the script and explore the possibilities that are in the music.

Packie Russell (1920–77) is a fine example of one who learned his music the old way but played like a demon. His **REEL AND JIG** is everything that Caoimhín admires: it's just one man and his instrument, but it's like the two are one – the mood is light and joyful, and he finds expression in the humble concertina that you wouldn't have guessed was there.

Packie may not even have been the best musician in his own family – his two older brothers were also gifted musicians. They grew up in the most romantic of settings, in a farm just off the Cliffs of Moher near the little town of Doolin in County Clare, looking out toward the Aran Islands. Music ran in the family: the father was a sean-nós singer, the mother a concertina player.

> "The concertina was Packie's instrument, Micho and Gussie played the timber flute and the tin whistle. In their early years music was not yet centred in pubs and the three brothers often walked or cycled miles to play together at house dances. Neighbours gathered together in designated houses telling stories, singing and dancing." [4]

When Packie was a boy of 12 his father died and he became an apprentice stonecutter. It wasn't the most rewarding of trades: the labour was hard and the work was irregular and low paid, but good jobs were few and far between in the west of Ireland back then. While others were emigrating the three brothers remained on their home turf. After Micho made a number of radio and TV appearances word slowly got around that there was this little corner of County Clare where you could still catch the purest traditional music (and not just music – Packie was a renowned storyteller). Sadly only a handful of recordings of Packie's music were ever made. This one was taken from Tuning the Radio, a recent compilation of recordings from the RTÉ radio archives from the 1940s and '50s of various folk musicians. Legend has it, according to the sleeve notes, that there are traditional music enthusiasts, "who may know little about Dublin but everything about Doolin!"

And here's the best part of the story, for it shows how much people still cherish the music to this day. Every year at the end of February there is a small festival in Doolin where the three brothers – and their two sisters – are remembered in music and dance and an anniversary mass.

My next selection, recorded 65 years later, tries to recapture some of that old magic. Louise Mulcahy plays her flute with a freedom and an agileness, and you feel her presence and her joy in the **REELS**, which are ended far too quickly. Louise listens to archival recordings a lot, and she's particularly fond of music from the 1920s and '30s – "The music at this time was predominantly played for dancers and was filled with great lift and expression. I like to recreate this feeling when I play music." [5]

Louise also takes great inspiration from her father, box player Mick Mulcahy. "I was born into music," says Mick. "My father played the accordion... I could never keep away from the accordion and the sound of it." [6] In his youth he used to find seasonal work on the west coast and play the Dublin clubs during the off-season. Along the way a couple of albums were made, but he just loved playing. Like his father he would play the accordion every day in his home, and when his daughters were born in his adopted home in Abbeyfeale, West Limerick they too learned what it was to grow up with traditional music all around them.

Louise moved quickly from the tin whistle to the flute, and by her teens she was learning the uilleann pipes. In 2000, the two sisters Louise and Michelle were still teenagers but Mick decided that they were good enough, so the three of them made an album. Today they're a stronger unit than ever: Louise is quick to praise

Michelle's harp and piano playing and to tell me about the "deep musical connection" which they have, [7] and the rapport is very much there on their fourth album, The Reel Note, released in 2016.

The track is taken from Louise's one solo album to date, Tuning the Road (2014), which "represents my musical journey to date". The names of the composers of the tunes don't mean much to me, but I'm impressed by the trouble to which she has gone to find them – "The Irish Traditional Music Archive was a great source of inspiration along with other online archives such as NPU, The Comhaltas archive and other recordings I have collected over the years." Although she's unaccompanied on this track the album is another collaborative family effort.

The uilleann pipe occupies a special place in Ireland's music. It's an entirely different instrument from the Highland bagpipe. Instead of blowing air through a mouthpiece, the piper uses his or her elbow to pump air using a bellows. Because the uilleann pipe has to be played sitting down, and it's not as loud as the Highland pipes, it's more suited to indoor performance. The uilleann pipe has a range of two full octaves – twice as many notes as the Highland bagpipe – and a set of three drones, and various other technical features, all adding up to making it possibly the most challenging bagpipe in the world to learn how to play.

A key date in the story of the uilleann pipe's revival was 1968 when the cream of Ireland's pipers (most notably Leo Rowsome, Willie Clancy and Séamus Ennis) all got together to set up a pipers' association, Na Píobairí Uilleann. Liam O'Flynn, who in the 1970s would help popularise the uilleann pipes when he was part of the band Planxty, well remembers those early days: "The instrument came very close to extinction… The lowest point came about 60 years ago when there were very few pipers left, maybe 50 at most, and no more than a handful could make a set of pipes." It was down to a handful of players, like those named above, to keep the torch alight – "For O'Flynn, these players, all of whom he knew and learned from, are heroic figures: wonderful musicians, vital bearers and advocates of their tradition, generous teachers and great men." [8]

Planxty, The Bothy Band and The Chieftains all had pipers. The pipe's versatility was a huge asset, and it also helped that they didn't drown out other instruments. As the profile of the instrument rose there was a welcome increase, not only in the number of players, but also the number of instrument makers and the standard of their work, as Lunása piper Cillian Vallely recalls: "With the instruments that are made now, I'd say there has never been an era like it. I clearly remember teaching 20–25 years ago, and the pipes that would be brought into the class would make you cringe. And now, you go into a class and everybody plays an A, and it seems to be in tune, and people can't blame the pipes anymore. There's also a great standard in reed-making." [9]

Dublin piper Sean McKeon uses the instrument to great effect on the traditional air BEAUTY DEAS AN OILEÁIN. A duet with Liam O'Connor on fiddle, it's a very beautiful and expressive piece and quite a contrast to the faster dance tunes which dominate the album. With the drone in the background it's like more than the two instruments are playing, it's a rich multi-textured sound.

Sean is yet another Irish musician who comes from a musical family. His father, Gay McKeon, is a piper who for many years was a mainstay of Na Píobairí Uilleann. His grandfather and his uncle also played the pipes, as does his brother Conor. Sean himself has shown prodigious talent since he was a teenager, and there will be many eyes watching to see where this takes him. He's spent a bit of time touring with the Damien Dempsey band, and it's yet to be seen whether he is more in his element as part of a band or as a solo artist.

Just as much a part of Irish tradition as the instrumental dance tune is the unaccompanied song. This requires some explanation. In the late 20th/early 21st century Irish song is big business: leading artists sell albums by the million all around the world. These albums all play on the stereotype of the Irish as a romantic people known for their beautiful songs, and are highly polished and produced. All of this is a world away from Ireland's sean-nós singing tradition. Sean-nós is unaccompanied singing, normally in the Irish language. There are almost as many different sean-nós styles as there are singers, but recurring features include natural unaffected vocals, a narrow vocal range, variations in the melody, and a stress on the words and meaning of the song. Sean-nós is so intimately rooted in oral tradition that its survival, and the fact that it's still widely taught today, is little short of remarkable.

Maighread Ní Dhomhnaill is one singer who has tried to knot together the broken thread of her past. She grew up in County Meath but her father's family was from Donegal and her aunt, Néillí Ní Dhomhnaill, was a real tradition bearer, a blind sean-nós singer who had learned and retained many of the old songs. In 1971, Maighread and two of her siblings were part of the seminal short-lived group Skara Brae who made just one album:

"It was made in an afternoon, with a microphone hanging out of the ceiling. I was 15, Triona was 17 and Micheal was 19 or 20. They were the first traditional songs done to guitars – it was the first time the pop music thing was brought to the Irish language." [10]

Triona and Micheal went on to form The Bothy Band, while Maighread, with help from her family, released a solo album. She then turned her back on a musical career, studying nursing, getting married and raising a family. When she returned to music it was with a renewed sense of purpose, a desire to preserve what she could of the Donegal song tradition. With encouragement from her husband, she trained her voice and began working on her own interpretation of songs from her aunt and others that she connected with.

"Gael Linn [record label] kept at me to make an album. Eventually, I rang up Donal Lunny and asked him would he be interested in producing it. Half an hour later he was on his bike outside my door. On his bike. I always remember that."

The album, which came out in 1991, included the song **THE GREEN-WOOD LADDIE**. It's a traditional song which may have originated in County Antrim and was certainly known to the Antrim singer and folklorist Robert Cinnamond. The song is about a forbidden love and some believe that "there may well be a deeper significance to the term 'Greenwood' suggesting that this song expresses an attachment that crosses the sectarian divide." [11] One of the best-known versions is by Shirley Collins, and it's instructive to compare the English folk singer's recording with Maighread's interpretation: while Shirley Collins' song is moody but understated, Maighread's is much more ornamented. She slows the song right down, lingering on each syllable, and every time I hear it my hair stands on end.

There have been a few Skara Brae reunions over the years: these continue despite the death of Micheal in 2006. In 2007, at a tribute concert for Micheal, a new group T with the Maggies was formed, with the two sisters Maighread and Triona joined by Altan's lead vocalist, Mairéad Ní Mhaonaigh, and Clannad's Moya Brennan. They have since released one album.

According to Louise Mulcahy, "Irish traditional music has certainly gone from strength to strength over the years and is currently thriving." [12] There are, she says, many reasons for this: many universities now offer traditional music courses; there are several organisations set up to promote Irish traditional music; archival recordings are widely available; and Irish music festivals the world over provide exposure to the music. Few would argue with any of this. Fiddle ace Martin Hayes sees this, though, as anything but a simple natural progression. You can reproduce the tunes, he would say, but you can't recreate the social and cultural context from whence they sprang. Before radio and TV and the internet people in rural Ireland were much more isolated within their communities, with relatively little contact with other cultures. Traditional music "can no longer exist as a folk music, in the very pure sense of folk music rising out of the people". [13] So it has to find new ways of making itself relevant and new ways of evolving if it is to survive and thrive:

> "I think the regional styles are dying out, and I don't think they can ever be revived. I think any resuscitation of them in that sense would be very mechanical, would be very premeditated, and of course this music never came out of a premeditated, orchestrated form. It would be imitation rather than a real expression. So the only hope I see is for people to find individual expression in it."

Martin Hayes has recently collaborated with Caoimhín Ó Raghallaigh in the ensembles Triúr and The Gloaming. Also in The Gloaming are Iarla Ó Lionáird, Dennis Cahill and Thomas 'Doveman' Bartlett. The band's experimental approach to folk music won acclaim from far outside the usual folk circles, and in March 2015 they fended off competition from U2, Damien Rice and Sinéad O'Connor to win the Meteor Choice Music Prize for best album of the year. But had they betrayed their roots? Actually, says Martin, "we're all really hard-core traditionalists ourselves". Their love of tradition runs deep, it underpins what they do; they're just enjoying the freedom to be creative. "For us it's just music and it's something that's deeply felt and meaningful." [14]

Four-piece Dublin band Lynched don't have the same folk pedigree as The Gloaming, but they're coming from a similar place. The band was formed by brothers Ian and Daragh Lynch who had been around the punk scene for a few years but had become drawn to traditional music.

"There was, and still is, a pub in Dublin called The Cobblestones. And they would have sessions on there every night of the week. We play a lot in there now ourselves but I used to live across the road and I'd go in and hear the music... I spend a lot of time listening to what you'd call in England 'source singers' – older traditional singers. And I think there's a certain earthiness and tone to the singing, even the approach to the songs you don't hear in modern singers." [15]

So the inspiration, if you like, came from traditional music, and from Dublin in particular; but the aim was just to make good music, not to conform to any one idea of what folk music should sound like. "We never sat down and decided on a specific sound we wanted or anything. We all just played together, adding or taking away elements until it sounded right. In this way, everything that makes up our musical consciousness must have made its mark in some way or another." [16] The band introduce their debut album Cold Old Fire (2015) with the bland description that it contains "a selection of traditional folk songs from the Dublin, English and Traveller traditions, as well as two original pieces." There's so much more to mention: the inspired song choices, the Dublin accents, the raw and compelling harmonies, the subtle arrangements and clever use of their instruments.

The standout track for me is **THE TRI-COLOURED HOUSE**, a traditional song clearly related both to Scarborough Fair and Elfin Knight. It's one of many songs that the folklorist Tom Munnelly collected from the travelling community in the 1970s. Lynched have this to say about it:

"The Tri-Coloured House is related to Child's Elfin Knight, a song in which one party... sets another a series of impossible tasks. Many different versions have been collected in Ireland,

as well as further afield, and Child noted that the basic plot occurs in narrative form in India, Russia and Arabia."

We're so accustomed to lone singers that the unrefined four-part harmony comes as a bit of a shock. It helps convey the sense that this is a song that's been passed down through the community over many generations. The arrangement must have taken a considerable amount of work, but it's a success: the mood grows more sinister and the track gathers power as it moves between its various phases.

NOTES

1. http://www.troublesarchive.com/resources/bobbiehanvey.pdf
2. https://comeheretome.com/2014/03/18/an-interview-with-christy-moore/
3. http://www.stateofchassis.com/08-01-14irishtimestext.htm
4. http://www.clarelibrary.ie/eolas/coclare/people/russell_brothers.htm
5. http://italish.eu/irish-musics-present-future-7-questions-7-louise-mulcahy/
6. http://www.limerickleader.ie/news/what-s-on/214414/from-the-heart-and-on-the-note-with-musical-limerick-family.html subscription required
7. Email 4/11/14
8. http://www.taramusic.com/features/lofpipes.htm
9. http://celticevents.com/2014/05/16/an-interview-with-lunasa%E2%80%99s-cillian-vallely-with-dirk-mewes/
10. http://www.irishtimes.com/culture/maighread-s-way-1.219234
11. Liner notes to Hen Party's The Heart Gallery, quoted at https://mainlynorfolk.info/shirley.collins/songs/greenwoodladdie.html
12. Email 4/11/14
13. http://ceolas.org/artists/Martin_Hayes/interview.html
14. http://irishpost.co.uk/martin-hayes-on-breaking-tradition-and-experimenting-with-the-gloaming/
15. https://lynchedmusic.com/press/
16. http://nodepression.com/interview/interview-dublin-roots-band-lynched

ITALY

In the 1960s something was happening in the port city of Genoa, and it was shaking Italian music to its foundations. The city was home to a generation of outstanding young singer songwriters who were bringing new ideas and new influences to their art: Fabrizio de André, Luigi Tenco, Umberto Bindi, Gino Pauli and Sergio Endrigo. Although each ploughed their own individual furrow, they were often collectively referred to as the scuola genovese (Genoan school).

These men were rebels by instinct. Politically, they all belonged on the left. They were influenced by the great artists and thinkers of Paris's Left Bank, and by modern French songwriters. They were against formulas, cliché, commercialism of art; and they weren't afraid to offend people at times. They believed that art should reflect real life. They wrote of love, and suffering, and struggle, and war. Lyrics were composed with a craftsman's skill: the music may have been folky, but it caught the zeitgeist of the time and found an appreciative audience.

If one artist epitomised the age, it was the romantic iconic figure of Luigi Tenco (1938–67).

His life was encircled by tragedy, from the death of his father when he was very young, to his own bewildering suicide at the age

VEDRAI, VEDRAI	*Luigi Tenco*
BUTTANA DI TO MÁ	*Rosa Balistreri*
RAGGIA DU MARI	*Matilde Politi &*
	Compagnia Bella
FIORASSIU E PUNTU 'E ÓRGANU	*Andrea Pisu &*
	Giancarlo Seu
PIZZICA DI ARADEO	*Canzoniere*
	Grecanico Salentino
LA BELLA MARIANIN	*Lombardo, Pinti &*
	Zambruno

of 28. His character was complex: a private, shy person given to severe self-criticism. In the months leading up to his death he had a brief but intensely passionate affair with the singer and actress Dalida. They'd planned to marry: an announcement was set to be made after the Sanremo festival. [1] The festival was meant to be a career high point, but Tenco's stage fright got the better of him, and he tanked. The disappointment was crushing. Luigi was found dead in his hotel room and Dalida never got a chance to say goodbye. A month later, consumed by grief, she tried to take her own life by downing some barbiturates.

Songwriting for Luigi was a form of catharsis, a way of releasing his own inner turmoil. "He was not interested in the fantasy of romance peddled by the pop industry but the stark reality," wrote Chris Campion in The Guardian. "His lyrics read like minimalist poetry; almost entirely shorn of ornamentation, they sometimes seemed curt to the point of being surly, but were emotionally devastating." [2] He was also known for his socialist commitment and his protest songs – a different form of truth telling. **VEDRAI, VEDRAI** is one of his melancholy love songs. He sings slowly, knowing that he can hold his listeners rapt with his strong, rich voice. The words of the song, assuring us that his life isn't yet over, were unintentionally prophetic: like a few other 1960s musicians I can name, he became more influential, more widely loved and admired, in death than he had been in life.

Italy is like a federation of mini-states. Instead of saying 'I'm Italian' people will often say 'sono toscano' (I'm Tuscan), or whatever the region is that they're from. For many, this is an important part of their identity. Italians even have a word for regional pride: campanilismo, which involves a deep attachment to local culture and traditions. And this is no accident. If you look at the different regions, each one has a unique history, a strong local dialect, its own cuisine, its own music, and so on. It's always been that way. Does this mean that the Italian state is weak and fragile? The visible tensions between North and South, and the recent rise of separatist movements such as the Lega Nord, would suggest so; but to me the picture is not so black and white. For many lifetimes Italians have celebrated their regional traditions without putting up a brick wall to shut out those of a different culture, and for good reason: these cultures didn't develop in isolation, but through interaction with multiple ethnic groups and many borrowed influences. Each regional identity can be seen as part of a larger mosaic, fitting into and complementing a multicoloured national identity, and this idea also has a powerful hold.

Sicily is a prime example of a region with its own history and identity, but an identity that has been shaped and coloured through exposure over the centuries to many other cultures. Part of this identity is the Sicilian language, which is recognised as a language in its own right, distinct from Italian. At various times

Sicily has been part of the Greek, Roman and Byzantine empires; it's been ruled by French and Spanish kings; by Christians and Muslims. Its situation, which makes it a natural port of call for sea traders, has prevented it from ever becoming isolated. Sicilian song carries in it Greek, Arab and Spanish influences to this day.

Rosa Balistreri (1927–90) grew up during a time when Mussolini was busy increasing grain production and reclaiming land: none of these big projects improved the situation of the rural poor, of whom there were a good many in Sicily. Rosa's family were too poor to send their children to school, so from a young age she worked in domestic service and as a seasonal farm labourer. The first time she went to church was as a singer: she was 15, and prior to this had never owned a pair of shoes. A year later she was pushed into an unhappy marriage. Her husband beat her, causing her to lose her first child. One day she defended herself with a knife and ended up in jail. She thought that she'd killed him, but she hadn't. So as soon as the opportunity arose, she fled to Palermo.

In Palermo life got no easier. She became pregnant again, stole money from the family she was working for, was discovered, fled and was arrested, and served out another prison term. Still pregnant, she was living on the streets of Palermo for a while. The baby was stillborn. How sad and desperate Rosa must have felt at that time is hard to imagine. But she had a living daughter from her husband, and this spurred her to carry on. Eventually she managed to get a school place for her daughter, and she herself learnt how to read and write. As a working woman in the city though, life was full of dangers. One day a priest tried to rape her at the place where she was staying. She emptied the alms boxes and bought herself a train ticket to Florence. Here she would live for the next 20 years. [3]

Finally Rosa began to build a life for herself. She became part of an artistic circle, taught herself to play the guitar and pursued her interest in traditional song. In 1966, Dario Fo gave her a lead role in one of his shows: she was then aged 39. The LPs started to come soon after. Rosa was a voice for the voiceless. She sang songs she'd learned when she was young and songs by long-forgotten writers, found through research, some of which have now become part of Sicily's heritage – folk songs, vernacular songs, lullabies. Songs of struggle and suffering, songs which always took the side of women and workers, protest songs which railed against injustice. **BUTTANA DI TO MÁ** is a howl of bitterness and rage: the guitar sticks like a broken record on the same note, while her voice soars and swoops, denouncing those whose actions have put her in jail.

"I'm not a singer," she once said, "I'm an activist who makes speeches on the guitar." She fought for people's right to an education, the rights of women, workers' rights and socialism. She fearlessly spoke out against organised crime, and its links with church and state. When she agreed to sing at the Sanremo Festival in 1973, it was because she wanted people to hear songs that protested against poverty and injustice. The Sanremo judges decided that people didn't want to hear songs like this, but it was they who were out of step with the times. The student movement which had erupted in Italy in 1968 had given rise to new movements in the 1970s. In this political environment Rosa's poor working class background became an asset. Even those who didn't know her story were impressed by her authenticity. Her voice, so steeped in the knowledge of poverty and pain, came to represent not only Sicily but the causes that she fought for.

Traditional folk music in Sicily is probably more marginalised now than it was in the 1970s, but one artist born in the 1970s still carrying the candle is Matilde Politi. Her childhood dream was to become an actress, but music was always part of her life too, and she enjoyed the performance aspect. She graduated in Cultural Antropology in Rome, got a diploma in Performing Arts at Pontedera, then began devoting her energies to the study of Sicilian traditional music. Among the fruit of these researches: a set of albums on which she's restored to life and interpreted many Sicilian folk songs. Matilde is no dogmatist though when it comes to folk music. In fact she loves working with musicians from other countries and cultures, and taking part in crossover projects. On her albums she's used to working with musicians who, like herself, play several instruments, and the old material is given a modern makeover with creative arrangements.

RAGGIA DU MARI is a maritime song, "è legata ad una sera dove sul mare si sentiva il Marocco." [4] The rapid chanting and pulsating rhythm make it very accessible to non-Sicilian speakers. It's from the album Vacanti Sugnu China – Sicilian folk songs; her brother Gabriele is part of the band. The album was produced in such a way as to try and impart the feel of live performance: Matilde wanted it to sound spontaneous and of the moment.

The 21st century has seen a huge increase in migration to Italy. For Matilde, this is something to be embraced. Already, when she returned to Palermo at the start of the noughties, "I discovered that my city in ten years had changed a lot, had become a multiethnic city." From the desire to share cultures and support migrants and asylum seekers at the same time was born the idea of the Sarabbanda project. Sarabbanda is made up of Ghanaian, Ivorian, Nigerian, Togolese, Moroccan, Tunisian and Bengali musicians, whoever wants to be a part of it – "almost no one has musical skills as a professional. They practise regularly, they play as an orchestra – sometimes they earn some money, but the biggest thing for them, they earn the right to tell their story and to be listened to on a stage with a microphone in hand, the right to have fun..." [5]

Sardinia is home to some of Italy's most distinctive and fascinating music, and star attraction is a unique woodwind instrument called the launeddas. A launeddas consists of three reed pipes of varying lengths, one of which is a drone (i.e. it plays a constant note). All three pipes are held in the mouth simultaneously and played using a circular breathing method. It's a very ancient instrument, but in modern times the greatest launeddas players were Efisio Melis (1890–1970) and Antonio Lara (1886–1979), who were both born in the small southern town of Villaputzu. Melis was an innovator, a virtuoso; Lara by contrast was solidly grounded in tradition. Luigi Lai, who grew up near Villaputzu and used to travel there for lessons with Lara, has huge respect for Lara, but Melis was something else, an "artistic, imaginative, creative force". [6] Melis had a couple of recording sessions in 1930 and 1937, and one with Lara in 1962, which have been remastered and are readily available today, and I strongly recommend that you seek these out.

Villaputzu is now home to an annual launeddas festival where Sardinia's finest come to play and to pay homage to past masters such as Efisio Melis. In 2016, the festival included a religious procession, workshops, local crafts, a mask exhibition, folk groups from Sardinia and overseas, but above all else, the amazing sound of the pipes.

An outstanding younger launeddas player, Andrea Pisu, was born in 1984 – it should come as no surprise by now – in Villaputzu. The launeddas master Aurelio Porcu taught him for a year and a half before his health gave up; after that Andrea worked alone, while immersing himself in recordings of Melis and Lara. Andrea's a creative individual who's keen on working with musicians from other genres, but he still yearns for the golden age of the 1930s when the launeddas was a vital part of every celebration: "Today the players are confined to working fixed hours as set by the rigidity of a concert program or a folk event; there is no room for improvisation (something that has always characterised the launeddas player)." [7]

FIORASSIU E PUNTU 'E ÓRGANU has no slow build-up: the noise hits you from the first moment. It feels like you're surrounded by pipers on all sides, playing for all they're worth (the launeddas can have this effect), but no, there's no orchestra, just two people. This is not relaxing music: it's street music, music to assault your senses and fill you with energy and excitement. Andrea, who's played in many Italian and European cities, says it's not only Sardinians who love this sound: "wherever I have gone the reception has always been incredible." He's delighted that Sardinia is at last beginning to take its heritage more seriously and to bring this music to a much wider audience.

Sardinian music's greater profile also owes much to two giants of Sardinian music, who deserve a brief mention here.

Maria Carta (1934–94) had a fairytale life: a provincial girl who grew up in poverty, who became a beauty queen, who became a film actress (she played the mother of Vito Corleone in The Godfather Part II) and who had an amazing singing career. She would sing all forms of traditional music, from gosos (devotional songs) and Gregorian chants to lullabies and Sardinian folk songs; it wasn't an obvious recipe for success, but the Sardinian people took her to their hearts. After her death the Maria Carta Foundation created the Maria Carta Award, a coveted prize for the best in Sardinian music.

Tenores di Bitti are the most famous representatives of Sardinia's ancient polyphonic singing traditions. Don't assume from this that they are tenors! Canto a tenore is the term for this specialised style of singing which actually involves four contrasting male voices – oche (solo voice), mesu oche (half voice), bassu (bass) and contra (contralto). The men sing standing in a circle. Tenores di Bitti have been going for over 40 years, during which time they've performed their powerful, intense, compelling song all around the world. Meanwhile, back in the tiny town of Bitti where they're from, there is now a museum of tenore singing, complete with a library and research centre.

Another group who recently celebrated their 40th anniversary are Canzoniere Grecanico Salento (CGS). As the name suggests, they hail from Salento, the peninsula which forms the heel of the Italian boot. Forty years ago Salento was not renowned for its music, but as we shall see, a lot has changed since then. The story begins with the unlikely figure of Rina Durante – novelist, poet, journalist, cultural activist. Her research into Salento's musical traditions, and in particular the history and legend of the pizzica dance, led her to form CGS in 1975. Although she did all the research for the group, she didn't play or sing. A cousin of hers, Daniele Durante, became the group's leader.

CGS spearheaded the revival of pizzica music in Italy. Pizzica originated as a ritual music and dance believed to cure the victims of tarantismo. Tarantismo is a pathological condition brought about by tarantula bites. The frenzied dance, it was thought, purged the evil spirit which caused victims to suffer seizures and hysterics.

As the music's popularity grew, the first La Notte della Taranta took place in 1998. First conceived as a series of concerts in different Salento towns at the same time, by 2000 it had become a fully fledged festival, and by 2015 some were describing it as "the largest traditional music festival in Europe." [8] A unique aspect of the event is the appointment of a guest director – "a Maestro Concertatore to arrange and interpret classics from the local musical tradition, directing a group of nearly thirty musicians from Salento together with exceptional guests from Italy and abroad. The Concertone alone attracts around 150,000 spectators, while tens of thousands follow the final rehearsals the day before." [9]

The history of La Notte della Taranta is dogged by allegations of commercialism. Behind the rows about the content of particular festivals lies a deeper concern: do the rapidfire club-friendly dance beats of the modern pizzica bands stray too far from the music's traditional roots? In the end, whether we call pizzica traditional or tradi-modern music is perhaps less important than the integrity with which it is played. And here CGS can still teach other groups a thing or two. Daniele's son, Mauro Durante, who took over the group from his father in 2007, says that while the band have never been afraid to try out their own ideas, "CGS has always been very respectful of the traditional repertoire. We always try not to betray the nature and the message of the songs by using overwhelming arrangements or interpretations." It's all about keeping hold of the music's essence:

> *"Pizzica has this magic; people can naturally get it. In our concerts the audience gets captured by the energy of this music and led somewhere else. We can't forget that this music originally had a therapeutic, exorcistic function, in the ritual of tarantismo. Pizzica can transcend linguistic and temporal borders. I hope that through the immediateness of pizzica, people can get closer to our whole culture." [10]*

To me this makes total sense when I listen to a song like PIZZICA DI ARADEO. It may be fast and loud, but the musical quality is undiminished: these are great musicians enjoying themselves and giving it what they've got, and that's what gives the music its special energy. I should mention that I've chosen – with no particular intent – a track recorded by the 'old' CGS. After Mauro took charge he recruited his own band, with some of the best young musicians in Salento, keeping only vocalist Maria Mazzotta from the pre-2007 lineup. Under Mauro, CGS has solidified its reputation as a major act on the world music scene.

Our final destination is a region in the northwestern corner of Italy. Visitors to Piedmont know it for its wine and its gastronomy, and possibly its famous football teams. Some may have explored the villages in its Alpine valleys – places where the vestiges of a traditional folk culture may still be glimpsed today. They may also notice that not everyone converses in Italian. The Piedmontese language is close to Occitan, and both languages are widely spoken in Piedmont. The regional parliament recognised Piedmontese as an official language in 2004, and as a consequence it is now taught in many schools.

In the 1970s, a few music groups were formed that took quite an interest in Piedmont's cultural heritage. One of these was Tre Martelli ('three hammers' – originally there were three in the group). Tre Martelli was the performing arm of the Trata Birata Cultural Association, which carried out serious research into the musical traditions of the local area. This was reflected in the band's albums, which were packed with traditional songs, ballads and dances. But for the best insight into what the band are all about, I refer you to an article on their website about the Sbrando. [11] After running through 500 years of the history of this circle dance, they explain how a piece of sbrando music came to their attention and was included on their album Trata Birata. Then a couple of years later the British band Tiger Moth did a cover of the tune. When Tre Martelli realised that Tiger Moth's audiences were doing their own steps to the music, this spurred them on to do more research. The sbrando was still being performed at some village festivals, and so they analysed it in all its different forms. Then the group's dancers developed their own choreography. So from then on the band got people to dance the sbrando at their concerts and gave many dance lessons. It caught on: the article ends by saying that every bal-folk event they attend, there's nearly always a sbrando to dance to.

Another young band, La Lionetta, released a traditionally inspired debut album entitled Danze e Ballate dell'Area Celtica Italiana, made up of songs collected in Piedmont by Costantino Nigra in the 19th century. Even then, though, La Lionetta were no folk purists: they were interested in the interactions between cultures and the effects of combining different influences.

Today there are any number of folk groups in Piedmont, each one following their own musical path in the instruments that they play and the style that they adopt, but collectively forming a characteristically Piedmontese mix of influences, from Piedmontese and Occitan and the dance and song traditions of the north of Italy to Celtic, French, and beyond. Many of these groups can be found on the Piedmontese record label FolkClub Ethnosuoni.

My selection is an album by three women, Paola Lombardo,

Donata Pinti and Betti Zambruno, each with a wealth of knowledge of Piedmontese folk tradition, yet each with contrasting backgrounds (classical, folk, jazz). It was a brief collaboration, and they've all moved on to other projects, but the combination of female harmonies with the accordion playing of Armando Illario works very well. The songs are all traditional, but we're advised against viewing this as a Piedmontese album: they are songs that speak to women everywhere. On **LA BELLA MARIANIN** Pinti is the soloist. As the other voices join in, the song grows in energy and transports us to another place.

NOTES

1. http://www.gala.fr/l_actu/news_de_stars/dalida_qui_est_luigi_tenco_l_homme_pour_lequel_elle_a_voulu_se_suicider_en_1967_383661
2. https://www.theguardian.com/music/musicblog/2008/jan/24/unsungheroesno4luigitenco
3. This account of her time in Palermo is based on http://www.palermoviva.it/rosa-balistreri-canta-cunta/
4. http://www.blogfoolk.com/2013/11/matilde-politi-vacanti-sugnu-china.html
5. http://www.blogfoolk.com/2010/08/matilde-politi-la-tradizione-musicale.html
6. http://tottusinpari.blog.tiscali.it/2013/06/16/intervista-a-luigi-lai-il-maestro-delle-launeddas-che-racconta-la-sua-vita/
7. http://tottusinpari.blog.tiscali.it/2015/07/03/il-virtuoso-e-%E2%80%9Canarchico%E2%80%9D-delle-launeddas-andrea-pisu-il-suonatore-del-simbolo-della-cultura-musicale-della-sardegna/
8. http://www.independent.co.uk/news/world/europe/la-notte-della-taranta-tradition-vs-contemporary-beats-brings-conflict-to-italian-folk-festival-10488924.html
9. http://www.lanottedellataranta.it/en/the-festival/festival
10. http://www.rootsworld.com/interview/cgs2012.shtml
11. http://www.tremartelli.it/index.php/lo-sbrando

KOSOVO

When Kosovo declared independence from Serbia in 2008 it signed up to a package of commitments brokered by UN envoy Martti Ahtisaari. Under the Ahtisaari Plan, Kosovo declared itself to be a secular multi-ethnic country with guaranteed minority rights. The Plan was based on the hope and belief that Kosovan Albanians and Kosovan Serbs could live together in a unitary state. This goal, however, could hardly be said to represent the aspirations of either the Albanian or the Serb communities. The Republic of Serbia has never recognised Kosovo's independence, and Krstimir Pantic expressed the feelings of many Kosovan Serbs when, having been elected mayor of the town of North Mitrovica in 2013, he refused to take the oath of office. Nonetheless Kosovan Serbs do engage in the democratic process and do take their places in the Kosovo Assembly. As for the ethnic Albanians, pollsters have consistently found that a majority would support some form of unification with Albania.

So Kosovo's future is up for grabs, and much may depend on emotional attachment. If you speak to a Kosovan now, they're more likely to identify as Albanian than as Kosovan. Can this change? Can the fledgling state succeed in instilling greater pride in Kosovo's own history and culture? And what role can music play in this?

The biggest difference between the Albanian-speaking populations of Kosovo and Albania is that the Republic of Albania was never a part of Yugoslavia. For most of the 20th century, the two populations inhabited very different worlds, living separate lives and fighting their own struggles. The Albanian state had been founded following a wave of insurgency in 1912. So when the borders of Yugoslavia were established the Albanian majority enclave that remained was seen as a problem and as a threat. The Belgrade government tried to reduce this threat through force and diktat. Thousands of Serb colonists were moved into Kosovo. They seized houses and land, and when villages rebelled against this, whole villages were razed to the ground. Children were first forced to attend Serb language schools, then allowed to attend so-called Turkish schools. Albanian language and culture was suppressed, but still people clung to their roots. By the late 1930s, seeing its policies failing, the Belgrade government began to look to more drastic solutions. In July 1938, a meeting took place in Istanbul where agreement was reached on relocating 40,000 Albanian families from Kosovo, Macedonia and Montenegro to Turkey. [1]

In Communist Yugoslavia Albanian identity was again viewed as a problem. Albanian language schools were shut down, displays of Albanian national symbols were banned. Albanians were discriminated against, shut out from jobs, and at constant risk of raids and arbitrary arrests by the security police. In 1968, students in Pristina organised a mass demonstration, and following this Belgrade gradually adopted a more liberal approach. The University of Pristina, which opened its doors in 1969, permitted students to study in the Albanian language. And the 1974 constitution gave Kosovo real autonomy in its own affairs. The changes weren't enough though to satisfy the hunger for freedom from Serb rule. Many people longed to be part of a greater Albania. And yet for all the common heritage Albania was by this time like a foreign country. Since 1948 the border had been firmly sealed, crossing it illegally a crime punishable by imprisonment. So most Kosovans had little idea that under Enver Hoxha Albania was suffering from prolonged economic and cultural stagnation.

After the war with Serbia ended in 1999 one of Kosovo's most urgent priorities was the restoration of the historic heart of the city of Gjakova, which had been destroyed by Serbs in apparent retaliation for Nato bombing. It had to be done. Gjakova is a remarkable place, home to a uniquely Kosovan cultural heritage. The jewel in the crown is its Grand Bazaar, unequalled anywhere in the Balkans. Since the 17th century the Bazaar has been home to the many trades and craft industries for which Gjakova is famous: gunsmiths, silversmiths, tinsmiths, metal workers, leather workers, saddlers, costume makers... The craftsmen were organised in esnafs, a guild system. Esnafs controlled economic activity, and much more. They were also a form of cooperative which supported those in need and were channels for social activities.

Today, Gjakova is being rebranded as a centre of cultural heritage. Every year it honours its cultural traditions in its sofra festival. A sofra is a round low table, and sofra music is folk music played in an informal setting by groups of male musicians sat down around these tables, which originally would have been organised within the esnafs. In the festival the music goes hand in hand with other aspects of Gjakovan culture: folk dancing, yes; but also food (plates of meze may be left on the sofra) and drink. The drink of choice is the local raki, which I understand is potent stuff, and many local craftsmen indulge in a bit of homebrew.

Gjakova may be overwhelmingly Albanian these days, but historically it's a place where people of different faiths have lived peacefully side by side, and that's an ethos which the festival tries to keep alive. Grupi Hadi Bajrami are seven Roma musicians from the area who like to play Gjakovan songs, and they've performed multiple times at the festival. The group's named after a legend of Gjakovan music: Hadi Bajrami was a sharki player, singer and raconteur.

Qamili i Vogël was a Gjakovan through and through who worked on the printing press right up to retirement, then died in 1991 when just in his late 60s. He had practically no formal education; his big break came when he joined Ymer Riza's ensemble. Ymer Riza, another sharki player, was instrumental in reviving Kosovan music and clearly played a big part too in Qamili's development: so much so, that when Qamili formed his own band, he named it after his mentor. It's his name though, even more than that of his mentor, which is revered in Kosovo to this day. He was a musical giant who performed with many other leading artists (including Hadi Bajrami). He also gave countless hours working with musicians, training them and producing them. He was very committed to preserving Kosovan and Albanian folk song: he published books of Albanian folk song which no one had done before, in addition to which he recorded and released as much as he could.

VAJTIMI I AVDISE is not your typical Balkan tune. There are Eastern Mediterranean, perhaps Turkish influences in there.

There's a freedom to Qamili's singing: one recognises right away that this is the kind of singer who will improvise, reinterpret songs and add to the emotional palette. What the future holds for Kosovo is hard to say – but it can certainly claim to have a past.

NOTES

1. http://sam.gov.tr/wp-content/uploads/2012/02/SuleKut.pdf

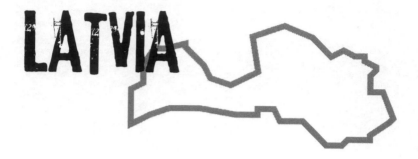

"To the Latvian the dainas are more than a literary tradition. They are the very embodiment of his cultural heritage, left by forefathers whom history had denied other, more tangible forms of expression. These songs thus form the very core of the Latvian identity and singing becomes one of the identifying qualities of a Latvian."

(Vaira Vīķe-Freiberga, Journal of Baltic Studies, 1975)

This was quite a bold statement to make in 1975 when Latvia was very much a part of the USSR and struggling to assert its cultural identity. Skandinieki, the group who started off the Latvian folk revival, were only formed in 1976. But a decade later the seeds of that cultural revival would coincide with a flowering political movement to the extent that the events leading to Latvia's independence would become known as the Singing Revolution. Hop forward another decade, and the young Latvian state would elect as president a woman with a background in academia and a passion for folklore. Dr Vīķe-Freiberga (for it was she) proved a very popular president and served two four-year terms.

Dainas were four-line poems and songs which had been

KIUKOJ, UORU DZAGIUZEITE	Saucējas
SVÁTKI GUOJA	Laiksne
LEC, SAULITE	Vilkači
SIT, JÁNÍTI, VARA BUNGAS	Valdis Muktupāvels & draugi

passed on orally from generation to generation. When serious attempts to document them began in the 1890s they seemed almost inexhaustible: hundreds of thousands were recorded. Mostly sung by women, the dainas depicted the cycles of nature, the everyday working life of farming communities, birth, love and death. Every important festival and ritual was commemorated, including weddings, coming of age, and the winter and summer solstices. And it was in the dainas that ancient folklore and stories of pagan gods were preserved.

Skandinieki was formed by Dainis and Helmi Stalts, and members of the Stalts family have remained at the core of the group ever since. Their trademark is polyphonic singing: they've always been a large ensemble, and many of their songs involve choral singing and chanting with no or minimal instrumentation. Some songs are sung in Livonian – a minority language that is in serious danger of dying out.

Traditional instruments were to feature very strongly in the Latvian folk revival, with pride of place going to the kokle. The kokle's quite a distinctive-looking zither-type instrument with a long crafted piece of wood, a hollow trapezoidal body and strings. It's played sitting down. According to Valdis Muktupāvels, "kokle tradition is believed to be more than two thousand years old. The oldest Latvian archaeological discovery related to the kokle comes from the 13th century, the first written testimony from the early 17th century, but the oldest physical instrument – the so-called Cours lute, held at the Latvian National History Museum – goes back to the year 1710... At the turn of the century, Latvian traditions of kokle playing were mostly lost and ancient instruments could be heard only in certain places in Kurzeme and Latgale." [1]

Valdis's name is now part of the story of the instrument: he brought his knowledge of the kokle to Skandinieki when he joined them in the 1980s, while his brother Māris played the kokle in Iļģi, the most successful of all Latvian folk groups. Valdis has also written extensively about the instrument.

After independence Latvia reclaimed the pagan side of its folklore and history. The summer solstice on 23rd and 24th June (in Latvia called Līgo and Jāņi) became a national holiday, celebrated as enthusiastically as New Year's Eve, while the winter solstice is celebrated by dragging the yuletide log. The majority of folk ensembles embraced all this as part of their culture and identity, but without self-identifying as pagans. Here's Ilga Reizniece, founder of the group Iļģi: "For many years I have been very interested in everything about the lives of my ancestors, their culture, religion. Iļģi's early repertoire included 'God Songs' and 'Sun Songs'. Through music I sought my way, but it did not lead me to religion. It did lead me to Latvian identity. I will stick with music. As I said, neopaganism in Latvia to me seems pleasant, but for me – too artificial." [2]

Valdis meanwhile had joined Ensemble Rasa who in the mid-90s released a landmark CD of winter and summer solstice songs, Latvia – Music of Solar Rites. The wonderful polyphonies were supplemented by Valdis's detailed liner notes which provided a mine of information about pagan rites and myths. Among the singers on the album was Iveta Tāle, who a few years later would found the group Saucējas.

The folk scene was quickly diversifying. Some introduced electric kokles, some tried to marry folk and rock. Iļģi experimented with a variety of styles. The women of Saucējas, by contrast, were strong traditionalists. They studied field recordings, and performing a cappella sought to imitate the singing styles and techniques. Their 2012 album Dziediet, meitas, vokorā was made up of songs from two regions in southeast Latvia where in 1891 and 1923 two of Latvia's most important folklorists, Andrejs Jurjāns and Emilis Melngailis, had collected dainas. Saucējas carried out their own fieldwork in the same villages, and the fruits of this can be found on the album and the book, written by Iveta Tāle, which accompanies it.

The 2016 album Trici, munu ustabeni! by contrast was based entirely on old research from 1958 carried out by a team from the Latvian SSR Academy of Sciences in the Latgale region in eastern Latvia. The women's aim once again was to render the songs as faithfully as possible as they would have originally been sung, without dressing them up in any way. The 29 songs selected include love songs, work songs, and songs about war and seasonal festivities. The multilayered polyphonic harmonies of KIUKOJ, UORU DZAGIUZEITE are a real highlight – this song is about a girl who starts crying when she hears the cuckoo singing, as she misses her brothers.

Another all-female ensemble, Laiksne, have been described as 'post-folklore', which, while it doesn't seem to describe a lot of their work does fit SVÁTKI GUOJA. This was the lead track from Es čigāna meita biju, an album of winter solstice songs released in December 2013, and features trance-like chanting to a driving rocking beat. Despite the modern arrangement this is a band dedicated to playing traditional instruments, and who set out to revive traditional songs in their original dialects.

Was it just me, or was there a lot of female-centred folk music in Latvia? The next band I encountered were very much a male group. It soon became clear that this wasn't the only different thing about them: "We were teenagers when we started out. We were fiercely opposed to the folklore movement, and the image of the average folklore enthusiast – unkempt, long hair and a categorical attitude towards everything. Tell me, how can you establish contact with someone like that? That's why we spent a lot of time thinking about our own image, to avoid resembling members of a sect and so that other young people wouldn't think of us as being odd." [3] The words are those of Davis Stalts, leader of the group Vilkači.

Vilkači (which means werewolves) had been inspired by another male band called Vilki (wolves). They set out to study and recreate how the ancient peoples of Latvia lived a thousand years ago. **LEC, SAULITE!** (Rise, sun!) is fairly representative of their sound: slow and solemn singing with atmospheric music in the background. As well as the music they were into crafts and battle reenactments. They weren't the kind of pagans who wore flowers in their hair: "Together we have felt the need to popularize the ancient culture of white society… We want to inspire contemporary Latvians, especially young people, to remember and feel their roots, their ancestors who once lived so simply and naturally, ancestors who once were forced to defend their loved ones, their land and the people against the foreign invaders, leaving their loved ones behind, and pouring out their opponents' blood." [4]

Davis Stalts was born in 1982, the son of Dainis and Helmi who had formed Skandinieki all those years ago. More recently his father served a couple of terms in parliament as a nationalist MP. The younger Stalts has already had a turbulent political career, falling out with former party colleagues both in the coalition government and on Riga Council. Davis Stalts represents a new breed of assertively right-wing politicians whose rejection of any accommodation with the country's Russian-speaking minority does not bode well for Latvia's future.

In 2012, Valdis Muktupāvels reappeared with a new group

of musicians and yet another solstice-themed album: Karsta bija Jāņu nakte (Midsummer night was hot). The album was conceived as a song cycle in which each song complemented the previous one. The dominant mood of the album is light and celebratory, and for me that's what comes across on SIT, JĀNĪTI, VARA BUNGAS with its male/female harmonies and tripping dance rhythm. Valdis doesn't just play kokles on the album – we find him playing bagpipes, traditional reeds, accordion and even the didjeridoo. In Latvia people celebrate the summer solstice by jumping over bonfires, which for Valdis just serves to prove that people have their own ways of turning up the heat.

NOTES

1. http://piekuns.com/?section=about-kokle
2. Michael Strmiska – Paganism-Inspired Folk Music, Folk Music-Inspired Paganism, and New Cultural Fusions in Lithuania and Latvia (2012), p376
3. Latvian Music Information Centre – Native Music (2006), p11 (thanks to Ilze Liepina for sending me this brochure)
4. Band website, retrieved, March 2014, http://vilkatis.lv/par-mums

LIECHTENSTEIN

The Principality of Liechtenstein is a tiny Alpine country wedged between Austria and Switzerland. With an area of just 160 square kilometres and a population of 35,000 you'd be entitled to wonder whether it can possibly have any unique culture to speak of.

It's true enough that the folk music of the Principality doesn't differ radically from that of its neighbours: Switzerland, Austria and Bavaria. It doesn't rank highly in global importance. If this is a problem for you, try putting out of your mind the fact that Liechtenstein is a self-governing country and think of it as a small network of settled communities – communities which, however small, have something to reveal to us when we look closely at the people and their music.

Josef Frommelt is a musician and amateur historian from the village of Triesen, and this chapter owes much to his painstaking research, as well as the work that he's done in preserving (and recreating) Liechtenstein's musical past.

In the first half of the 19th century, Frommelt found little written record of the music. Folk dances such as polkas and schottisches were popular and these would typically be accompanied by the violin, which until the latter part of the century was much the most important instrument. Frommelt does find several references in the mid-century to Josef Banzer who made records of the music to a number of these dances and was known as the Bard of Triesen. Sadly he ended up murdering his wife with an axe and getting locked up for insanity. [1]

In the 1860s, the quiet harmony of Triesen was transformed when a Swiss firm opened a cotton mill. Even more than the church, the mill became the focal point of the town's life. Hundreds of weavers were employed there, including some from neighbouring villages, and a smaller number of skilled workers began arriving in the town from far and wide.

As the mill was opening its doors, five men from Triesen formed a brass band. The ensemble was led by elementary school teacher and organist Franz Oehri, and theology student Florian Kindle wrote new arrangements of dance tunes and hymns and composed a number of pieces himself. [2] As well as performing at dances and events in the village, before long they were performing around the region as their reputation grew. When war came in 1914 the dances were stopped and they had to put away their instruments, but the band reformed in 1923 under a new name, Harmoniemusik Triesen. (Unfortunately,

Frommelt tells us, after the war the string band tradition never fully recovered.)

Frommelt himself became the band's musical director in 1964. Over the next two decades the band grew to considerable size. When new uniforms were ordered in 1967 there were 40 members, including five women who'd recently joined the Liechtenstein Music Association. And by the early 1980s, numbers had increased to more than 50. The band had outlasted the old mill, which closed its doors for the last time in 1982. The land on which the mill had stood passed into the hands of the local community, and (no doubt after much effort and fundraising) a new cultural centre was opened on the site in 2006. Called The Gasometer after the old gasometer tower that used to overlook the mill, its design includes a new tower containing several exhibition areas.

On 11th May 2013 a concert in The Gasometer explored Liechtenstein's musical past. Harmoniemusik Triesen (who'd recently celebrated their own 150th anniversary) played tunes by their founder Florian Kindle. Two more local ensembles, Tresner Huusmosig and the Triesner folk music quartet, played a few old string numbers, while young soprano Nadia Nigg raided Josef Banzer's songbook. The programme of music was very similar to the CD compiled by Josef Frommelt, Volksmusik aus Liechtenstein: Langgässler Schottisch (unfortunately the concert schedule doesn't tell us whether Frommelt was there in person, organising behind the scenes, playing music or selling CDs). The featured track is from this album, a slow-paced and very elegant MASOLKA (Alpine dance) by Tresner Huusmosig.

Liechtenstein's national day is 15th August, and Josef Frommelt likes to mark this day, whatever the weather, by climbing a mountain and lighting a bonfire. The steep slopes of the Mittagsspitz lead up from the Rhine Valley, and from the summit of the Mittagsspitz on a fine day a whole panorama opens up of mountains familiar to him: "the Falknis, the Schwarzhorn,

the Plasteikopf, the Rappastein, Langspitz and Goldlochspitz…
when I come back from a trip abroad, I only feel really at home
when I see these mountains around me." [3]

NOTE

1. http://issuu.com/medienbuero/docs/lie_zeit_7/9
2. http://www.hmt.li/archiv/
3. See note 1

LITHUANIA

I f you'd like a taste of Lithuanian culture, google search for 'Trys Keturiose Lino Laikas YouTube'. The two-part video is an audiovisual project by the folklore group Trys Keturiose.

You might get a few strange looks if you start sharing these videos – not because they're improper, but because they turn modern aesthetic ideas on their head. We see five women garbed in plain robes and headscarves suggestive of some religious order inside a building which, from its stained-glass windows, appears to be a church. Like the costumes, the production is without any artifice or showiness: there is just one camera, and the camera moves around very little. Strangest of all is the singing. It's mostly just chanting, without any instruments, and they're not trying to dazzle you or impress you with their voices. Each of the songs has a narrow melodic range, and instead of harmonies we get polyphonies, where the singers are following different melodic lines. Throughout the performance the singers remain solemn and serious, and the first smiles that we see are right at the very end when the ensemble are being applauded by the audience.

The choreography, the attention to detail, is all there. Not all the women join in on every song: there are three-part, four-part, five-part songs, and each song is carefully arranged and has its

KAS TAR TEKA PAR DVARELI, RYGAILIO

Trys Keturiose

APEJA SAULIUTE

Kulgrinda

GERVELE

Atalyja

own dynamic. At times we cut away from the footage inside the church, and patterned graphics move down the screen.

This form of song is called sutartine and it's unique to Lithuania. Daiva Račiūnaitė-Vyčinienė, as well as being the driving force behind Trys Keturiose, is one of the world's leading experts on sutartines and she's written extensively on the subject. (For those musicians among you, one particularly unusual characteristic of sutartines which she talks about is the dissonant intervals in the harmony.)

Sutartine singing is an ancient tradition with roots deep in Lithuania's past, but by the middle of the 20th century this tradition seemed to be fading into oblivion. A leading musicologist of the time, Jadvyga Čiurlionytė, commented dismissively that "sutartines have become museum-pieces in today's musical culture. They sound really strange to ears more accustomed to contemporary music." [1]

Collection of sutartines from rural sources didn't take place until the early 20th century, when the tradition was already dying. A few collections of these songs were published, and there were also some phonograph recordings made. In the 1950s, Zenonas Slaviūnas carried out extensive research on sutartines and in his work reprinted a lot of the earlier material. Slaviūnas' book was all very interesting – but what did these old songs actually sound like? One of the earliest revival groups was Sadauja, formed in Vilnius in 1971. "Sadauja stands out among other ensembles," claims Daiva, "because Emilija Kuzavinienė (1903–92) was involved with it from its inception and the songs and sutartines were passed down from her mother," who was born in 1863. But they were the exception at the time:

"Most songs were learnt from Slaviūnas' three-volume set of sutartines. Only in exceptional cases were they learnt from the archive sound recordings at the Institute of Lithuanian Literature and Folklore, to which few people had access. It is therefore unsurprising that when groups began to sing sutartines, they had no idea how they should sound. Their singing was musical and pure, but bore little resemblance to the traditional articulation of sutartines." [3]

Knowledge was increasing all the time. Two of those who helped guide Sadauja in those early years, Kazimieras Kalibatas and Laima Burkšaitienė, were to teach Daiva a few years later. With their example and encouragement, she became very interested in performance. In the early 1980s she formed the group that later became Trys Keturiose; around this time she also began organising a sutartines evening as part of the annual Skamba, skamba, kankliai folklore festival in Vilnius.

Trys Keturiose don't release many albums. This may be partly because they have academic careers to pursue, but it's not just that: they see recordings as a poor substitute for a live performance where they can make a deeper connection with their audience. The group are very committed to capturing in their music traditional modes of sutartine chanting. However, they recognise that tradition is not static, that people have to interpret it for themselves and find their own truth. And live performance always gives that little bit more creative freedom.

In 2012 they did bring out an album, and KAS TAR TEKA PAR DVARELI, RYGAILIO appears on it. The song has a lovely, easy flow, making it one of their more accessible numbers. We can hear three separate voices (or sets of voices); the song is just a repeated refrain, the words convey no meaning, and yet it has its own energy, its gentle ebb and flow. Allow yourself just to listen attentively and without expectations, and see where the music takes you.

Kulgrinda also sing sutartines, but they don't confine themselves to bringing the past back to life. Kulgrinda songs, according to Daiva, "are freely interpreted or newly created, often with completely new texts". [4] The aim: a newly created, constructed tradition, basically a mythologised view of past tradition. I use the word mythology advisedly: Kulgrinda are the standard bearers for the Romuva religion, and bandleaders Jonas Trinkūnas (1939–2014) and his wife Inija Trinkūnienė (born 1951) are its high priests.

Lithuania was the last European country to be Christianised. Fragments of old pagan beliefs survived, passed on through the language and the culture. There had been previous attempts to revive the Romuva faith, before Jonas Trinkūnas gave it that much sought-for quality, credibility. Its credibility also suffered no harm from the state's heavy-handed attempts to suppress it during the Soviet years. Back in the late 1960s, Jonas had started up a folklore movement which thrived for a few years before the authorities got nervous and shut it down. Jonas lost his job as a lecturer at Vilnius University, and for 15 years he was banned from engaging in any scientific research work. Naturally, he carried on with his private research into the cultural and musical traditions of the Baltic states.

And then came perestroika. Jonas was taken back on by the university, he formed Kulgrinda, and the foundations of a new pagan movement were laid. As Lithuania moved rapidly to regain its independence in 1990 to '91 it openly declared itself a religious movement and adopted the name Romuva ('temple', 'sanctuary'). A high value was placed on ancient stories and songs that illuminated the beliefs of Lithuania's pre-Christian past. Inija Trinkūnienė believes that the association with sacred ritual was what made folk music essential to people's lives. The loss of this link was instrumental in folk's long-term decline: "Living folklore beyond any doubt was made poorer by such a process. Traditional folklore was not able to compete with modern forms of urban entertainment; therefore it was condemned to die out." [5]

So Jonas and Inija ensured that song and dance were an integral part of all their rituals and ceremonies. Most important of these was the fire ritual, an ancient Baltic tradition. There is chanting as the fire is lit on a stone altar, and singing and dancing continues as the devotees tend the fire and make ritual offerings to it. Kulgrinda released a series of themed CDs which evoked ancient history, myth and ritual. Ugnies Apeigos ('Rite of Fire', 2002) came with liner notes in Lithuanian and English introducing the Baltic fire ritual and explaining which gods were honoured by which songs. Perkuno Giesmes ('Hymns of Perkunas', 2003) was dedicated to the god of thunder, strength and wisdom. Prusu Giesmes ('Prussian Hymns', 2005) was sung in Old Prussian, an extinct Baltic language. Giesmes Saulei ('Hymns to the Sun', 2007) was a collection of songs to the sun goddess Saule, while Laimos Giesmes ('Hymns of Laima', 2014) was dedicated to Laima, the goddess of fate. Even if the songs themselves were often newly created, authenticity was added by the seriousness of the research that went into each album, the use of traditional instruments such as the kankles (zither) and skuduciai (panpipes), and the link to a new living tradition. Kulgrinda perform at annual festivals, marriages, funerals and public ceremonies. They're a part of the summer camps that have attracted many young people to the Romuva movement. Usually they're close to the nature that they revere, outdoors in the countryside, dressed in unprettified traditional costume.

I have to confess though, for me it's the modern elements in the music that make Kulgrinda's sound so powerful. In the past there was a strict division of labour: there would be vocal sutartines, sung by women, and instrumental sutartines, with men playing the instruments. On Kulgrinda's albums the singing is often accompanied and is enhanced by modern production skills. So on the sun song **APĖJA SAULIUTĖ** the simple call and response chanting is given real drama by the bagpipe sound at the beginning, and the drone and the low drumbeat that can be heard in the background.

I'm not alone in this: musically, Kulgrinda's main legacy has been to help inspire a new wave of post-folklore bands, based in cities rather than the countryside and much more diverse in their musical output. Žalvarinis was a direct offshoot, a collaboration between some of Kulgrinda's younger members and the pagan metal group Ugnelakis. While Žalvarinis looked to the folk tradition for their material, out-and-out pagan metal bands were writing songs from a mainly male perspective about Lithuanian gods, mythology and historical battles. Returning to the post-folk groups, as far as such labels have any useful meaning, one could describe Spanxti as neofolk, Pievos as folk rock, and Atalyja, for want of a better term, as folk fusion.

On **GERVELĖ**, Atalyja take a sutartine and add to it with layers of instrumentation, trying to make it sound as good as possible. This is traditional folk remixed for the big festival stage. Atalyja are a large band with nine members including four vocalists. The vocals do remain important, but they're no longer the sole focus, the track builds in intensity, more instruments come in, one (perhaps a skuduciai) introduces a lovely melodic line, and after this there's a whole instrumental section.

That was released in 2004 and Atalyja have come a long way since then, they've never lost that desire to experiment and to expand their musical palette. "The ancient melodies," they claim on their website, "are enriched with elements of rock, jazz, funk, blues rock, metal and Indian music." What the ancient musicians would have made of this we'll mercifully never know, but 21st-century festival-goers love it. Ernest Jepifanov (aka Nadaprem), a longtime band member and multi-instrumentalist, is a student of Indian classical music: 2015 saw the release of an album in his name in collaboration with Atalyja (Virsmai ir Versmes) which is a long way from folk music. It's a world music project, a cleverly constructed soundscape of unlikely instrument combinations and all manner of exciting grooves.

NOTES

1. Quoted in Daiva Račiūnaitė-Vyčinienė – The revival of Lithuanian polyphonic sutartines songs in the late 20th and early 21st century http://www.academia.edu/9177468/Daiva_Ra%C4%8Di%C5%ABnait%C4%97-Vy%C4%8Dinien%C4%97, p101
2. Ibid, p102
3. Ibid, p107
4. Ibid, p109
5. http://www.marasloks.lv/public/?id=99&ln=en

LUXEMBOURG

On 10th May 1940, Hitler's troops entered the neutral state of Luxembourg, taking it under German control. The following year it was decided to hold a census to legitimise the occupation. It was a familiar enough Nazi tactic: in 1938 a referendum in Austria on the Anschluss with Germany had returned a 99.73% result in favour of German union. The census asked just three questions:

1. Current nationality?
2. Mother tongue?
3. Volkszugehörigkeit (of what people are you part)?

The German-controlled media bombarded the people with messages explaining that Luxembourgish was really a dialect of German and trying to get them to write down 'German'. Moreover, this was not a secret ballot: every questionnaire had to be signed and there were open threats of reprisals against anyone who voted the wrong way. Nonetheless, the Resistance ran a campaign asking every citizen to write down three times Luxembourgish. Once the German authorities got wind of the fact that over 90% of the population was likely to vote this way, the census was hurriedly cancelled.

ISLÉKER LEET

Dullemajik

The episode is important, not just in itself, but because it's entered into national mythology. You could be forgiven for assuming that Luxembourg's sense of national identity would not be very strong. A micro-state wedged between France and Germany, it's not isolated from its neighbours by either geography or ethnicity. Its population is diverse, with the highest rate of migration per head of any European country, and that's not taking account of the more than 160,000 who commute there every day from Germany, Belgium and France. What culture it has of its own is heavily influenced by its larger neighbours. And yet, and yet... in 2007, Luxembourg became the first city to be designated European Capital of Culture twice. Clearly, this meant something. Luxembourgers are comfortable with the idea of Luxembourg as a nation rooted in hundreds of years of history, and there's a strong sense of confidence, or pride, that their country has something special to offer.

Luxembourg's musicians have long looked beyond the borders for inspiration rather than to any identifiable Luxembourger culture. The great majority of pop and rock bands sing in English. [1] Luxembourg's five Eurovision Song Contest wins (the most recent being in 1983) were all sung in French. Despite it being the most widely spoken language, only a small scattering of bands sing in Luxembourgish.

Dullemajik, formed in 1975 by Guy Schons, are exceptional in many ways: they're a Luxembourger band who play traditional folk music, who sing in Luxembourgish and who research Luxembourger culture. Dullemajik is a Luxembourgish term for a hurdy-gurdy, and Schons is a hurdy-gurdy player, but the band isn't set up to follow any one genre. They started with six musicians and a range of instruments, giving them flexibility to explore different aspects of Luxembourg's musical past. You don't quite know what you're going to get from Dullemajik; it could be anything from medieval ballads and forgotten dance tunes, to chansons from the early 20th century, or their own compositions.

From the band's first album, **ISLÉKER LEET** is a delightful teaser which makes you wonder if more musicians explored Luxembourg's heritage what treasures might they find. I don't know if this actually is an old song, but the flute melody sounds medieval, and I love the lightness with which it dances along.

NOTES

1. http://www.luxembourg.public.lu/en/publications/a/apropos-musique-amplifiee/ap-musique-amplifiee-2007-EN.pdf

MACEDONIA

acedonia's most celebrated singer was born in 1943 to a poor Muslim family from Skopje's Roma community. "My father was a shoeshine man," Esma Redžepova told Songlines magazine, "and he lost a leg when the Nazis bombed Skopje. This did not stop him working and he never begged." [1]

Esma knows all about inner strength and willpower to succeed. "At the age of nine," she claims in the same interview, "I realised I was different." She began singing and composing songs: her most famous hit, Chaje Shukarije, was written when she was just 12. Her parents, though, wanted her to marry early and bring up a family – it was common at the time for Roma girls to be married off when they were just 12 or 13. She told them she wanted to sing: she'd been offered training by the bandleader Stevo Teodosievski. Of course her parents were opposed to this too as women singing in public was considered shameful. But Teodosievski won them over, promising them that he would make young Esma into a real artist, not just a nightclub singer.

Stevo Teodosievski soon had more battles to fight. He was thrown out of Tito's Communist Party because of his cultural beliefs; he clashed with the party-controlled Radio Skopje over

HAJRI MATE DIKI DAJE Esma Redzepova & Usnija Jasarova
ISTAMBOL KOCEK Kočani Orkestar & King Naat Veliov

their reluctance to play gypsy music. Even his fellow musicians questioned whether it was a good idea to promote this Roma girl. But he believed in Esma, and he believed that he could get non-Roma to listen to Roma music. He took her to Belgrade where she studied at the Academy of Music. By the age of 18 Esma was touring internationally with the Ansambl Teodosievski, and the hit records soon followed. Esma was Yugoslavia's first real Roma singing star.

The old prejudices, though, didn't simply disappear. It was almost unheard of for Macedonians and Roma to intermarry... until in 1968, in the flush of their early success, Esma and Stevo did precisely that. "We were the first mixed marriage! That was a big deal!" remembers Esma. "Can you imagine how many people were at our wedding... Ten to fifteen thousand people came to see if it were true that the two of us were getting married." [2]

Esma knew all too well how fortunate she had been to avoid becoming a child bride, wed to a man who would have insisted that she give up any ambitions of being a singer. The song HAJRI MATE DIKI DAJE (I curse you, Mother) is the words of a young girl sold off by her parents to a rich man she doesn't love. Esma's voice cuts in about a minute into the song: it's incredibly beautiful, but you feel the sadness in her voice, and it becomes all the more poignant I think when you're aware of the subject matter.

The young couple had begun adopting homeless street children and giving them a musical education. Eventually they opened a school where 48 boys were raised. By all accounts the boys had great affection for Esma and Stevo and several became part of the band.

Esma had this dual role – an ambassador of Roma culture, but also since independence in 1991, increasingly an ambassador for the young Macedonian state. She presents the Roma as an unassuming peace-loving people who believe in live and let live: "There is one sentence which is very common for Gypsies: We came naked into this world and we will go back naked. And we don't want to have a homeland. All the world is our homeland." [3] In the same breath, she lavishes praise on Macedonia. She knows about the bad things that have happened to her people, she's heard and seen it all, but she doesn't like to speak of the Roma as victims, and besides she is genuinely proud of the status that they enjoy in Macedonia.

"Macedonia is the least oppressive place for Roma; it was one of the first countries in the world that early on had a radio show in the Romany language, with singing and music. One of the first Romany leaders was a mayor [of Sutka]. We have Romany members of parliament, we have two private Roma channels on TV and several radio stations in the Romany language, and on national TV, there are two half-hour weekly shows so all of Macedonia can watch us." [4]

In theory the rights of minorities are protected under Macedonia's constitution, but the practice is more problematic. Albanians are by far the largest minority: the 2002 census reported a Roma population of only 53,879 (2.7% of the population). The real population according to some estimates may be as much as three times higher, which tells us something in itself. Marginalisation and social exclusion of Roma people is evidently not a thing of the past. So Roma children have the right to be educated in their mother tongue, but this has not been backed up by teacher training programmes for Roma teachers. Worse still, the undocumented status of many Roma prevent them from enrolling their kids in school at all, and the state has dragged its feet in combating this issue. The Roma can have their TV stations – but it's up to them to find the funding for it, there is no state support. Šuto Orizari, the Skopje district where many Roma were resettled in the wake of the 1963 earthquake, is Romany speaking, is self-governing and has a Roma mayor. But it's hardly a success story: levels of poverty and unemployment are through the roof. As a consequence it's very difficult for the municipal authority to collect the tax revenue that it needs in order to function. There are not even many businesses because the whole area is residential.

Undoubtedly, though, Macedonia was a place where many gypsies felt able to settle down and make a life for themselves. For over 100 years the Veliov family have been part of a Turkish-speaking Roma community in the town of Kocani. When Naat Veliov left his mother's womb in 1957 he entered a thriving musical tradition. His father headed up a family orchestra that played the wedding circuit, and which was previously directed for many years by his grandfather. Under his father's tutelage it became clear that Naat had an exceptional aptitude for the trumpet. At the age of 18 he was already leading the orchestra. They would have played all the folk dances of the region, but as a lover of jazz Naat brought a new kind of energy to the music.

In 1988, Emir Kusturica made an award-winning film called Time of the Gypsies with a soundtrack by Goran Bregović which had Veliov playing trumpet. The film and the soundtrack helped to popularise Balkan brass band music. It wasn't long before Naat had signed a contract with the Belgian producers Stéphane Karo and Michel Winter, who were also managing the Romanian Roma band Taraf de Haïdouks. At first this seemed to be working, and the international sales of L'Orient est Rouge (1997) put the Kočani Orkestar name on the map. Then in 1999 came the split.

The split wasn't graceful and it wasn't amicable. Naat claims that the Belgians took advantage of him over money; there were also arguments about musical direction. In the midst of this, imagine his dismay when he found out that the Belgians had registered 'Kočani Orkestar' as a trademark, so he was legally barred from using the name of his own family band. He recruited his father and other family members and they became the Original Kočani Orkestar.

ISTAMBOL KOCEK is a joyous cacophony of tuba, trumpet, sax, clarinet and drums, and a tribute by the band to their Turkish origins. The album Gypsy Mambo was released just before the split and it has Naat's fingerprints all over it in its celebration of the music he loves from jazz to Turkish to South American. Today Naat still plays the music he loves, but he's not recorded since 2003. "He now shares his time," reports Michele Gurrieri, "between tours all around Europe and a quiet life in the Roma neighbourhood of Kočani – playing in local restaurants, at weddings or at bachelor parties that last until morning." [5] As well as his father, two sons and a grandson have played recently in his band.

The other Kočani Orkestar, started up by saxophonist Ismail Saliev, has had a successful run with Stéphane Karo on the Crammed Discs label, but the music has changed quite a lot: for my money too much global fusion, and too much of a departure from the Balkan dances and rhythms that inspired me to listen in the first place.

Ismail Saliev could retort that Roma music has always embraced other cultures and reached out across national borders. It's only very recently that we've become used to Roma music being represented by brass bands, although brass bands have been around in the Balkans for many decades before that. Jim Samson identifies three types of urban Roma music in Macedonia:

- *The zurla-tapan ensemble (zurla being a double-reed oboe-type instrument, and tapan, a drum)*
- *The calgija, an ensemble which mainly plays music of Turkish origin (typical instrumentation: violin, oud, kanun, and the dajre and tarabuka drums, though many more instruments got added in later years)*
- *Muzica lautareasca or gypsy fiddle music.* [6]

These urban genres were well suited to Roma musicians who gravitated towards larger ensembles that could lead the dancing at weddings and festivals. So the music of the Macedonian Roma always fell on the urban side of the urban/rural divide. I've no space here to explore rural Macedonian folk music, but I would recommend the twin CD set Music from Macedonia on Caprice Records. The compilation is a good introduction to the range of folk instruments and folk singing styles in Macedonia. Three wonderful instruments, the gajda (bagpipe), zurla (oboe) and kaval (flute), feature on various tracks, but pay attention too to the sparkling accordion playing of Goran Alachki, to the impressive Romany brass band music from Orkestar Ace and to the singers who represent different ethnic groups.

NOTES

1. Songlines 107 (April/May, 2015)
2. Carol Silverman – Romani Routes: Cultural Politics and Balkan Music in Diaspora (Oxford University Press, 2012), p205
3. http://matadornetwork.com/abroad/a-modern-history-of-macedonia-through-music/
4. Silverman, p213
5. https://www.ulule.com/the-king/
6. Jim Samson – Music in the Balkans (BRILL, 2013), pp293-297

MALTA

It's one of the wonders of the world, a World Heritage site since 1980. But for centuries all trace of its existence was hidden beneath the earth.

The Hypogeum was discovered entirely by accident in 1902, when stonemasons cutting cisterns in the rock for a new housing development broke through its roof to find underground tunnels. This was to prove just the starting point of a system of vast underground chambers, carved out of the limestone rock over a period of centuries between 3,600 and 2,500 BC with the aid of only flint and stone tools. Built on three different levels, its carved walls recreate many of the features of ancient Maltese overground temples. Many burials were made there and many religious ceremonies carried out, the exact nature of which we can only guess at.

The great civilisation that built the temples disappeared to be replaced by others. Over the millennia Carthaginians, Romans, Vandals, Byzantines, Arabs, Sicilians and the British have all laid claim to the island, and all have left their stamp on it.

Malta takes its cultural history seriously. Political parties compete for who can offer the strongest cultural programme. In 2002, the Cultural Heritage Act was passed which led to the

L'ISTORJA TA'ARTURO U MARIA, PT1 *Emmanuele Cilia*

setting up of Heritage Malta, and a new revamped national Arts Council. By joining the EU in 2004 Malta also gained access to European funding for cultural projects. In 2010 and 2011 the government announced significant increases in the cultural budget at a time when arts and culture were being squeezed in other countries because of the recession. In 2012, Valletta was selected as European Capital of Culture for 2018.

It's surprising then that Malta's musical heritage has been so long neglected. Traditional Maltese singing – ghana – is hundreds of years old. It comes in various forms, but two of the main ones are ghana tal fatt, a narrative poem in verse, and spirtu pront, which typically involves a couple of ghannejja (singers) taking on each other in a song duel, improvising verses as they go along. Some of the notable 20th-century ghannejja were Fredu 'l-Everest' Spiteri (1929–65), Mikiel 'il-Bambinu' Abela (1920–91) and Frans 'il-Budaj' Baldacchino (1943–2006). From what I can tell, they've left few recordings behind, and outside of Malta CDs of ghana singing are not easy to obtain. For now, the best advice I can give to those interested is to seek out those villages in Malta and Gozo where ghana singing is still popular.

Steve Borg was making world music programmes for Maltese

radio when he realised: "I was playing all types of music except Maltese." [1] His research took him to King's College Cambridge, where he found 18th-century Maltese musical scores which had been published 200 years ago by Edward Jones. Borg enlisted the help of ethnomusicologist Guzi Gatt to reconstruct traditional Maltese folk instruments that nobody played anymore. Ruben Zahra was then asked to develop a repertoire using the source material and the old instruments.

In 2000, the group Etnika was formed and released their first record. Producer Andrew Alamango was the fourth founding member of the group. "Most of the group's instruments," he says, "were made of cane, animal skin and horn. Examples are the zaqq, a form of bagpipe with a single-drone chanter; the zummara, a cane single-reed flute; the zafzafa, a cane and skin friction drum; and tambourines made with goat skin played in a dance-like fashion. These instruments belong to a much older semitic tradition and some are still in use in trad feasts like carnival. Others like the bagpipe have been given a new lease of life through use in Etnika band." [2] Alamango understates just how radical and important Etnika's contribution was. Gatt worked long hours to make several zaqqs himself. This remarkable, distinctive instrument is now being picked up by other folk groups. Zahra: "People hadn't actually heard these instruments. When they did, it was a revelation. The music is vivid, not nostalgic." [3]

Etnika's lineup was to go through several changes in the next few years. But Alamango remained part of the project, and was delighted to see not only that Etnika was gaining a higher profile and more respect, but that as a direct result more people were starting to take an interest in the traditional folk music of the islands. Alamango was also responsible for setting up Filfla records. Filfla is like a cross between a record label and a mini national music archive (in fact one of Alamango's aims is to bring about the setting-up of a national sound archive). It aims to preserve the very earliest recordings of Maltese music, recorded in Tunis and Milan in the early 1930s, and to clean them up, digitalise them and make them publicly accessible.

How, I wanted to know, had the Etnika and Filfla projects changed perceptions of traditional music in Malta? People are now more aware, Alamango tells me, "of a lost heritage of music, instruments, musicians, composers and poets which had been forgotten for decades. The music portrays a strong sense of identity and characteristics of the language which we'd long forgotten. These projects have helped in redefining the concept of tradition and its application."

It is thanks to Filfla that we can now hear the haunting voice of Emmanuele Cilia. **L'ISTORJA TA'ARTURO U MARIA, PT1** is a cleaned-up 1931 recording on which the guitar's slow pace leaves the nasally vocals hanging tremulously in the air. Some recordings of his were later released in the 1960s, and Alamango says that, "people today still remember him for his clarity of voice, musical aptitude and satirical wit."

NOTES

1. http://www.maltatoday.com.mt/2001/0923/tw/waw.html, retrieved September, 2013
2. Email 30/9/13
3. http://www.rootsworld.com/reviews/etnika.shtml

MOLDOVA

Reunification is on the agenda.

In March 2016, thousands of Moldovans marched through Chisinau, some carrying Romanian flags, calling for Moldova to unite with Romania. What was behind this? Moldova, already one of the poorest countries in Europe, had just lost an eighth of GDP to a massive fraud in the country's largest banks. The crisis highlighted the fact that two decades on since independence, problems of corruption had not gone away. Some believed that the answer lay in closer ties with Europe and preventing Putin's Russia from gaining any further influence. However, hopes of future EU membership had failed to materialise, with political divisions preventing this from getting off the ground. In the meantime Romania was enjoying the benefits of EU membership, its economy booming.

The key question here is how strongly are Moldovans tied to a sense of a unique national identity? Since the state was formed debates have rumbled on about what it means to be Moldovan: apart from the river Prut, what is there to divide Moldovans and Romanians? Is there an ethnic difference? Don't they share the same language and culture? To the outsider it's all a bit confusing: Moldova is adamant that Moldovan is a separate

MELODII DE NEUITAT *Nicolae Botgros si Orchestra Lautarii*

SARBA *Orchestra Fratilor Advahov*

language, but foreign analysts and travel guides say that it's almost indistinguishable from Romanian, or at most it's a dialect.

It's my conviction that Moldova will choose to remain a country. To understand why, we need look no further than the relationship the people have with the culture of their region.

Hora dance takes its name from the Greek language while Sirba dances, if their name is anything to go by, may well have originated from the Serbian people. These are the two best-known Romanian/Moldovan dances, evidence that for centuries dance has been a great cultural unifier. Over the years shoes have also tapped to Russian, Armenian, Bulgarian and gypsy folk dances. The effect of all this interchange was not to diffuse local identity, but to enrich it. There are all manner of different forms of hora and sirba dances, and some of this is down to villages and communities interpreting them in their own way.

Every folk dance or folk music group wears traditional folk costumes, and these again are an assertion of local identity. The female costume consists of a number of standard elements – shirt (gathered at the neck), skirt, apron, narrow belt, leather vest – but there is huge variety in its design. Each costume with its bright colours, its patterns and its ornamental motifs is a little piece of regional culture, likely to have been laboriously sewn by village women.

Somewhat confusingly for English speakers, Moldovan folk music is known as 'muzica populara'. Traditional ensembles have long rows of fiddlers blazing away: many of the dances are fast, so the music has to be fast and furious too. The most successful and most admired of all these ensembles, popular on both sides of the Prut, is the Orchestra Lautarii din Chisinau. Lautari means fiddlers. It's a term often used for gypsy musicians, but I have it on authority that anyone who takes their fiddle to weddings and plays traditional dances is a lautari. Lautarii were formed in 1970 by Nicolae Sulac, but their story really begins in 1978 when another Nicolae, Nicolae Botgros, joined the ensemble and became its director.

Nicolae's father, Dumitru Botgros, was a musician of rare talent and an uncompromising teacher. He taught his children that they needed to work if they wanted to eat the next day. And work they did. At music school in Cahul, Nicolae and his brothers were given permission to skip classes on the Friday so they could spend their weekends with the family ensemble playing at weddings and parties. This was no soft option; their father rehearsed them hard, they played all night and got no sleep, and they would return home on foot carrying their instruments even in the middle of the Moldovan winter. [1]

Nicolae Botgros brought to Lautarii his work ethic and his professionalism, also his passion for making audiences happy and keeping alive in every sense the music that he'd grown up with. The group went from strength to strength, they played in all the big European capitals and the list of artists who played with them over the years was like a who's who of Moldovan music (there've been over 300, reckons Nicolae, from the famous to the novice. [2]) As I write this, Nicolae has been with the band almost 40 years. It's like a family; the love and the loyalty are just as strong – "nobody leaves us," he says proudly. [3] Leading the group now is Nicolae's son Corneliu, who married the folk singer Adriana Ochisanu, and already their son, Christian, practises the fiddle many hours a day, preparing for the day when he will become the next tradition bearer.

The solo violin at the start of **MELODII DE NEUITAT** is a treat. After a couple of minutes the rhythm section kicks in – and from here it's an exhilarating ride as the music and dancing slowly become faster and wilder. For Nicolae and his group what matters is connecting with people in that moment of performance; music that's recorded to be played on the radio can never quite have the same immediacy.

Orchestra Lautarii have made albums, but getting hold of any of them is not an easy task. It's the same story across the board, not just with folk music but other genres too. As far as I can make out, very few CDs actually get made in Moldova because the public are simply not prepared to pay for them. And sadly one of the consequences is that Moldovan artists rarely get their work reviewed by blogs or magazines, and the music doesn't become known internationally. Perhaps the best-known Moldovan group is the rock-oriented world music group Zdob si Zdub, who've made recordings for Warner Music, and on Romanian, Russian and German record labels. One traditional album that's widely available and which I can recommend is Art of the Lautar by Marin Bunea. The mustachioed Bunea is a fifth-generation musician from a proud family of fiddlers, a graduate of the Chisinau conservatory and currently conductor of the Presidential Doina Orchestra. One can only hope, though, that in the future more international labels will take a close look at Moldova, and in particular at Moldovan muzica populara.

One candidate for their attentions would be Fratii Advahov, represented here with a short, fast and furious **SARBA** dance. Fratii means brothers, and Vasile and Vitalie Advahov are two brothers who grew up in the town of Cahul in southern Moldova. Their parents were both highly accomplished musicians and they soon picked up the bug. Music took them to Chisinau, where they spent 12 years at the Ciprian Porumbescu music high school and a further five years at the state conservatory. In Moldova it's seen as a natural thing for folk musicians to have a classical training – "popular music orchestras in Moldova are on a level with classical music." [4] But it can't be easy for these folk orchestras to survive, given their sheer size and the fact that there's no money to be made from selling CDs. Vasile and Vitalie made a decision early on: they didn't want to be just another wedding band, they wanted people to take them seriously. So for their first CD, recorded in 2005, they recruited a very distinguished guest singer: Zinaida Julea, who'd sung with a few of the big folk orchestras.

The term 'orchestra' is not used lightly:

"Today, the Orchestra led by the Advahov brothers has about 30 instruments – two nais [pan flutes], two clarinets, a saxophone, two trumpets, a double bass, a tambal [dulcimer], a braci [viola], a guitar, two accordions, a drum and 17 violins... But the great dream of Vitalie and Vasile is to sing with all the folk musicians on both sides of the Prut." [5]

That was in 2012. By that time Vasile and Vitalie already had taken their mighty ensemble to perform in concert halls around Europe. Since then they've expanded the orchestra some more and played with quite a few more musicians from both sides of the Prut. "We work in a family atmosphere," says Vitalie, who attributes the group's togetherness to the fact that so many of them went to music school together. [6]

NOTES

1. http://arhiva.vipmagazin.md/profil/Nicolae_Botgros/
2. http://www.moldova.org/de-muzica-nu-ma-satur-niciodata-interviu-cu-maestrul-nicolae-botgros-241285-rom/
3. http://adevarul.ro/moldova/actualitate/interviu-nicolae-botgros-conducatorul-orchestrei-lautarii-concurez--insumi-1_50ad0f567c42d5a6638e0cf9/index.html
4. http://arhiva.vipmagazin.md/profil/Vitalie_si_Vasile_Advahov/
5. Ibid
6. http://www.evzmd.md/special/cultura/273-cultura/18948-dinastia-de-virtuozi-o-via%C8%9Ba-de-muzica,-zece-ani-de-orchestra.html

MONACO

It seems like the result of a curious accident. The Principality of Monaco is the second smallest country in the world covering an area of less than one square mile, and is a small enclave on the French Riviera near the Italian border. How did France, a republic with several overseas territories, lose control of this small outcrop of rock on the Mediterranean coast?

In fact the history of Monaco is no more or less accidental than the history of the European land mass which, over the centuries, has seen whole nations rise up and disappear, and borders redrawn on countless occasions.

When France fell in 1940, Monaco was ruled by Prince Louis II, who was born and raised in Germany but had served in the French army. Its population had divided sympathies: some were French and some Italian. The German military occupation only extended to the northern and western parts of France. The remainder of the country, together with Monaco, fell within the zone libre. The one thing the zone libre was not was 'libre'. It was controlled by Vichy, who also controlled the news media and airwaves. Louis accepted Vichy rule but tried to keep Monaco neutral. It was a forlorn task. The Vichy regime had no desire or ability to thwart Hitler, and on 11th November 1942 this was

LE CHANT DES PARTISANS   *Léo Ferré*

underscored when the German army occupied the zone libre. On the same day, Mussolini's troops occupied Monaco. They remained there until September 1943 when Germany seized the Principality.

Official histories tend to airbrush over the extent of collaboration with the Nazis. Of course Louis collaborated. He knew that failure to do so could mean a bitter end, not just for him but for Grimaldi rule in Monaco. But the extent of his collaboration still has the power to shock. From the beginning of the war rich German money launderers began to settle in Monaco. Some of their money was blown in the casino, which saw a sharp increase in revenue during the war years. But they also set up dummy companies to help them avoid tax.

Louis seems to have been happy to encourage the arrival of well-connected Germans and their ill-gotten money. In November 1942, he wrote to the German authorities reminding them of his record of loyalty and cooperation and inviting them to eject the Italian troops – which is precisely what they did less than a year later. [1] The Germans arrived with their own agenda – and I'm not just referring to the Jews. By now Émile Roblot, one of Louis's ministers, was in negotiations with German banking authorities to create a secret bank in Monaco. This bank, Banque J.E. Charles, was created with the purpose of enabling top Nazis to stash away their money after the war on territory which they hoped would remain neutral.

In July 1941, Louis passed a law to register all Jews in Monaco, and several German and Austrian Jews that had fled to Monaco were handed over to Vichy France. After September 1943, all Jews in Monaco became targets of the Gestapo, and many hundreds were rounded up for deportation. Did Louis try to warn Jews who were about to be deported, as has been claimed? I'm somewhat sceptical; I'd like to see some evidence one way or the other. Some policemen did prewarn Jews, at great personal risk, when a Gestapo raid was imminent. But it seems implausible that Louis himself would have had much pre-knowledge or involvement in this.

An extensive Wikipedia entry tells us this about Léo Ferré's life during the war years:

"After graduating from Sciences Po, he returned to Monaco in 1939 before being mobilized the following year. During World War II he was assigned to the infantry and led a group of Algerian 'tirailleurs'... in 1943, Léo Ferré married Odette Shunck, who he met in 1940 in the city of Castres. The couple moved into a small farm at Beausoleil, on the hills of Monaco." [2]

So whether or not he was an active member of the Resistance he had opportunity to witness at first hand exactly what was happening in Monaco at that time. Whatever memories he took away, they stayed with him. **LE CHANT DES PARTISANS** was the anthem of the French Resistance, a song with enormous resonance. As well as this, Ferré wrote a song called Affiche Rouge, a musical version of a poem by Louis Aragon. The poem/song commemorates the Manouchian Group, a network of Resistance fighters based in

Paris, 23 of whom were captured by the Nazis at the same time before being tortured, interrogated and executed.

NOTES

1. http://sudwall.superforum.fr/t1973-monaco-occupation-allemande-1943-1944
2. https://en.wikipedia.org/wiki/L%C3%A9o_Ferr%C3%A9, retrieved June, 2018

MONTENEGRO

One of the world's youngest nations (it declared independence in 2006, following a referendum), Montenegro is still wrestling with issues of national and ethnic identity. Are they a region of Serbia or a separate nation? Do the people define themselves as Serbian or Montenegrin? You can't take any one opinion poll because people's views keep changing. The key to winning this debate is likely to lie in successfully reclaiming the past. And after its colourful history, the spotlight is bound to fall on Montenegro's cultural heritage. So I shall make no apology for looking back in time in this chapter at a couple of remarkable figures from Montenegro's past.

Avdo Mededović (1875–1955) has been called the Balkan Homer. He was a guslar: a singer who recites long epic poems while accompanying himself on the single-stringed gusle. Although he never learned to read or write he had a prodigious memory and a knack for improvisation. In the summer of 1935, Milman Parry of Harvard University's Department of Classics showed admirable perseverance by recording nine of Avdo's songs onto phonograph discs. The songs alone took up 53 hours of recording time, and many further hours were taken up by recorded conversations with Avdo.

DREMA MI SE *Ksenija Cicvaric*

This wasn't just a feat of memory. Every time he performed a song, Avdo would embellish it, adding depth to his characters and reams of scene-setting description to the basic narrative which increased its length.

"Parry made trial of Avdo's ability to learn a song that he had never heard before. Among the singers from whom Parry collected while Avdo was dictating or resting was Mumin Vlahovljak of Plevlje. Parry arranged that Avdo was present and listening while Mumin sang Beciragic Meho, a song that Parry had adroitly determined was unknown to Avdo. Mumin was a good singer and his song was a fine one, running to 2,294 lines. When it was over, Parry turned to Avdo and asked him if he could now sing the same song, perhaps even sing it better than Mumin, who accepted the contest good-naturedly and sat by in his turn to listen... The pupil's version of the tale reached to 6,313 lines, nearly three times the length of his original, on the first singing!" [1]

Incredibly he was still able to perform the song for Parry's former assistant 16 years later – "he assured me that he had not sung it since that time, nor had he heard it in the intervening years." Parry was not just a passive observer. Some of the embellishment may have been for his benefit, as appears to have been the case with The Wedding of Meho Smailagic: after Parry requested a longer piece Avdo spun the song out to 12,323 lines.

The music can be found in Harvard University's Milman Parry Collection, but it's probably not going to be top of many people's listening list. Even if you understand the language the sheer length of the songs coupled with the non-melodic style is daunting enough, and the poor recording quality may also be offputting. Avdo Mededović never achieved fame or fortune during his lifetime. He died in the same small village where he was born (Obrov, near the town of Bijelo Polje in the east of what is now Montenegro) and his reputation as a great guslar barely extended beyond his home region. After serving several years in the Ottoman army, he worked as a tradesman and as a farmer, and raised a family, happy to lead a simple life while the outside world was becoming ever more violent and bewildering.

For Ksenija Cicvaric (1926–97), as a teenager in wartorn Podgorica, there was no escape. The Germans and the Italians had carved up Yugoslavia between them, leaving the Italians occupying Montenegro. In 1941 there was an uprising against the Italians. Two ideologically opposed armies were involved: Tito's Partisans and the Serbian Chetniks. After the uprising was defeated at heavy human cost the Chetniks entered into an agreement with the Italian occupiers whereby the Italians would supply them with arms and supplies to fight the Partisans. This bought the Italians some time, but in the end it was not to be enough. In September 1943 Italy surrendered to the Allies and Montenegro was occupied by German troops. Within weeks, the Allies had carried out the first bombing raid on Podgorica. The raids – which had been sanctioned by Tito – soon intensified with devastating effect. The small city was reduced to rubble and 4,100 people lost their lives, among them some of Ksenija's brothers and sisters. [2] Finally, in December 1944, Partisans took over the city. But for some, like Ksenija's family, this was only the beginning of a new kind of terror. Fearful of being branded as collaborators they fled their home, walking into further trouble: Ksenija's father died en route and she herself had an alarming encounter with Ustaše troops in Croatia.

Ksenija's first husband was employed by JAT as an airline pilot. He was arrested on grounds of collaboration and put in a camp, and Ksenija never saw him again. According to my sources, thousands of people believed to be collaborators and traitors were summarily killed by Tito's Partisans after the war, or left to die in camps. Ksenija was left doing whatever work she could find to feed her young children, but eventually life improved: she was taken on as a singer by Radio Titograd, and she married again, to another pilot. Then came the most unkindest cut of all: her five-year-old son died following a road accident outside her apartment. To escape from the pain she decided to move from Podgorica to Belgrade. As fate would have it, this was to be the making of her career. Radio Belgrade straightaway got in contact with her; it was a great opportunity, and during her time at the radio station she would get to perform with some of the greatest musicians in the country – and to outshine them all.

What she's achieved as a singer, says Ksenija modestly, she owes to her mother – "She taught me all the original Montenegrin songs and developed my love of singing." [3] Of course she sang songs from other parts of Yugoslavia too; but she kept returning again and again to songs of old Montenegro. One of her great regrets was that she'd never been to a music school, but her voice is none the worse for this. It's a mellow, mature voice: there's great skill and technique in her singing, and a smouldering passion and sadness. DREMA MI SE (I'm ashamed) is a folk song from Podgorica: the mood of regret is conveyed by a battery of strings and the pain that reverberates from the vocals.

Adaptations of folk songs like this for full orchestra were light years away from how the same songs would have been performed a few decades earlier, usually accompanied by little more than the single-stringed gusle. Thanks to Ksenija many people fell in love with the songs, and she could have asked for no greater reward than this.

NOTES

1. https://chs.harvard.edu/CHS/article/display/6181
2. http://www.fokuspress.com/top-story/3469-dusko-novakovic-sin-ksenije-cicvaric-majku-je-zivot-surovo-kaznjavao-tugu-je-lijecila-pjesmom
3. http://www.yugopapir.com/2013/04/ksenija-cicvaric-ambasador-stare.html

NETHERLANDS

"The river Rhine is to the Netherlands what the Mississippi means to New Orleans. In these 'low lands' – the delta of Western Europe – multiple streams of cultural influences have both come down the river and in from the sea. They flowed in from Eastern and Southern Europe; since the 17th century from its maritime links with Africa, Asia and the Americas. During the 20th century political and economic changes led to a new massive influx of migrants. This added legacy profoundly colours the contemporary Dutch music world. Besides hosting the biggest Eurasian festival on the globe and the biggest Caribbean festival on the European continent, you will not only find a hybrid of musics from the former colonies Indonesia, Suriname and the Dutch Caribbean but also from the Balkans, Cape Verde, Latin America and the Mediterranean. In short, Dutch delta sounds." – Dutch World, promotional booklet for Womex 14. [1]

"Several theories exist as to why Dutch people lack interest in their own culture. Really, I do not know. By all means, they have never had to fight to preserve their culture as the Flemish, Irish or Basques had to do. This might

SIL IK DY RIS	*Kapriol'!*
'T HEERENHUUS	*Pekel*
DE ROMMELPOT	*Madlot*

explain why people do not really value it. I think it is OK that the Dutch have an open mind for other cultures, which might account for avoiding right-wing tendencies like those in other countries. On the other hand, I think an interest for one's own culture and an open mind for others' can exist next to and with each other." –

Hans Hoosemans of the group Wè-nun Henk. [2]

The authors of these two quotes don't disagree that traditional forms of folk music that existed in the Low Countries in past centuries have become marginalised. Where they differ is in their attitude to this. To put it simply, one is saying, 'let's celebrate the rich and diverse music that we have', while the other bemoans the loss of something valuable.

Mola Sylla, Fernando Lameirinhas and Farida Mohammad Ali are foreign-born musicians who moved to live in the Netherlands at various points in their lives, and whose music is rooted in the culture in which they grew up. So while they are part of Holland's lively world music scene, there's not a lot that they can tell us about Dutch music. The Amsterdam Klezmer Band, on the other hand, are not so easily dismissed. When they started out in the mid-90s, there were already a couple of Dutch klezmer bands (Di Gojim and Ot Azoj). Though not part of any established tradition, Holland had always been open to East European music, and around the same time Dutch people were listening to the gypsy jazz of the Rosenberg Trio and Mazzeltov's Yiddish songs. Thanks to bands such as these, klezmer and East European music generally have found a new lease of life here, perhaps for the first time since the waves of immigration from Eastern Europe in the 19th century.

Does it matter that some Dutch people are listening to klezmer? Isn't this just another imported music style, like hip hop or reggae? Over recent years the question has taken on a sharper, more political edge. For social liberals an openness to, and acceptance of, other cultures is like an article of faith, an expression of the tolerant, inclusive society that they believe the Netherlands to be. But the last decade has seen the rise of Geert Wilders' Party for Freedom, which has exploited fears about immigration from the Muslim world, and from Central and Eastern Europe. Here as elsewhere, anti-immigration attitudes often go hand in hand with a hostility towards multiculturalism. A lack of cultural reference points, of things that people can call their own, can help to foster feelings of powerlessness and fear.

Is there an unspoken assumption here that there's something almost reactionary about promoting 'white' Dutch culture? If you think about it, traditional Dutch folk music (volksmuziek) and klezmer music have quite a bit in common. Both were performed by ordinary people for ordinary people; and whether the performers were wandering klezmorim, farm labourers or Dutch sailors their musical knowledge was something that would have been passed on within their community. The musical heritage is this: not just a body of music, but a way of making music through which traditions were kept alive for hundreds of years, and which may be able to teach us one or two things today. Connecting with this kind of tradition isn't an insular act, rather an appreciation of a culture that's been enriched by thousands of individual contributions.

Ate Doornbosch (1926–2010) was a folk collector and broadcaster whose labours were key to making possible the Dutch folk revival. From 1957 to 1993 he presented over 1,300 programmes of the radio series Onder de Groene Linde in which he played old Dutch folk songs, mostly from the north of the country. Some of these were taken from music archives, but a great many were recordings that he'd made himself. He'd had to fight to make the show happen, his bosses weren't too enthusiastic, but their attitude changed when the numbers started coming in: it's estimated that for a time, at least, the programme was attracting audiences of 350,000.

The Dutch folk revival was relatively weak and short-lived, but what was significant about it was that it didn't look to America for inspiration, but found inspiration in the kind of songs that Ate had been playing all these years. The more traditional bands, such as Fungus and Dommelvolk, sang in Dutch and covered a number of songs that they'd learned through Ate's recordings. As a lot of these recordings were of amateur musicians performing unaccompanied, it doesn't need much imagination to realise that much work went in to rearranging all the tunes.

Like many others, Henk Scholte had started out covering a lot of English language folk songs. One thing that helped change his perspective was hearing songs in the minority Frisian language: "I had many contacts in Friesland… It was great to see how these people were busy with their own culture. The Frisians are proud of their own identity, their own language. The group Irolt started there and they did not sing in the Dutch language but in Frisian. That was the time I started thinking about making music from Groningen." [3] In 1975, he met Eddy de Jonge and they formed the group Törf. "We discovered that there existed quite a lot of material from Groningen. Already in 1930 a book was published with old songs in our own language. I also visited people to record the songs they could remember. Of course, I could sing in English, but I was not British. I felt that I wanted to stay close to my roots and this was my identity. Not only the songs interested me; I wanted to know the background of the songs as well. For instance: what was the importance of such a song in the time it was written?"

The Gronings dialect can be difficult for Dutch speakers to follow; not many groups had recorded songs in Gronings, so there were no models to copy. Törf raided old songbooks and filled their first couple of albums with interpretations of traditional songs. By the early 1980s the new folk scene was dying, there were no longer the opportunities to play, however, "we ended up in the Groningen language movement… Groninger evenings were organised everywhere." [4] The focus of the band shifted and they began writing music to poems by Groningen poets. There were many lineup changes, different instruments introduced. But Henk and Eddy both carried on, symbols of the band and of its association with Groningen tradition. Flip Rodenburg is a multi-instrumentalist specialising in medieval instruments who plays bagpipes and a variety of wind instruments. He it was who walked into a museum and came across by chance an old manuscript sitting on top of a piano. Written by a Groningen schoolteacher, Jacob Pieters Beukema, in the mid-19th century, it contained the score to a number of dances, but none of the melodies was familiar. Gradually he realised that he had something unique and valuable. "That man had an eye for what was good music. He probably built a much larger collection and this script was a selection which he had made for his grandson." [5] A few years later Törf released their own collection of Beukema's dances, Törf speelt Beukema (1998).

One of those bands playing Dutch and Frisian music in the 1970s was Perelaar. Two of the band members, Marita Kruijswijk and Marian Nesse, had studied musicology at the University of Amsterdam; however, as Marita explained to me, this didn't necessarily lead to a familiarity with volksmuziek. During her time at university she was doing fieldwork in Scotland when she was asked one evening to entertain the group with a Dutch song. She struggled to come up with anything, and: "I realized that all my teachers and fellow students in the Netherlands were only interested in music cultures of exotic countries far away and never studied the music of their own culture." [6] As her own interest grew, before long she was looking up ancient Dutch manuscripts and songbooks herself. A primary source for Perelaar was Ate's folk song archive, as was the Boerenlieties, a vast collection of 1,000 dance tunes published in the early 18th century.

In the 1980s, Marita and Marian both moved to Friesland where they started up a new group, Kat yn 't Seil. After the group became Esperanto enthusiasts they released several albums under the name Kajto.

Kapriol'! is a new ensemble formed by Marita and Marian in 2008. The band's 'programme options' reflect the breadth of their interests – and talents, encompassing singing, storytelling and instrumental music:

- *Alternating programme in Dutch and/or Frisian*
- *Fries programme with the writer William Schoorstra which tells stories of Friesland in the early Middle Ages*
- *Programme in Esperanto*
- *Swinging balfolk programme, optionally with dance interpretation of European balfolk dancing*
- *Maritime programme with shanties and songs about life at sea*
- *A lively programme for historical (e.g. medieval) events, complete with historical clothing.*

This is education as entertainment (or should that be the other way round?). It's about preserving knowledge and tradition, but also making the music fun and accessible. The album Niewelnacht

Lieten (2015), which is dedicated to Frisian music, came about as a result of a request by an EU organisation. The band had already collected many old songbooks by this time, but they took the project very seriously:

> "We went to the library of Tresoar which is the Frisian historical and literary centre in Friesland. There we got a lot of photocopies of music notations and song texts. And of course it took us some months till we had decided which songs and which tunes we would select for the album and then it took some more months till we had arranged and practised the music."

There are several dance numbers from the 17th, 18th and 19th centuries. The instrumentation is non-traditional, and they mix it up a bit, and add vocals here and there, to create the variety that a 21st-century audience demands. SIL IK DY RIS is even older – "in The Hague we found a manuscript from 1602 with the oldest Frisian songs which also have music notation, written by Jaques Vredeman. They are a nice mixture of civilized-sounding music with very naughty words." One female voice is joined by another, and then by a male voice, in a perfectly orchestrated short piece of polyphonic singing.

Two other Perelaar musicians, Peter Moree and Erno Korpershoek, became one half of the group Pekel, who remain active to this day though their most productive time was in the 1990s. Pekel's fascination with Dutch maritime history is a theme that runs through all their albums; but although the songs have a traditional flavour many are self-written. Peter's cousin, Perry Moree, is a historian who's written extensively about the Dutch East India Company (VOC), and his research provided the band with an abundance of raw material for their songs. Their 1996 album, From the Maas to the East, tells the story of the crew on the first voyage of the VOC ship de Bevalligheidt in 1748. 'T

HEERENHUUS is a jolly shanty about the pleasures of shore leave: the heerenhuijs of the song is a place where the girls know how to give sailors a good time.

"Traditional Dutch music," the band acknowledge on their website, "is no longer commonly played." Trying to rectify this is hard: they are perpetually swimming against the tide. Elsewhere, I read that while the band have frequently been invited to perform at European festivals, it's a different story in their home country. There seems to be a perception that Dutch language folklore music is insular and conservative.

Balfolk on the other hand is thriving. The informality of the event helps it escape any stigma: people can turn up and take part, they don't have to wear costumes and the dances are not over-formalised – there's room for improvisation in the music and in the dancing. There's no expectation that events will have a regional or even a Dutch character – they're more like Euro ceilidhs at which live bands will play a range of European dances. Much as Marita welcomes the success that balfolk has had, she is guarded when asked about its possible impact on Dutch folk music. "It gave birth to many great new folk groups with enthusiatic, gifted young musicians. Also balfolk nights certainly helped to reawaken the interest in traditional culture, that is to say in the West European traditional folk music, but not particularly in the Dutch or Frisian traditional folk music."

Shanty singing is also surprisingly popular. One shanty site claims there are about 1,200 shanty choirs active, mainly in the north, but also in towns with no maritime connection. On another site I read that 'every village in Friesland has a choir and a shanty choir'. Such claims are impossible to verify, but there are definitely a lot of choirs, and a fair few shanty festivals – evidence, on the face of it, that Dutch folk music has more life in it than some people think. There's just one problem: they mainly sing English-language shanties. This isn't for any lack of interest:

*"There simply were not many Dutch shanties. The
Netherlands lost their position as a leading seafaring
nation in the beginning of the 19th century because of the
Napoleonic wars. There were few ships and the ships that
were available were idle in the ports. This is the reason
most of the Dutch songs and traditions disappeared. After
the French domination, the Netherlands built up their fleet
again. However, these ships often sailed with a foreign crew.
They mostly sang English, German or French shanties...
new Dutch songs were not necessary."* [7]

Peter Koene's path (1948–2013) to folk music began when as
a teenager he heard Pete Seeger singing Little Boxes on Radio
Caroline. There followed a period of discovery: more American
folk singers, and folk rock bands. Seeger, though, he says on his
website, "has always been my mentor and inspiration". So when he
heard Seeger advising singers to sing songs in their own language,
he took this advice seriously. "It was hard to find good Dutch
material these days. I started with singing family repertoire. I asked
my grandmother, some aunts and the grandparents of my girlfriend
if they still knew some old songs." [8] He sought out songs about
everyday life and songs of protest, that was what he wanted to sing.
He sang in folk clubs and in a few different bands, but the records
he made back in the 1970s and '80s are difficult to obtain now.

Between 1978 and 1995 Koene was editor of the Dutch folk
magazine Janviool, later to become New Folk Sounds. After
this he served as a board member and President of Foundation
Folk Netherlands; he also had his own radio programme. But he
still believed that he had something left to contribute, and still
had the drive to start new projects. One of these was the group
Madlot, who hosted regular balfolk events in the university town
of Wageningen. Accordion player Judica Lookman was the caller,
Bert Lotz blew it away on his bagpipes. People young and old
were coming to dance to old tunes.

Ik hoorde dees dagen was released by Madlot in 2005. The 19 tracks are all selections from the Boerenlieties which, to remind you, was the great collection of dance tunes from the early 18th century. They picked out songs they enjoyed singing and tunes which gave opportunities to the band to showcase some of their many instruments. So Marche van Koehoorn is an unusual and rather special duet of two koehoorns (blowing horns). Poolsche duttel sack/Poolsche Sara and DE ROMMELPOT are bagpipe dances. On De rommelpot the bagpipe plays to a soft thudding beat: this is Ariëtte Zuidhoff on the rommelpot, or friction drum. The basic criterion is what works, rather than what is most authentic, so for instance, the modern-day accordion also stars on some tracks.

MARITA KRUIJSWIJK'S DUTCH GROUPS TO WATCH:

- *Madlot*
- *Henk Scholte with his group Törf*
- *Jos Koning with his groups 't Speelhuys and Twee violen en een bas*
- *Pekel*
- *Frisian group Baldrs Draumar*
- *Balfolg groups Lirio and Té*

NOTES

1. https://issuu.com/wmfnl/docs/dutchworldwomex14wmfnl
2. http://www.folkworld.de/29/e/dutch.html
3. http://www.folkworld.de/26/e/dutch.html
4. http://www.streektaalzang.nl/strk/gron/pers/p074tor1.htm
5. Ibid
6. Email 3/9/16
7. http://www.liereliet.nl/index.php/en/geschied-en/119-shanties-en
8. http://www.folkworld.de/24/e/dutch.html

NORWAY

The Hardanger fiddle – or hardingfele – is an elegant little instrument. Its body is similar in shape to the violin, though it's usually very decorative and topped with a carved head of a dragon or other folkloric creature. When you hear it played you'll see that the differences run deeper than this: the hardingfele is, and always has been, a folk instrument, that plays music for dancing to. Norway has a number of regional dances: down the south of the country each west-coast town has its own version of the region's springar and gangar couples dances; and these dances are inseparable from the music of the hardingfele.

For those musicians among you, what gives the sound of the hardingfele its unique quality are four or five 'sympathetic strings' that run underneath the fingerboard and add echoing overtones. So the same instrument can produce a melody and a drone sound at the same time.

In the mid-19th century, Norwegian culture was flourishing as part of the romantic nationalism movement. Although mainly confined to an educated elite, the movement embraced an idealised view of Norway's rural heritage. Commissioning a painting of fjords was one thing, inviting an unkempt folk musician to ply his trade in one's home quite another. Prejudice ran deep, and it would

KVENNESLÅTTEN, MYLLARSPRINGAR
(KJELDERHELGELAND OG TELEMARKSTRAD) *Hauk Buen*

EG ER FRAMAND   *Sondre Bratland & Annbjørg Lien*
BJØLLESLÅTTEN   *Gro Marie Svidal*
MANEVISE   *Eplemøya Songlag*

take many years before rural fiddling would receive the respect that it deserved. This was the environment in which Norway's greatest fiddling legend, Torgeir Augundsson, lived his life. Torgeir was better known by the nickname Myllarguten (miller boy), which would have been a constant reminder to urban audiences of his humble origins. His introduction to urban audiences came about as a result of a chance meeting with the classically trained fiddler Ole Bull in 1831. Ole Bull had been hankering for the chance to bring a more Norwegian flavour to his repertoire, and hearing Torgeir play was a revelation that would remain with him for the rest of his life. For several days after that meeting the two musicians played tunes for each other. After this, with Ole Bull's backing, Torgeir was engaged to perform across Norway, and even further afield, in Gothenburg and Copenhagen. More than just a brilliant fiddler, he was an innovator who reshaped the way in which traditional music was performed.

And yet in his lifetime Torgeir never achieved the status and recognition of musicians such as Ole Bull. A legend grew around his name: that he had acquired his magical skills by selling his soul to a fossegrimen, the mythical fiddle-playing water spirits who live in waterfalls. Does the story sound familiar? A century later the bluesman Robert Johnson was reputed to have sold his soul to the devil. Such stories can do much to enhance the reputation of an artist by creating an aura of myth about them. At the same time, they reinforce prejudice. Chris Salewicz writes that, "the very notion of the black man selling his soul to the Devil at the crossroads is a white man's superstition." [1] Likewise, the fossegrimen legend was a convenient way of avoiding the question of where this music actually did originate from. Torgeir had learned from his father and from other fiddlers in a community that was rife with music. From a young age he performed regularly at feasts and weddings in the Telemark region, trying to outdo other fiddlers with his virtuosity, but also learning from the best. Later in life, as the concerts dried up, he bought a farm and tried to settle down, but he was no farmer and it didn't work out. Broken and dispirited, in 1872 he died of tuberculosis, leaving his family in poverty. In the years to come his music would have a profound influence on the culture of the emerging nation, most notably in the works of the composer Edvard Grieg who introduced folk music themes into classical music.

The national fiddlers' association was founded in 1923. For much of its first 50 years it must have seemed to those aware of its existence to be a small anachronistic organisation standing against the tide of history. But then between 1973 and 1985 the number of registered fiddle clubs almost doubled, from 60 to 111, while membership of the association rose even more steeply, from 600 to over 3,000. [2] Interest in folk music both old and new was being rekindled. Folk festivals were springing up: the Folkemusikkveka at Hallingdal started in 1976. A music academy devoted to folk music, the Ole Bull Akademiet, was founded in 1977. And the symbol of the new folk movement, its great uniting theme, was the hardanger fiddle.

Despite being a national symbol, the hardingfele retains its rural character: most master fiddlers grew up in small towns with strong fiddle-playing traditions. Since the early 1950s, brothers

Hauk Buen (born 1933) and Knut Buen (1948) have lived in the tiny village of Tuddal. Their family had been musical for many generations, and their aunt, Bergit Tjønn, who raised them both from a young age, was herself a capable fiddler. The legacy continues: sister Agnes Buen Garnås (born 1946), a traditional singer who's also released many CDs, has three children who've all pursued successful careers in folk music, including the fiddler Per Anders Buen Garnås.

KVENNESLÅTTEN, the title tells us, is a **MYLLARSPRINGAR**: a springar (dance) written by the miller boy himself, our friend Torgeir. It's from an album Slåttar på Myllarfela, originally released in 1991, of tunes played by the two brothers in honour of Torgeir Augundsson. The music soars and leaps: with each chord change you catch your breath in anticipation of the next delight. Of the two brothers, Knut is the better known: a voice of authority on all things traditional, who's written books and numerous articles, appeared on TV and received many awards. He's also a skilled ornamental wood painter in the rosemåling style. But I wouldn't like to say who is the better fiddler: both possess the natural brilliance of a fossegrimen.

Though the brothers do compose a lot of their own material, they're firmly in the traditional camp, believers in keeping the past alive. Annbjørg Lien (born 1971) by contrast, thinks that hardingfelespillere (Norwegian fiddlers) could do with being a bit more creative. Folk music, she says, shouldn't be put on a pedestal or treated as a treasure that can't be touched: musicians should be able to play with freedom, following their own instincts. [3]

I'm sure that Annbjørg would be the first to acknowledge that this freedom should be grounded in familiarity with tradition. She herself had some classical training but made the choice to become a folk musician: partly because she felt a strong attachment to the music that she'd grown up with (her parents were folkies), but also because folk music was less rule bound. She then took private lessons with several fiddlers, including Hauk

Buen. She cites Hauk Buen and another old-time fiddler, Torleiv Bjørgum, as inspirations, alongside Sigbjørn Bernhoft Osa, a hardingfelespiller who changed perceptions of Norwegian music through his involvement in the progressive rock group Saft. [4] Over a period of three decades she's released many albums: as a solo artist, with the folk group Bukkene Bruse (Billy Goats Gruff) and in collaborations with other musicians.

In 1994, Bukkene Bruse played at the closing ceremony of the Lillehammer Winter Olympics. Four years later, they were in Mozambique, as part of an initiative for Save the Children. Interviewed afterwards, she said, "We worked with children and they were dancing and singing, so natural. We [in the North] think too much. Everything is planned; everything is decided. We are trapped by all of the things we have. What's important to us is valueless. They have nothing and they are happy and are dancing from day to day. I think everybody should take a trip like that once a year..." [5] Her next album, Baba Yaga, was something of a celebration of musical free spirit. From the opening track, which samples children's chanting, the traditional and the modern meet in many different ways as instrumentation and mood shift constantly throughout the album. There are quite a few firsts – Annbjørg has never worked with a Moog synthesiser previously – but it never feels like a clash of styles, Annbjørg finds the harmony in the diverse elements.

The hardingfele is so rich in its sound, it fills out a tune so well, that the musician who combines it with other elements is always taking a risk; but Annbjørg believes that such risks are more than worth it if hardingfele music is to be fully embraced by modern audiences. EG ER FRAMAND is a religious folk song with lyrics that express yearning – 'I seek the City of God where sorrow and death are no more. Dear Lord, lead me to Heaven's shore.' This is captured in the slowed-down tempo, the elongated notes and in the deep, honest voice of Sondre Bratland, a leading traditional folk singer.

Today there are several record labels turning out dozens of high-quality CDs every year: Etnisk Musikklubb, Grappa, ta:lik and Knut Buen's own Nyrenning label. Many of the artists and groups signed up to these labels and headlining folk festivals are young. Erlend Viken and Olav Luksengård Mjelva are two hardingfele players born in the 1980s who are striding out in new directions. The Erlend Viken Trio are an unconventional combination of fiddle, guitar and cello, two of whom also play in a bluegrass band, the Earlybird Stringband. Olav Luksengård Mjelva found joy in the creative collaboration between Norwegian and Swedish musicians in the band Sver. This led to a couple of further projects: Olav and Andres from Sver got together with Kevin Henderson from Shetland to form The Nordic Fiddlers Bloc; and Olav has also released a couple of CDs with Swedish nyckelharpist, Erik Rydvall, as Rydvall Mjelva. Langeleik music is not as popular as the hardingfele – the Norwegian zither has just one melody string and up to eight drone strings – but Lise Lunde Brennhagen believes the old instrument has a future: she recently released an instrumental album of langeleik tunes.

My next featured artist, Gro Marie Svidal, grew up in the beautiful countryside of Jølster in western Norway, and studied music at the Ole Bull Akademiet and the Norwegian Academy of Music. From when she was a small child she's admired the dazzling skills of competition fiddlers, never imagining that she could be among them. But, in 2014, she beat off competition from 13 other elite musicians to take first prize in the elite fiddle category at the Landskappleiken festival. How did that make her feel? "It is huge," she says simply. [6]

On **BJØLLESLÅTTEN** the hardingfele imitates the sound of pealing bells as the changes are rung. The tune's taken from Gro Marie's second album, Eilov. As on her debut album, Gro Marie has elected to stay with traditional material, fiddle tunes collected from the western provinces of Sogn og Fjordane and Hordaland. The creativity lies in the way she's interpreted them. I get the impression from her interviews that she'd like to stretch herself in different ways – she says she has worked with other musicians in the past, so I wouldn't be surprised to see a bit of a change in approach on future albums.

Unaccompanied singing – sometimes called kveding – has deep roots within traditional culture. Forms of song include ballads, some of which date back to medieval times; lullabies; skillingsviser, so called because they used to be sold for a shilling, which were topical poems set to existing melodies; and stev, which have short verses of four lines and can be quite witty.

Kveding is certainly alive and well in the southern district of Telemark. This is the home of Agnes Buen Garnås and Sondre Bratland, two influential singers who we've met already. Sondre helped to set up a Kvedarskulen (singing class) at the nearby Ole Bull Akademiet in Voss. Another graduate of the Akademiet is Jon Anders Halvorsen who's released several fine CDs of vocal music. "The songs I enjoy the most," he says, "are the medieval ballads. They became popular in the late 1200s and have been very popular in Telemark up to our time. Telemark is even thought of as the region in Norway – and probably in Scandinavia – with the longest living tradition for these songs." [7] Asne Valland Nordli is from the west coast; she started tutoring at the Ole Bull Akademiet when she was only 14! Her 2014 album, Over Tones, with the fiddler Benedicte Maurseth, is well worth checking out.

The Sami are an indigenous people who live in small communities in the arctic climes of northern Scandinavia. Their territory extends from northern parts of Sweden, Norway and Finland to the northwestern tip of Russia. To them, singing is more than just a form of entertainment. Joik (or yoik) singing is a very personal form of expression, it's about honouring someone, or something, in one's life. There are no rules, no parameters: each individual develops their own joik style which becomes like a personal statement. Normal practice though is that joiks are either unaccompanied or sung to the beat of a drum, and that they contain no words, only sounds. The place to go for Sami music is the DAT record label, and I've been listening carefully to a compilation album that they put out with the catchy title Guovddut Juoiga – Yoiks from Guovdagequidnu. I find it difficult to relate to, but it is remarkable, distinctive music, and may suit those who delight in offbeat sounds.

Eplemøya Songlag have created their own brand of a cappella music – and it's been getting quite a buzz, winning friends in unexpected places. Kieron Tyler of Mojo magazine says that, "seeing them in Oslo a few years ago left an indelible impression." [8] They are an all-female trio. Liv Ulvik, whose background is in folk music, has teamed up with two jazz singers, Wenche Losnegård and Anja Eline Skybakmoen. Möya Og Myten (The maiden and the myth) is their second album, and it's a collection of songs about women, some traditional, and some self-written. Anja elaborates:

"We searched for old myths, urban myths and mythical characters in traditional Norwegian history and culture. We used about a year to find the right stories and melodies for us. We search online, in archives at the libraries, talked to storytellers here in Oslo and so on. On our first album we searched for stories about strong women taking responsibility for their own lives no matter what. For example, the story about the girl who didn´t have a man. She was so desperate to find a man that she eventually made herself a man out of branches from trees and intestines from one of her dead sheep. And this self-made man was as good as any other man. That´s something to think about." [9]

MANEVISE ticks all kinds of boxes: it's fresh and inventive; it's beautifully arranged, with exquisite harmonies; it's full of female energy; it's soothing and relaxing. The debates about to what extent Norwegian folk musicians should keep it traditional will go on. But Möya Og Myten is a valuable reminder that sometimes it's necessary to break a few rules to create something that's really special.

NOTES

1. Chris Salewicz – 27: Robert Johnson (Quercus 2014)
2. Chris Goertzen – Fiddling for Norway: Revival and Identity (University Of Chicago Press, 1997), pp36–37
3. http://www.ballade.no/sak/en-godt-bevart-hemmelighet/
4. Ibid
5. http://www.rootsworld.com/interview/lien.html
6. http://www.nrk.no/sognogfjordane/ho-er-best-pa-hardingfele-1.11809291
7. http://www.folkworld.de/30/e/nattsang.html
8. http://kierontyler.blogspot.co.uk/2013/01/eplemya-songlag-moya-og-myten-interview.html
9. Ibid

POLAND

In Poland the folk revival began late: it only really got going in the early 1990s. Yet in little more than a decade the Warsaw Village Band had emerged from this scene to become one of the most popular and talked-about bands on the world festival circuit. They were at the forefront of a wave of bands who'd fallen in love with the wildness and energy of Polish dances such as mazurkas and obereks, and were reinterpreting them for the 21st century. At full throttle, the Warsaw Village Band play with the power of a rock group. This isn't appreciated by everyone: one reviewer complained that, "these folk melodies are simply beaten to death". [1] It's a familiar debate: are the band revitalising tradition with their high-energy urban style or killing it off?

Piotr Zgorzelski doesn't have your typical folk musician's CV. Born and raised in Warsaw, he didn't have any formal musical training, and didn't play any instruments as a child. His first band played Latin American music – "music from Peru and Bolivia was very popular in the early '90s in Poland." [2] Polish folk music was at the time something he actively avoided. It had a negative image, bound up with the state-sponsored folk and dance ensembles of the Soviet era who would dress in matching costumes and sing a sanitised folk repertoire.

MAZUREK KAWALERSKI "OJ, WSTAN DZIEWCZYNO RANO"	*Kazimierz Meto & Józef Meto*
PIOSENKI ZE SLOWACJI	*Orkiestra sw Mikolaja*
OBER ZAPUSTNY	*Kapela Brodow*
ROWNY KRETOWICZA	
(KRETOWICZ'S ROWNY)	*Janusz Prusinowski Trio*
HEJ, BIDA MENE Z HYZY ZENE	*Kapela Drewutnia*
LAZY JOHNNY DANCE	*Warsaw Village Band*

Despite this, Piotr was beginning to listen to Carpathian and Ukrainian tunes and to perform them with his band. They seemed to offer something more real, more grounded. Then, in 1993, he met some members of the band Bractwo Ubogich (The Brotherhood of the Poor, who I'll refer to as The Brotherhood) and friendships were formed that would last a lifetime. The Brotherhood were only together for a couple of years, but they were playing village music before anyone else, they were searching the collections of Oskar Kolberg and Andrzej Bienkowski for authentic material, and they united under one roof many of the people who would go on to play pivotal roles in the folk revival: fiddler Janusz Prusinowski; singer Agata Harz; accordionist Jacek Halas; Anna and Witold Broda of the band Kapela Brodów; and Remigiusz Mazur-Hanaj, a co-founder along with Janusz of the dom tanca (dance centre) movement in Poland.

Andrzej Bienkowski had arrived at the same place, coming from a very different direction. Since 1979 he'd been carrying out fieldwork and making recordings of village music. He couldn't understand why no one was interested in his work. The great Polish composer Frédéric Chopin had been inspired by village music, even composing dozens of mazurkas based on the traditional dance, and surely Chopin knew a thing or two! For him, meeting The Brotherhood changed everything: "For the first time I met someone who thought like me. People for whom obereks and mazurkas by Józef Kedzierski and Marian Bujak are as precious as preludes by Chopin and Lutoslawski. Meeting them gave our research new meaning. Finally, I knew for whom I was doing it." [3]

For The Brotherhood, the meeting was equally fortuitous. Through Andrzej they got to hear (and see films) of village musicians of remarkable quality; such as the violinists Józef Kedzierski, Marian Bujak, Piotr and Jan Gaca, and Kazimierz Meto. Andrzej would have described, as he has done many times since, what a revelation it was to hear these artists for the first time:

"I bought cheap liquor and went to Mr Józef. He said that he hadn't played since his wife's death a few years ago. So, I opened the bottle and then another one, and finally Kedzierski did want to play. I had never heard anything like that before, it was as if I discovered Atlantis."

"Kazimierz Meto... was born strange, and lived in an enclosed world, he became a bachelor... Kazio starts playing, and his hands are as huge as loaves of bread, and I

just cannot understand how he is able to produce sounds on a violin. Wonderful singers arrive, very warm women, and every 30 seconds or so they say to him 'Get married, Kazio, get married'. And it's like that throughout his entire life." [4]

These men were a dying breed. Yet when they held their violins in their hands they played with the vigour of 20-year-olds. This was folk music unlike anything that most Poles had heard before. It was fast and furious and wild and unrestrained. It was dance music, but not of the polite costumed variety: this seemed to be aimed more at young people who were out enjoying a few drinks. A couple of decades later, after starting his own record label (Muzyka Odnaleziona), Andrzej began releasing some of this music to an unsuspecting world. 3xGace (2012) is a set of recordings of the Gaca brothers (Piotr, Stanislaw, Jan and Stefan). Mety Graja (2008) is the brothers Kazimierz and Józef Meto; and there are several compilations of field recordings in similar vein.

On MAZUREK KAWALERSKI "OJ, WSTAN DZIEWCZYNO RANO" there are just two instruments: Kazimierz's violin and Józef's bass. The violin resembles an assault weapon, insistently summoning people to the dance, while the bass is used like a drone instrument. It's an arresting, unnerving sound.

Underpinning all this music was Poland's rich folk dance traditions. There are five Polish national dances: the Mazurek, Oberek, Krakowiak, Kujawiak and Polonaise. Of these, the first three are fast dances. 'Oberek' means spinning; couples will spin around in the same direction as they dance. There are also numerous dances associated with specific regions. Of particular interest are the highlanders' dances from the Tatra Mountain region in the south of the country. The male dances feature a good deal of jumping and air kicks, and often use as a prop the ciupaga, or shepherd's axe.

The Lublin-based group Orkiestra Swietego Mikolaja (Saint Nicholas Orchestra), formed in 1988, found inspiration in similar places. The city of Lublin sits between Western and Eastern Europe with a foot in both camps. Jews, Rusyns and Ukrainians have lived there over the centuries, contributing to its multicultural identity. Pockets of an older Rusyn (or Ruthenian) culture still existed in eastern Poland. The Ruthenian people of the Carpathian region encompass Lemko, Boyko and Hutsuls. Having never fully assimilated, their culture still has Eastern European characteristics, and it was these Carpathian styles of dance music and singing which attracted the interest of Bogdan Bracha and the Orkiestra Swietego Mikolaja.

"We do not aim to modernise the folk source," say the band on their website, "but rather to create its continuation... It is our own tale of the world that has faded away but is still extremely significant for us." It's a subtle distinction: they want to explore and reinterpret traditional material, but not to transform it so far that it loses its essential quality. The seven musicians aren't exactly a traditional ensemble. They play violin, nyckelharpa, dulcimer, mandolin, hurdy-gurdy, guitar, double bass, flute, and most surprisingly, the Asian dutar. They've revived bialy glos (white voice), a powerful and startling form of shouted singing which was apparently once used by Polish mountain shepherds. Since 1991 they've organised an annual folk festival in Lublin: Mikolajki Folkowe, which claims to be the oldest folk music festival in Poland. And since 1996 they've also published the folk magazine Gadki z Chatki.

Each CD is a record of their personal explorations of the source material, and a door into little-known parts of Polish culture. O Milosci Przy Grabieniu Siana (2004) consists mainly of poems by Wanda Czubernatowa, a contemporary folk poet from the Tatra Mountains, set to music. Huculskie Muzyki (2006) – an album of Hutsul music – was a joint project with Roman Kumlyku (1948–2014) and his Czeremosz band. And Lem-Agination (2007) is an album inspired by Lemko songs and folklore.

Hutsul and Lemko culture had suffered during the Soviet era.

In 1944, Poland and the Soviet Union agreed upon a series of population exchanges that saw nearly half a million Ukrainians and Lemko-Rusyns relocated to the Soviet Ukraine. However, thousands more Ukrainians and Lemkos exercised their right to remain living in Poland. In 1947, these people were accused of giving support to Ukrainian insurgents, and Operation Vistula was launched. The southeastern corner of Poland where the Lemkos lived was forcibly depopulated, whole villages were emptied and Lemkos were scattered across Poland. Hutsuls living in Soviet Ukraine also knew what it was to feel unwelcome and undervalued in their own country. Roman Kumlyku's father was killed by the Soviets, his mother evicted from the mountain farm that she called home. Many years later they resettled in Verkhovyna: a town that the Soviets had stripped of any vestiges of its former Polish identity, including the town's name (until 1962 it was called Zabie, which means frog!). Here Roman established a Hutsul museum and promoted Hutsul culture.

PIOSENKI ZE SLOWACJI actually means songs from Slovakia, but it's on the Lem-Agination album. It's a delightful piece of dance music with an irresistible melody, and alternating female and male vocals.

Village dance music continued to enjoy a starring role in the Polish folk revival. As we've seen, members of The Brotherhood were among the main initiators of the Dom Tanca movement. Based on the dance house movement in Hungary, it was an attempt to answer the question, how do you go about making traditional music popular? In Poland, as in the rest of modern Europe, people had become estranged from their own traditional culture. Just getting up on stage and playing mazurkas wasn't going to change that. But if more people had seen a mazurka dance, or better still tried it out themselves, they might be more receptive. So Dom Tanca organised workshops, concerts and summer camps, all aimed at introducing people to traditional song, music, dance and crafts in a fun, informal setting.

As might be expected with such a strong collection of characters, after the split of The Brotherhood everyone followed their own musical direction, but their love of dance music kept them anchored to their roots. Jacek Halas has been a part of several of Poland's more interesting bands: Muzykanci, Lautari, Nomadzi Kultury, Transkapela. This has given him many opportunities to work with musicians from other genres, something he obviously enjoys. Equally important to him, though, is his work with the Dom Tanca Poznan, getting people to connect with traditional music and song. You can find him now teamed up with his wife in Kapela Halasów, playing old dances and ballads.

OBER ZAPUSTNY is from Tance Polskie (Polish Dances), a lovingly assembled album by Kapela Brodow. Many but by no means all of the tracks are lively instrumental dance music. There are a handful of slower pieces – a walking dance, a waltz – and several short songs with no musical accompaniment. Despite being billed as an ober dance, my feature track doesn't sound like any other obereks I've heard. It's like a marriage of folk and classical music: a brief refrain, repeated again and again with little variations. Witold Broda's violin playing on it is simply magnificent.

The latest Kapela Brodow album, Muzikaim, was released on Andrzej Bienkowski's Muzyka Odnaleziona label. Recorded live in October 2014, it's the product of years of research by Witold into Jewish music from Polish villages.

Remember our young initiate Piotr Zgorzelski, who came to folk music from Latin American music? He helped to set up the Dom Tanca Warsaw, where he's been a dance teacher for 20 years, passing on knowledge that he's gained from rural dancers. He's performed with Kapela Brodow and Adam Strug, but it's as the bass player of Janusz Prusinowski's band that he's really come into his own. The Janusz Prusinowski Trio (now called the Janusz Prusinowski Kompania) don't just turn up and play a concert here or there: wherever possible they hold workshops as well in the cities where they're touring, which I can't imagine is a very financially profitable activity. Piotr's the main man for the dance workshops.

Above all though it was Janusz's enthusiasm, his vision and his capacity for organisation that drove them forward. That excitement that he felt when he first saw one of Andrzej's films has stayed with him: "What he showed us was a revelation – for me it was like an experience that all is one, a unity of what I was looking for in rock'n'roll – freedom of improvisation – on one hand, and on the other what I have from my home, what keeps me together with my family, the people I love. And that was mazurkas; improvised, free, very sophisticated in a rhythmical sense, and used for the dance, and expression of body." [5] In the mid-90s he threw himself into the Dom Tanca project, persuading dozens of village musicians to come and play in Warsaw so that others could experience what he'd experienced, and learn what he'd learned. Then he took a job as an English teacher, trying to bring in a regular income. But after a near-miss in the car with his whole family he decided, "We have the gift of our lives – let's use it." He began recording again, and one thing led to another. Even as the Janusz Prusinowski Trio began to establish themselves there were always other cultural projects that demanded his skills and attention. In 2010, he launched the Wszystkie Mazurki Swiata (Mazurkas of the World) Festival in Warsaw.

The time was right for a mazurka festival, and there was no one better than Janusz Prusinowski to make it happen. A couple of years earlier, he'd released a critically acclaimed album of mazurka music. And though the numbers of village musicians had dwindled, more and more young bands were including mazurkas and obereks in their repertoire. In Janusz's view, this is because "more and more people are looking for something special and local." [6] The mazurka has that rootedness, that Polishness, which modern culture can't offer, and a history which goes back hundreds of years. Importantly too, according to Janusz, there are still many traditional instrument makers in Poland – "without them our music wouldn't exist." [7]

On 12th May 2015, Poland's Minister of Culture presented Janusz with a lifetime achievement award for his contribution to folk culture. But his story is far from finished yet. Just three days earlier, his band had been in Germany, staging a mazurka flashmob. At the time of writing, I'm waiting for news of the band's fourth album. In the meantime, I offer you a tune from the third. Po kolana w niebie (Knee-Deep In Heaven, 2013) is almost entirely made up of songs and dances from the Polish villages. There are again a number of mazurkas, but the track I've chosen for you to hear is the somewhat slower ROWNY KRETOWICZA with its haunting melody.

Janusz talks about a 'culture of participation' in which people come not just to listen, but to dance. When you dance the mazurka your whole body, all your senses are engaged. With 'fusion' music this organic connection becomes weak, or disappears altogether. As lines are crossed, and the music becomes more akin to rock or electronic dance music, people respond differently, dance no longer has that bonding effect.

The next track on my list is by a group who've kept their feet firmly planted in the traditional camp: Lublin band Kapela Drewutnia. Singer Olga Iwanicka talks about how the band was inspired by hearing traditional Lemko music – "the closeness between man and nature, expressed through melodies and rhythms." [8] There's no doubting the truth of what she says: they sing in the Lemko language, as well as in Polish and Ukrainian; they've performed numerous times for Lemko festivals and events. But it's not the whole story. They also play many forms of Slavic folk music from the wider region, performing old songs, trying to keep the original lyrics and melodies intact, while reinterpreting them for a modern audience. They've made a conscious decision to avoid the use of electronic instruments, which sets them apart from many other contemporary Polish folk and world music artists. But they allow themselves ample scope for creativity in the instruments that they use. Every band member is a multi-instrumentalist; they play over 20 instruments between the eight of them. And a few of these instruments are rather unusual to say the least: the suka bilgorajska (an ancient type of fiddle, played in an upright position), the reco reco (a Brazilian scraped percussion instrument) and the topshur (Mongolian lute).

In the hands of Kapela Drewutnia, the Lemko song **HEJ, BIBA MENE Z HYZY ZENE** is a fast, explosive dance tune, a folk punk style footstomper for the post-Pogues generations. A small word of warning: this is no more representative of their set than the slow ballads or the polyphonic singing that they perform equally well. If you go to a Drewutnia concert or buy a CD, expect to get acquainted with folk music in a variety of different guises.

Today, Poland has many successful bands which owe a debt to Andrzej Bienkowski and the pioneers of the folk revival, but who have progressed beyond mazurkas, defining their own space in the folk spectrum. Their output is very diverse. Caci Vorba concoct an intoxicating mix of gypsy, Balkan and Carpathian music spiced with elements of swing and rock'n'roll. Sutari are three young women whose polyphonic singing is overlaid with a musical backdrop of sounds from everyday life. "All of the material," they say, "is a living dialogue with Polish traditional music." Zgagafari's debut album is a collection of Slavic folk songs which they've rearranged and played around with to try and make something interesting. Unlike Sutari, they make no claims to be a traditional band. [9]

For Transkapela the inspiration was klezmer: "We are inspired by nomadic Jewish groups from the late nineteenth and early twentieth centuries whose music we know from recordings and sheet music." [10] It's good to know that Poland's Jewish music heritage hasn't been forgotten. But there isn't quite the same frisson that Bienkowski found with the old village musicians, some of whom are still living today. And while Transkapela make beautiful music, much of it is their own compositions – a creative take on the sounds of a century ago. By contrast, Kroke are a trio from Krakow who started out playing klezmer, but now combine this with jazz and other genres – they claim to "create their unique style which floates across borders, forms and time".

Meanwhile one group was creating radical, exciting music which wore its debt to Bienkowski on its sleeve. This group was the Warsaw Village Band.

"When I was young, I wasn't listening to traditional music at all; I was listening to music from the U.S. and other cultures," says Wojtek Krzak. "But at 16, I was really impressed by the music of a Polish traditional fiddler. For me, it was like discovering Jimi Hendrix. It was like discovering Ali Farka Touré from Mali." [11] The musician's name was Kazimierz Zdrzalik. Kazimierz became the young man's teacher, and taught him how to play in the old rural style, introducing him to polkas, obereks and mazurkas. Wojtek moved to Warsaw where he joined the Warsaw Village Band. Here he found kindred spirits: men and women who'd been to music school but whose search for musical roots had led them to start travelling to rural Poland and study the art of village musicians. "It was a rebellion of sorts," says Wojtek, "a response against narrow-mindedness and surrounding us mass-culture, which in fact leads to destruction of human dignity. The band is a radical return to sources in search of musical inspirations and immemorial virtues. It's also an exploration of folklore and archaic sounds. It's also fun, joy and spontaneity." [12]

When the Warsaw Village Band burst onto the international scene, they were playing old songs from the Mazovia region, using a weird and wonderful collection of instruments that included violin, dulcimer, hurdy-gurdy, cello, frame drums and the ancient suka fiddle. But it was how they played them that made such an impact, strings at high voltage, drums in full effect, and those female vocals: sometimes sung, sometimes chanted, sometimes half-shouted; modelled on the 'white noise' tradition that I described earlier. Yes, this was motivated by the desire to appeal to a younger audience, but there was more to it than that. Here's Wojtek again: "Creating a sort of trance was really important in this music. Old people talk about this. At traditional weddings they forgot about everything, they would drink vodka, eat kielbasa (sausage), and go on and on." [13]

On Uprooting (2004), they recorded a few of the old village musicians who had inspired them so much, and you can hear brief clips of these recordings in between the songs on the album. Kazimierz Zdrzalik makes an appearance, as do Józef Lipinski, Marian Pelka and Janina i Kazimierz Zdrzalikowie. It's an interesting juxtaposition. These are our musical roots, they are saying. Yet what they've created is something altogether new, a testament to how far Polish music has travelled from the days of one man with his fiddle.

From the album Infinity (2008), **LAZY JOHNNY DANCE** is a driving, powerful track. There's a lot of production that's gone into making this. It's a rich, multilayered aural experience, with instruments arriving and leaving all the way through. But at its heart: the repeated melodic line, the forceful female chorus. And at the heart of the Warsaw Village Band project, a passion for the source material, an intelligence and a sense of fun and adventure, all of which tells me that there is much more that they have yet to achieve.

NOTES

1. http://www.rootsworld.com/reviews/nord-13.shtml
2. http://www.akademiakolberga.pl/project/w-tancu-i-o-tancu-piotr-zgorzelski/
3. http://www.akademiakolberga.pl/project/andrzej-bienkowski/
4. http://culture.pl/en/article/the-folk-in-other-words-the-slaves-a-talk-with-andrzej-bienkowski
5. fRoots 338/339, August/September, 2011
6. http://wyborcza.pl/1,75475,11663836,Tancz_mazurka__To_nie_obciach_.html

7. http://wiadomosci.onet.pl/warszawa/festiwal-wszystkie-mazurki-swiata/x0gwbf
8. http://www.kulturasiedlecka.pl/branch,glowna,article,822,magiczna_kapela.html
9. Interview with Robert Gorgol – http://gramuzyka.redblog.gk24.pl/2012/09/12/robert-gorgol-zgagafari-kontynuujemy-ludowa-zywiolowosc-i-spontanicznosc-wywiad/
10. http://culture.pl/pl/wydarzenie/10-lecie-transkapeli
11. http://archive.rockpaperscissors.biz/index.cfm/fuseaction/current.articles_detail/project_id/206/article_id/4637.cfm
12. http://archive.rockpaperscissors.biz/index.cfm/fuseaction/current.articles_detail/project_id/138/article_id/1519.cfm
13. 'The Polish Pogues', Songlines 28 (January–February 2005)

PORTUGAL

"A shawl, a guitar, a voice and sincere emotion. These are the ingredients of Fado, the celebrated form of world music that captures what it is to be Portuguese.

Fado is the song that harnesses the Portuguese soul. Summed up by the Portuguese word saudade, the Fado can be about deep-seated feelings, a sense of sadness and longing for someone who has gone away, disappointments in love, everyday events, and the ups and downs of life. Inspiration for Fado can come from almost any source." [1]

The text was written by someone who works at Portugal's National Tourist Office, but you can find similar sentiments almost anywhere on the net. The not-quite-explicit suggestion is that this music could not have developed anywhere other than Portugal; the word 'saudade' has no exact equivalent in the English language; the mood and temperament of the Portuguese people is uniquely suited to the emotional demands of being a fadista, a fado singer.

POVO QUE LAVAS NO RIO	*Amália Rodrigues*
CANTA CANTA AMIGO CANTA	*Dona Rosa*
DE QUANDO EM VEZ	*Ana Moura*
JOTA DE L TIU GUEITEIRO &	
ALVORADA SANABRESA	*Velha Gaiteira*
SENHOR GALANDUM	*Galandum*
	Galundaina

Fado has always cultivated its own myths, which have become very much part of its fascination, its appeal. Count Vimioso was an aristocrat who in the first half of the 19th century scandalously fell in love with Maria Severa Onofriana, a singer of fados in taverns. The affair burned itself out and Severa died young of tuberculosis. But the story survived to be retold with endless embellishments: a legend that will be forever associated with the birth of fado.

During the second half of the 19th century the essential elements of what we now recognise as traditional Lisbon fado came together: the focus on the (solo) singer; the strumming of a guitar; and the sung poem (the quatrain). Its use of the poetic form and vocal embellishments distinguished it from folk music, but before we over-romanticise it, let's remind ourselves that it was in lower class districts of Lisbon, in working class taverns, brothels and prisons, that the fado first become popular. And, so I understand, a good many early fados dealt with the realities of working class life. This began to change as the Teatro de Revista, a popular theatre company in Lisbon, introduced fado music into their shows. And over a number of years more and more fadistas found themselves performing in theatres to audiences more affluent and with different tastes to those who frequented working class taverns. Many of the songs they sung had universal themes such as lost love. Some fadistas though to choose a different path: writing songs that were highly politically committed. [2]

Between 1926 and 1974 Portugal was ruled by dictatorship. In 1927, laws were introduced subjecting all lyrics to censorship. Songs that had not been approved could not be sung in public. This was partly aimed at fado: the regime distrusted what it viewed as a lower class entertainment. Fado continued to flourish in the 1930s and '40s, but gone was something of the diversity which had previously existed: fadistas steered away from anything that might be deemed too controversial. After a time the regime came to embrace fado tradition, and it assumed national song status.

The dictatorship years saw the rise of arguably Portugal's two greatest artists of modern times: Amália Rodrigues (1920–99) and José 'Zeca' Afonso (1929–87).

Amália was fado's first and most enduring superstar. Her songs and performances came to define what fado music was all about, and you will be hard pushed to find a leading fadista today who doesn't think of Amália as one of their main inspirations. Yet she was no diva. She didn't regard herself that way: perhaps this was part of the secret of her success. She came from a poor family and as a small girl for a time she sold fruit down at Lisbon's docks to help supplement the family income. She never lost her attachment to Lisbon and to the people. Her life and her art were connected: she sang songs that she loved, and did so with an emotion in her voice that felt natural and unforced.

On stage, she had a magic all of her own:

"Only those who saw her live know the magic of Amália. When the lights went down, a deep silence would descend on to the theatre. As the curtain rose her guitarists would

play for about ten minutes some variations on classic Portuguese guitar, only to create the right atmosphere and anticipation for her appearance, as she slowly came from the back of the stage... Then, she would be free to improvise with her guitarists, singing differently the same song every night, depending on her moods, and depending on the response of the audience she would change and adapt her repertoire. The guitarist would naturally follow her, such was the chemistry between them... Quite often she would divert from the original structure of a song to navigate or fly freely, inventing a new song, only to return in fantastic harmony to the original melody. In these moments, the public would go absolutely wild. This is not the Amália of the studio recordings." [3]

Her artistry is also present in the studio recordings. Of these there are many, but some of the most notable are those in the years from 1962 onwards, when she began working with Alain Oulman. The first of these was an untitled album which became known as Busto, after the bust of Amália's head on its cover. Most of the tracks were poems by contemporary Portuguese poets which Oulman had arranged to music. In other words, it was material that fado singers hadn't touched before, but which Amália instinctively understood. She sang with exceptional grace and sensitivity, and a new maturity in her voice. **POVO QUE LAVAS NO RIO** takes a typical urban scene, women washing their clothes in the river, and conveys a sense of the spirit of the women and the certainties of the life that awaits them. This is my featured track: like several of the songs on Busto it's now a fado standard. Abandono is quiet and full of suggested meaning. Estranha Forma de Vida is a poem written by Amália herself and married up with a melody by Marceneiro (another of fado's greats), on the subject of an uncontrollable heart.

This was the start of a fertile creative period for Amália and

Oulman during which Amália continued to perform around the world to huge success. But just as the world was embracing fado, Portugal was going through a period of revolutionary upheaval; and as people were caught up by the politicised atmosphere their musical listening habits also began to change.

Zeca Afonso began his career as a Coimbra fado singer. Coimbra fado is more restrained, less melodramatic than the Lisbon style, and has stronger associations with folk music. Zeca's socially aware lyrics and obvious folk music influences gave Coimbra fado something of a facelift – although he himself shied away from selling himself as a fado singer, giving his albums titles like Baladas e Canções, Cantares do Andarilho and Cantigas do Maio. A song he wrote in 1964, Grândola, Vila Morena, was to change his life forever. The song was adopted by the revolutionary movement, not just as an anthem but as a code sign for the uprising. When it was broadcast by a Lisbon radio station just before midnight on 24th April 1974, this was the signal for the tanks to roll into Lisbon.

After 25th April politically committed folk music known as Música de Intervenção flourished in Portugal with Zeca as its leading light. José Mário Branco and Luís Cília were among those who rushed back from exile to join the revolution. At the same time a new generation of political singers was emerging. Branco formed the GAC (Cultural Action Group), a collective of musicians, poets and composers united by a sense of mission, a dream of playing to the people, educating through song and transforming society. Alas, they were also riven from the start by sectarian divisions, and the group split apart within a few years.

Meanwhile, fado was in decline, tarnished by its associations with the Salazar regime, and diminished because it had little to say about the great issues of the time. Even Amália was not immune from this: "She was falsely accused of being an agent for Salazar's secret police, a slur that stuck for many years, while many were suspicious of her association with Salazar's minister of culture, Antonio Ferro, who championed her work and presented her around the world as an ambassador for Portugal." [4] Her sales figures fell. In time, people would come to recognise that she was a genuinely independent artist who'd had the courage to sing the words of left wing poets before it became popular to do so.

Fado's recovery was gradual. "Ten years ago," said Misia in a 2001 interview, "publishers would say 'fado doesn't sell'. It wasn't like it is today, when publishers want artists to sing fado, since it sells not only in our country but especially abroad." [5] Misia defied the doubters, basing her work on the traditional format, but embellishing it by the use of non-traditional instruments such as the accordion and violin, and by seeking out new material. When Amália died in 1999 three days of national mourning were declared, but for fado music this moment was a springboard to levels of fame and popularity that were to eclipse anything that had gone before. Misia and Mariza both recorded tribute albums to Amália. Fado em Mim was Mariza's debut album: born in Mozambique in 1973, she had no memory of the dictatorship years, or of the excitement and turmoil that accompanied the restoration of democracy. With her cropped platinum-blonde hair and designer gowns, she repackaged fado music for a new generation. Over 140,000 copies of Fado em Mim were sold, and since then Mariza has gone from success to success, becoming the face – and more often than not the voice – of contemporary fado as it's conquered international markets.

I don't entirely share the general enthusiasm for the new fado. Yes, it has its powerful and talented singers: there's intensity, passion and drama in the songs; and yet I find myself missing the sparser, quieter sound of earlier recordings, and the freedom that this gives the singer to express herself in different ways. The move away from melodic styles, the high production values, the focus on vocal performance, all make for an experience that feels less natural.

Besides the vocal improvisations, there is a lot of creativity here. Misia and Mariza are just two of many multitalented female fadistas currently active, and these women of fado feature on a good few compilations. All love to try out new things, new ideas. And yet collectively they all sound quite similar. The powerful voice, the pained emotion, the saudade – it's all a bit expected.

One artist who certainly stands out from the crowd is Dona Rosa. Born in 1957 to a poverty-stricken Lisbon family, she contracted meningitis at the age of four, resulting in complete blindness. Not wanting to be a burden, as soon as she was old enough she left her family to make her own way working the streets by selling magazines and lottery tickets, and begging. She found that with her good voice she could earn money by singing, so she became a street singer, accompanying herself on a triangle. And so for many years she lived her life; but the word fado translates as destiny or fate, and destiny was to take a hand in what happened next:

> "In 1999, a Portuguese production company needed a Fado singer for an Austrian Television Company production to be recorded in Marrakech. The program's musical director, the well-known Viennese artist and impresario André Heller, had a particular blind street singer in mind. Many years ago he had heard a blind street singer; a woman whose voice had moved him so deeply that she haunted his memory ever since. The search for her implied some difficult detective work, but finally she was found – Dona Rosa." [6]

She recorded an album and was invited to perform at Womex in Berlin. Suddenly, in her 40s she was in demand: the media wanted to hear her story, and people across Europe would pay good money to hear her sing. Working with musicians for the first time, her true talent became apparent. Her group isn't a traditional fado ensemble: accordion and percussion are added to the guitars for an unexpectedly lush sound. Occasionally the band take over and play instrumental tracks. It's when you hear

Dona Rosa's earthy vocals though that you feel the emotional punch: it's as though her defences have been stripped away and she's performing her life for you on the stage.

On **CANTA CANTA AMIGO CANTA** (sing my friend, sing) the sound is stripped down to just her voice and a guitar, with a hint of percussion coming in. It's very beautiful and melodic; and the words, written by António Macedo at a time before the revolution when the country's universities were convulsed by protest, are brimful of revolutionary optimism.

While Dona's song brushes against other genres, Ana Moura's **DE QUANDO EM VEZ** is a fado through and through. The song begins with the rippling sound of the 12-string Portuguese guitar, played by Custódio Castelo. There is no chorus to the song. In each verse Ana Moura starts singing with restraint, then in the last three lines raises her voice and vents her emotions. The sense of passionate longing, of love denied, is all there. The lyrics were written by Mario Raínho, one of the most celebrated contemporary fado poets.

Born in Santarém in 1979, Ana Moura's voice has a maturity and a smoky soulfulness that belies her years. "In Portugal we say that you don't choose to be a fadista. You are born one. And I was born a fadista," she claims. "I can never change that, or wish to do so." [7] She sees fado from a modern perspective. In interview after interview, she explains that the music is about feelings and emotions, as articulated by the singer. Yet as we've seen, this aspect of fado is not a constant: its importance has varied over time, and even today there are male Coimbra fado singers who place less stress on the expression of feelings. The album from which the song is taken, Leva-me aos Fados, isn't exactly a spontaneous release of emotion: the album took three months to record. Happily Ana Moura's creative judgement is excellent, and the production values don't interfere with our enjoyment of the songs. How safe is fado's integrity in an industry where so many techniques are to hand to enhance or exaggerate vocal performance? The answer I think lies in the strong bonds between professional singers, poets and musicians, and their mutual love and respect for traditional fado. It's they who will ensure that the songs are allowed to breathe.

Portuguese folk music is rooted in regional tradition.

Folk song collectors have long been interested in the traditional music of Beira Baixa. In 1896, Pedro Fernandes Thomas published 58 folk songs from Beira for people to sing 'in all their simplicity'. Decades later the Coimbra-based Brigada Victor Jara, one of the leading folk groups to emerge from the heady period of the 1970s, sought out and rearranged many traditional songs and dances from the northern regions on albums such as Danças e Folias. Velha Gaiteira are a traditional music project formed in 2007, that aims to keep alive some of the folk culture which once flourished in this mountainous region. Their name also gives a clue to the kind of music we can expect: gaita-de-foles is the Portuguese bagpipe. Despite the proximity to Spain's Galician region with its famed piping traditions, Portugal has an independent bagpiping tradition going back hundreds of years.

JOTA DE L TIU GUEITEIRO & ALVORADA SANABRESA is a dance tune: after 40 seconds the drums kick in and the piping becomes faster and more urgent. Velha Gaiteira's repertoire also includes work songs, religious songs and ritual dances. The moda dos bombos, which they perform with flute and drums, is, so they tell us, one of most recognisable aspects of local culture – "each village has its version." [8]

From the small medieval town of Miranda do Douro, Galandum Galundaina are ambassadors of Mirandese culture. Situated at the edge of the northeastern region of Trás-os-Montes, nestled by the Spanish border, Miranda has its own history, its own dialect, and of course its own culture, which remains part of the life of the villages of the region, each of which has its own fete. The band's four members include two brothers, Paulo and

Alexandre Meirinhos. Their mother and grandfather belonged to a local folklore dance troupe, and much of the brothers' knowledge of Mirandese culture, as well as some instruments, was inherited from them. Mirandese culture is noted, among other things, for the gaita mirandesa (regional variant of the Portuguese bagpipe) and for the Pauliteiros: a dance from the same family as Morris dancing, performed by costumed men carrying two sticks which they clack together while dancing in set patterns to the rhythm of bagpipe and drums.

Galandum Galundaina are not your average village bagpipe and drum ensemble. They research their history. They make their own instruments, which include ancient instruments like the hurdy-gurdy and the psalterium. They rearrange traditional songs and dances to allow them to make the most of instruments that they've grown to love, while also seeking to revive the region's old vocal music traditions. Mirandese music has strong Celtic influences, but Galandum Galundaina also add a flavour of Arabic music to the mix. The result is a rich and fascinating concoction that goes down a treat with young festival-goers the length and breadth of the country.

This mixture of the old and the new is evident on the track SENHOR GALANDUM: starting with male choral singing in Mirandese dialect, it soon becomes a dance tune as the instruments chime in. Barbara Alge, in her valuable study of the band, quotes them as saying: "we construct a bridge from nostalgic music to a lively music and a music with future." [9] They also bridge the gap between traditional rural folklore and modern urban folk music.

The band are also looking to leave a more permanent legacy. Their website contains a lengthy account of the work they've been doing over many years to safeguard the future of the gaita mirandesa, work carried out under the auspices of the Galandum Galundaina Cultural Association which they helped to found in 1996. At this time there were only a couple of gaita mirandesa makers still left in the region, but there was also a more fundamental issue: no two bagpipes were made in exactly the same way, varying in specifics such as pitch. Paulo Preto, a member of the band, was assigned to take the lead on developing a proposal to standardise the instrument. In 2007 he published a document which set out all stages of the process and presented instruments already built to the proposed criteria. After some further work a forum of gaita mirandesa experts took place in Miranda do Douro in 2011 where the proposals were ratified.

NOTES

1. http://www.tangodiva.com/culture-portugal-fado-the-music-of-portugal/
2. http://www.newstatesman.com/music/2007/10/portuguese-fado-lisbon-regime
3. http://www.furious.com/perfect/amaliarodrigues.html
4. http://www.theguardian.com/music/2007/apr/27/worldmusic
5. http://discodigital.sapo.pt/news.asp?id_news=655
6. http://www.jaro.de/artists/dona-rosa/
7. http://www.voicesofny.org/2014/11/ana-moura-brings-world-fado/
8. http://festluso.blogspot.co.uk/2013/08/velha-gaiteira-abre-programacao-musical.html
9. Barbara Alge – Os 'mirandeses' as cultural capital: Galandum Galundaina and the (re)construction of the 'música mirandesa' (2008) http://www.academia.edu/2035634/Os_mirandeses_as_cultural_capital_Galandum_Galundaina_and_the_re_construction_of_the_m%C3%BAsica_mirandesa

ROMANIA

In the 1930s, Bucharest was the place to be, dubbed the 'Paris of the East' thanks to its tree-lined boulevards, fin de siècle architecture and lively nightlife. And among Bucharest's brightest rising stars was Maria Tanase. She had a few sides to her. She was a diva, a striking beauty who lived life to the full and had a series of passionate love affairs. But she was also blessed with a powerful voice, a strong stage presence and a remarkable knowledge of Romanian folk songs. She was greeted as a star wherever she performed, but first and foremost it was Romanian people rich and poor who took her to their hearts; and when she died in 1963 her funeral was a day of national mourning. Tens of thousands of workers left their factories and the streets and balconies were lined with people.

It was an age of romance. Ioana Radu was married to a music teacher called Romeo, but one night in 1936 she walked out while he was sleeping, never to return. She headed straight to the bright city lights of Bucharest, hoping that one day she could make it there like her idol Maria Tanase. It didn't happen overnight, but her dreams did become true: she got to perform with the big orchestras, and even to share a stage with Maria Tanase herself.

September 25th, 2013, was the hundredth anniversary of

PE VALE	*Oana Catalina Chitu*
MOLDAVIAN SHEPHERDS' DANCE	*Taraf de Haïdouks*
DOINA PENTRU UN FRANT INIMA	*Fanfare Ciocărlia*
SUPARATA SUNT PE LUME	*Gabi Lunca*
DOÍNA LUI EFTA BOTOCA	*Efta Botoca*

Maria's birth. To mark the occasion, Asphalt Tango records released a tribute album entitled Divine. The singer, Oana Catalina Chitu, had grown up in the small village of Humuleşti where folk traditions were a part of everyday life. Inspired by her father to a love of tango music, she left home to pursue her musical studies, eventually ending up in Berlin (where the Berlin-based Asphalt Tango label would find her). Aided by her classical training, she has an uncanny ability to capture the essence of that golden age music. It is very much her own interpretation though, and on PE VALE I like her slow, languid singing and the drone effects on the double bass.

In 1991, a then little, known Belgian record label, Crammed, released an album that would lead in the space of a few short years to Romanian gypsy music becoming hugely popular around the world. The album came about as a result of the enthusiasm of two young Belgian music lovers, Stéphane Karo and Michel Winter. Realising that what they'd found was something special, they invited several musicians from the village of Clejani, where the tradition was particularly strong, to form a group. A troupe of lautari (traditional Roma musicians) is called a taraf, so the band became known as Taraf de Haïdouks. Stéphane Karo became the band's manager, promoter and producer, arranging first a short tour in Belgium then making the first of many albums with the band.

According to Romania's 2011 census, there were 621,573 Roma living in the country. As with most aspects of Roma life, this figure is heavily disputed. Amnesty International estimates the true number to be around 1,850,000. Feelings run strong. In 2009, when Madonna was giving a concert in Bucharest, she invited Roma performers on stage and spoke out against discrimination. Her words were met with boos. But discrimination is a fact. Again, according to Amnesty, "About 80 per cent out of the Roma in Romania live in poverty. Close to 60 per cent of them live in segregated communities without access to basic state services. 23 per cent of Roma households – in comparison with about 2 per cent of non-Roma households – suffer multiple housing deprivations, including no access to improved water sources, sanitation and lack of security of tenure." [1] Levels of violent attacks against Roma in Romania are not as serious as they are in Hungary, Slovakia, or the Czech Republic. But according to Roma rights campaigner Marian Mandache, the relative absence of organised far right thuggery in Romania has its dark side – "there isn't really much need for extreme-right groups because you find racism and stereotyping in all the mainstream parties." [2] Local politicians routinely portray the Roma population as lazy and prone to violence.

In 25 years, Taraf de Haïdouks had travelled many a long mile, and I'm not just talking about their global tours. Their music had changed, drawing in fresh influences as they tried to anticipate the ever-shifting interests of the world music market. Also a few of the original band members had died. So when it was decided to mark the milestone with another album, Stéphane knew that he had to make it a good one:

"Crammed asked me to recreate the atmosphere of the first

album. I went back to Clejani to recruit young musicians from among the children of those who had died. And we set out to make a record that would be like the really early days of Taraf." [3]

MOLDAVIAN SHEPHERDS' DANCE is a tune from the album Of Lovers, Gamblers & Parachute Skirts. In this tune you can hear all the reasons why the group have become so adored by so many. The strings are incredibly fast and furious. It's exhilarating stuff. It's trad music for the punk generation – but don't mistake them for a garage band. These are musicians who've cut their teeth playing at ceremonies and weddings, who remain grounded in traditional music, and whose musicianship is of the highest order.

On his death in 2016, Stéphane Karo was buried in a Brussels cemetery: "A group of mourners looked on while six Romanian Gypsy musicians played fiddles, accordions and a cymbalom as the coffin entered the earth." [4] It was a modest but fitting tribute to a man who'd done so much to promote Roma music.

He wasn't the only one at it. Asphalt Tango, the Berlin-based label which has become a byword for Balkan brass music, came into being as a result of a chance meeting.

"I was talking to a farmer, buying gasoline, and it came up that I liked the music of Romania very much. He told me, 'Hey man, go straight ahead and there's a tiny village called Zece Prăjini, where Gypsies live who play brass music.' This was totally new to me, so I say, 'Yes, cool,' and go there to have a listen." [5]

What Henry Ernst found in the village was the most exciting music that he'd heard in his life:

"It was like nothing I'd ever heard before – a wall of sound, such speed, I couldn't believe it was real – this was brass

*music which sounded more like techno or rock. I was
totally blown away. Very soon I knew I had to bring these
musicians to more people." [6]*

Doing this would involve big risks for a middle-aged sound
engineer. He sold everything he owned to finance a tour of
Germany and France, and set up Asphalt Tango as management
agents for the band, who he named Fanfare Ciocărlia. They never
looked back. In the two decades since, Fanfare Ciocărlia have
established themselves as possibly the most famous gypsy band
in the world. Key to their sound is a formidable array of trumpets,
tubas, horns and saxes. This set-up though is far from unique.
What gives them the edge over their equally talented rivals comes
down to a certain attitude and spirit, and a reputation for playing
with the speed of an express train.

Balkan Brass Battle (Asphalt Tango, 2011) is an attempt
to bottle the exuberance of the live shows. The 'battle' is a
competition between Fanfare Ciocărlia and the Boban i Marko
Marković Orkestar from Serbia: it's great fun, but shouldn't be
taken too seriously. It's something of an exercise in showmanship.
Both bands are trying to fire the audience up, outdo one another
for speed, and make an instant impression. Thus the Fanfare
Ciocărlia songs on the album include a cover of the James Bond
theme!

More representative, though, is their 20th-anniversary
album, Onwards to Mars! (2016). It has its turbocharged dance
numbers and exotic rhythms, but there are also plenty of nods to
traditional culture. Trenul, Masina Mica is an old Maria Tanase
song, performed in the band's inimitable style; there are a couple
of horas (a Romanian folk dance); and one doina, a melancholy
eastern-style song form specific to Romania. On DOINA PENTRU
UN FRANT INIMA we get to see a less well-known side of Fanfare
Ciocărlia. The band show their reverence for the traditional
form by slowing their music right down and playing the tune as

it's meant to be heard. On this occasion the alto sax is the key instrument, packing an emotional punch to convey the song's theme of heartbreak.

Asphalt Tango have done Romanian music another great service with their CD series Sounds From a Bygone Age, compiled from old Communist-era recordings for Romanian state radio. The artists featured include some of the greatest names in Romanian music: Romica Puceanu, Toni Iordache, Gabi Lunca. The track I've chosen is by the smoky-voiced gypsy singer Gabi Lunca. The arrangement on **SUPARATA SUNT PE LUME** is pure delight: there's a lightness and fluidity to the accordion playing by Gabi's husband, Ion Onoriu, and the accordion and vocals seem to just effortlessly interweave.

Once a favourite of Nicolae Ceauşescu, after the Ceauşescu regime was deposed Gabi turned her back on the songs that had made her famous and devoted herself to the Pentecostal Church, singing exclusively Christian music.

If you're content with one CD compilation, Tziganes Roumanie on the French Atoll label is not a bad introduction to Romanian gypsy music. There are songs by Romica Puceanu and Gabi Lunca, but don't stop there: there are several numbers by Simion 'Syrinx' Stanciu who's a virtuoso on the nai, a Romanian pan flute often used by lautari bands; cimbalom king, Ion Miu, contributes a few tracks; and best of all, there's a tune by the violinist Efta Botoca.

All accounts describe a musician of rare skill. There are stories about when Efta was growing up in western Romania: in 1936 the 11-year-old kid picked up his violin while at the Jebel Fair and started playing, and as word got around the cream of local musicians came by to listen to him play. [7] After the war he lived in Bucharest where he got to play in some of the leading state orchestras. It was during this time that Gheorghe Zamfir first heard him perform. For Gheorghe this was an unforgettable experience. He was still young at the time and could hardly have imagined himself playing with the great soloist, but a few years later he headhunted Efta to play in his band, and they were bandmates for a couple of decades up to Efta's death in 1991. Gheorghe remembers him as a good, honest man and an extraordinary talent.

And so here he is, playing **DOÍNA LUI EFTA BOTOCA**. Like the other doïna in this list, it's a slow, melancholy number, but the similarities end there. If Fanfare Ciocărlia's Doïna is more of an overt display of emotion, this is more restrained. It's moody, and it's haunting.

NOTES

1. https://www.amnesty.org/download/Documents/12000/eur010082013en.pdf
2. http://www.independent.co.uk/news/world/europe/the-truth-about-romanias-gypsies-not-coming-over-here-not-stealing-our-jobs-8489097.html
3. http://www.bruzz.be/en/music/taraf-de-haidouks-back-roots, retrieved September, 2013
4. http://www.theneweuropean.co.uk/culture/a-belgian-man-changed-folk-music-forever-but-you-ve-probably-never-heard-of-him-1-4824081
5. https://www.philharmonie.lu/media/content/download/documents/Publications/Abendprogramme_Abendzettel/saison_15-16/160315-ADM-Fanfare_Ciocarlia-.pdf
6. https://www.thenational.ae/arts-culture/after-20-years-the-kings-of-balkan-brass-fanfare-cioc%C3%A2rlia-still-reign-supreme-1.190665
7. http://www.banatulazi.ro/efta-botoca-violonistul-de-legenda-al-banatului/

SAN MARINO

When the Republic of San Marino became a World Heritage site in 2008, Unesco said that it was "testimony to a living cultural tradition that has persisted over the last seven hundred years." [1] Being hardwired by now to hunt out living cultural traditions, this line gave me encouragement. Alas, I was to be disappointed. Neither Unesco nor anyone else could point me to centuries-old cultural traditions. What I found instead was something just as interesting in its own way: a tiny country with a firm handle on its own identity, and a yearning for authentic cultural connections to the past.

What is true is that the tiny country has a very long history. It trades on this history: on its myth of origin, its claim to be Europe's oldest republic, its museums and architecture. And it's a fascinating story, how this small enclave of 32,000 people living around Mount Titan, entirely surrounded by Italy, has survived as an autonomous entity right into the 21st century. What the tourist brochures don't tell you is that, although some old churches may still be standing, San Marino has transformed from the place it once was. Where once families depended on sheep farming or quarrying for an income, now the tourist trade dominates the economy. Given the country's size, this explains the absence of traditional music and culture.

EMILIANO *Emanuele Rastelli*

San Marino's location makes it perfectly suited to draw on the rich culture of northern Italy. For instance the town of Pesaro just a few miles away on the Adriatic coast was birthplace of the great opera composer Gioachino Rossini. Rossini's dying wish was for a music school to be started in his home town: he bequeathed his properties to the town council, and the Conservatoire Rossini ran its first courses in 1882. One Sammarinese man who studied at Rossini's Academy and later became a professor there was Cesare Franchini Tassini. There must have been many a time when Tassini took a long hard look around him and dreamed of a school for Sammarinese musicians. Eventually, he realised his dream. The Istituto Musicale Sammarinese, as it's now called, was founded in 1975 under the auspices of the Società Corale San Marino, which Tassini had formed several years earlier. The importance of its work in training young musicians was recognised some 20 years later when it became a public institution.

Unlike other government initiatives – such as opening concert venues and museums, or promoting music festivals – which were aimed at turning San Marino into a cultural centre with tourism in mind, the music school was seen as something that could give the Republic's own culture a lift. The 1990s also saw the creation of a Sammarinese orchestra, L'Associazione Musicale Camerata del Titano, who in dozens of events and concerts have brought back to San Marino something of the range of classical music to which it's been exposed over its long history. They released a rather lovely CD, Concerti Spirituali, which is based on one of the few known works originating from San Marino: it was composed in 1637, during Italy's Baroque period, by the then Kapellmeister of San Marino, Francesco Maria Marini.

But what of music that ordinary people with no formal training could create and sing for themselves? Again, it's instructive to take a look at the wider region. Further down the Adriatic coast in Castelfidardo the first Italian accordion makers emerged in the mid-19th century. By the end of the century there were several workshops operating in the Marche region employing hundreds of workers. According to Beniamino Bugiolacchi, this new industry: "in a short period of time succeeded in transforming the local economy from one based on agriculture, to an industrial one open to the international market." [1] In the first half of the 20th century the export trade grew and grew: Italian accordions were reputed for their quality, and there was no better assurance of quality than the words 'made in Castelfidardo'. By 1953, Bugiolacchi tells us, "this small town in Marche, with a population of just 9000, gave employment to over 10000 workers in the musical instrument sector alone' with exports of over 190,000 units." Since then there've been many closures and the industry has declined, though Bugiolacchi still reports 30 companies based in Castelfidardo at the time of the article.

The accordion's not an old or a high-prestige instrument. It may not fit comfortably with the image that San Marino is trying to promote. But it's a living tradition, and as enthusiasm for the instrument swept across eastern Italy, Sammarinese people joined the fun. The accomplished accordion player Emanuele Rastelli was born in the Republic in 1968, and still lives there today. He studied at an accordion school in nearby Rimini founded by Laura

Benizzi. He's a versatile player who's taken on a range of projects over the years, but I enjoyed the crisp, cheerful tune of EMILIANO, which conjures up for me an idea of how the music would have sounded in its heyday of the 1920s and '30s.

NOTES

1. https://whc.unesco.org/en/list/1245
2. http://www.accordions.com/index/his/his_it.shtml

SERBIA

f you thought Serbian music was a bit obscure, think again. In 2013, readers of the US-based website worldmusiccentral.org voted Gipsy Manifesto by Boban i Marko Marković Orkestar their world music album of the year (it collected over 46,000 votes). Boban and Marko are the biggest stars in the Balkan brass band scene which in the past decade or two has swept all before it. In 2011, their album Balkan Brass Battle with the Romanian band Fanfare Ciocărlia spent months in the world music charts and filled venues across Europe. And the biggest and boldest celebration of Balkan brass band music is in the tiny Serbian town of Guča, where hundreds of thousands of music fans descend every year for its increasingly popular trumpet festival.

Boban and Marko, like the great majority of performers at the trumpet festival, are Roma. Boban believes that the success of the event has helped to counteract prejudice: "With our music, I think that we surely help people leave behind their prejudices about our region. I see many people coming to our concerts dressed in Gypsy style. They ask many questions, they approach our culture enthusiastically." [1] Certainly the fact that Serbs and Romas can come together in a festive spirit is something to be celebrated. But it would be wrong to deny that underlying tensions remain.

KHELIPE E CHEASA	Boban i Marko Marković Orkestar
MLADINO KOLO	Orkestar Dejana Ilica
SINCE MY FLUTE RINGS NO MORE	Bora Dugić
STO SE BELI GORE SAR PLANINA	Belo Platno
DEMIRANOV ČOČEK	Demiran Ćerimović Orchestra

The Serbs are a fiercely nationalistic people, and recent years have seen a resurgence of far right groups who target much of their vitriol on the Roma population. The Roma claim that they also suffer from institutional discrimination: they're largely shut out from public sector jobs, many live in unhealthy conditions and 30% have no access to drinking water. Thousands are not officially registered – have no ID card – and as a result have no access to state education, social services or welfare benefits. The state has to take a lot of the responsibility for this: "In order for Roma people to get official documentation, they need to know their birthdates and the birthdates of their parents. However, many Roma people do not know these dates. In response, the Serbian government recently allowed for a special procedure for Roma to obtain documentation without knowing their birthdates. However, [Roma rights workers] maintain that many local authorities in Serbia still do not recognize this new procedure." [2]

So how did this unlikely musical explosion come about? Why trumpet music? And why the Roma?

The musical traditions of Serbia's Roma enclaves were centuries old. Music was part of the life of the community, instilled in children from an early age. The region has an abundance of traditional forms of music and dance, and from what I can tell early musicologists didn't attribute any special importance to Roma music. What set the Roma apart was their role as public performers. Many of them relied on music as a source of income. Playing music was considered to be a low-status occupation. It meant working in bars and restaurants, or at weddings, and relying on tips. For women musicians in particular this was looked on as shameful: Roma women who performed to male audiences in bars were stigmatised as little better than whores. At the same time, if you were planning a wedding, you would make sure that you booked Roma musicians, because they were the best. Not only did they know all the essential kolo dance tunes, they could also play a lively trumpet.

Nowadays, says Boban Marković, "On all important occasions, they call for the trumpet and the brass band. Everyone wants to play the trumpet and to be in a brass band because that means work and money and you can be a star. You can live, it's a living. Other bands, violin bands, don't have a job." [3]

The trumpet is not a traditional Balkan instrument. It was first seen in the military brass bands of the 19th century, and its co-option into folk culture only began in the early 20th century. As enterprising Roma musicians taught themselves to play folk melodies on the trumpet, they must have soon realised that they were onto something. The trumpet's versatility made it ideal for occasions such as weddings.

The Guča Trumpet Festival began as a small affair in 1961 and grew slowly. It was a time of opening-up of gypsy culture in the former Yugoslavia. The Roma became an officially recognised national minority in Macedonia in 1971 and across the whole Yugoslav state in 1981 – this recognition extended to their language and culture. At that time the greatest stars of Roma music were Esma Redžepova from Macedonia and Šaban Bajramović from Serbia. Conscripted into the army as a teenager, Šaban deserted so he could be with the girl he loved, for which he was sentenced to three years of hard labour – a sentence raised to five years after he told the court that not even a penal colony could hold him. While in prison he learned to read and formed his first band. He went on to compose more than 600 songs, and his interpretation of the gypsy anthem Djelem, Djelem is regarded as a classic.

For visitors to the festival, the experience is all about shacking up with the locals, grilled meat dishes, drinking rakija (plum brandy) and dancing the night away. For performers it's a rather more serious affair: they're all competing for the prestigious awards of Top Trumpet (jury) and Golden Trumpet (audience). Well, most of them are. Boban Marković has won so many times at the festival that he doesn't bother to compete anymore.

Boban and his band are from the small town of Vladicin Han in the south of the country near the border with Kosovo. An extraordinary number of brass bands are from Vladicin Han and the neighbouring town of Vranje. Boban started playing trumpet at the age of six and turned professional at 16, but never learned to read music. His international breakthrough came after his friend and fellow musician Goran Bregović introduced him to the film director Emir Kusturica. Goran and Boban collaborated on the soundtrack of the films Arizona Dream and Underground, the second of which won the Palme d'Or at Cannes. Boban's son Marko (born in 1988) began performing with the group in 2002 and soon became its main soloist.

Boban and Marko respect their musical roots, but don't venerate them. For them it's not just healthy but essential that brass band artists express their creativity and allow the music to take on new influences and directions. On their albums we find them weaving various global sounds into the already rich tapestry that is Balkan brass music. KHELIPE E CHEASA is no homage to the past. It's a witty, chirpy number intended to bring a smile to people's faces and to get them tapping their feet.

Dejan Ilic of the Orkestar Dejana Ilica tells us on his website that he was born in 1977, that he's a nephew of the Marković family and that he learned to play the trumpet from his father, Novica Ilic, who now plays in his band. His album Balkanske trube (Balkan trumpet) was premiered at the Guča festival in 2013, and from it I've selected MLADINO KOLO (The Bride's Dance). It's a traditional tune, but Dejan gives it the modern Roma treatment, playing it faster and louder than it would have sounded before the days of the gypsy brass band.

Bora Dugić sees the rising popularity of the trumpet as detrimental to Serbian traditional music. "The worst thing," he says, "is that children grow up with the knowledge that the trumpet is their national instrument." [4] To expand the point: kids are ignorant about the real traditional instruments of the country, and of the character of most traditional music. Bora's own contribution to this collection, SINCE MY FLUTE RINGS NO MORE, is a beautiful moody melody which sounds uncannily like Pink Floyd. It's performed on the flute. Bora is a virtuoso flautist who's equally comfortable performing folk and classical music and who's performed solo around the world in such venues as Sydney Opera House. Somewhat incongruously, he also performed at the 2008 Eurovision Song Contest accompanying the Serbian singer Jelena Tomasević. It wasn't his best decision: the Serbian entry was a big power ballad in which Bora's flute contributed little.

The group Belo Platno have two passions: Serbian folk music and Byzantine chants. The Orthodox Church (to which 85% of Serbs claim allegiance) has powerful associations with Serbian history. The giant iconic Church of Saint Sava, one of Belgrade's main landmarks, is still under construction over 100 years since the first contest for architectural plans was held. Saint Sava was the founder and first Archbishop of the Serbian Orthodox Church.

In the 1590s, three centuries after his death, when Serbian rebels rose up against Ottoman occupiers, they carried the image of Saint Sava on their flags. The Ottoman commander's response was to have the remains of Saint Sava dug up from the monastery in south Serbia where he was buried, taken to Belgrade and ceremonially burned. And it's on Vračar hill where the pyre was lit by the Ottomans that the Serbs decided to erect their temple.

Vladimir Simic remembers that the group was assembled by Predrag-Stole Stojković in Belgrade in 1997, initially to sing in the church choir. Predrag-Stole taught him to play the kaval, a type of flute traditionally played by Balkan mountain shepherds. Within a year they'd formed into a musical group which they named Belo Platno after the white linen used in religious ceremonies.

I've chosen a chant, **STO SE BELI GORE SAR PLANINA**, to represent the group's music because it's very well arranged, and the women's voices are so clear and striking. But I have to report that they've also done some great work in reviving folk songs. As well as kavals they play the tamburitza, the gaida (Balkan bagpipe), tambourines and a variety of drums. They were given their first instruments by the award-winning church vocalist Dragoslav Pavle Akesntijevic; since then they've manufactured a few instruments of their own. Dressing in traditional costumes they perform songs and poems from around the region, but with a particular focus on Kosovo and Metohija.

While I understand the concerns of the folk traditionalists, I find it very positive that Balkan brass music is in vogue. The music is vibrant and life-affirming and transcends cultural barriers. Should you be so lucky as to make it to the Guča festival, spare a thought for the Roma bands who've come from towns like Vranje and Vladicin Han. The last decade has seen rising unemployment in the region as state-owned factories have been privatised and closed. Fewer residents now can afford to hold celebrations or hire Roma musicians. The money that bands are able to earn at Guča and by selling a few CDs isn't enough at a time of dwindling gigs, so they've had to find other ways of supplementing their income. 2013 saw the release of the documentary film Brasslands directed by the 10-person Meerkat Media Collective. The film told the story of three bands going to compete at Guča, one of which was Demiran Ćerimović's Vranjski Biseri Orchestra from Vranje.

The film's press release sets the scene:

"Every competitor seeks to win, but the film's characters are all making their trumpet pilgrimages for very different reasons: 25-year-old master trumpeter Dejan Petrović— the reigning Guča champion—returns to defend his championship title, while Demiran Ćerimović—a world- class Roma Gypsy trumpeter—struggles against deeply ingrained racism for the opportunity to make money for his family. Through it all, a fish-out-of-water American band plays to validate their very existence in front of a population still scarred by US bombs."

DEMIRANOV ČOČEK is from the Brasslands soundtrack: it's a wild, exhilarating cacophony of brass. Čoček dances are a very interesting marriage of modernity and tradition. Čoček developed in the Balkans from military brass band music of the 19th century, and it was Roma musicians who popularised the dance and gave it its character. The word čoček comes from the Turkish köçek, a term used for dancing boys who dressed in female attire. While the Turkish influence can be heard in the music, čoček group dancing seems to involve a sequence of small dainty steps.

NOTES

1. http://wild-rooster.com/we-are-the-best-dont-doubt-it-guca-legend-boban-markovic-says/
2. http://www.yale.edu/accent/ACCENT/TRANSLATIONS/Entries/2012/11/15_Roma_in_Serbia__Marginalized_and_forcibly_evicted_from_their_homes.html retrieved September 2013
3. http://www.bosnia.org.uk/bosrep/report_format.cfm?articleid=977&reportid=157
4. http://arhiva.kurir-info.rs/arhiva/2004/novembar/27-28/ST-08-27112004.shtml, retrieved September, 2013

SLOVAKIA

Košice, the 2013 European Capital of Culture (an honour that it shared with Marseilles), is a city of contrasts. A Gothic cathedral competes with a giant steel mill for its most notable landmark. The city is anxious to shed its reputation as a Soviet-era industrial hub. As Slovakia's second city launched its Capital of Culture year, project director Jan Sudzina declared that, "we want to transform Košice from a heavy industrialised city to one focusing on creative industries." [1] But despite a rapidly growing IT sector, creative industries have a long way to go before they replace the steel mill, since 2000 under the ownership of US Steel which employs some 11,000 workers. The Capital of Culture money has enabled the city to give itself a facelift, with a derelict swimming pool being replaced with a centre for contemporary art. To the dismay of the organisers though, one local council erected a two-metre-high wall which partitioned off a Roma neighbourhood, drawing international attention to the squalid condition of Košice's Roma slums and to the hostile attitudes of some people toward the Roma.

FS Železiar (the FS just means 'folk ensemble') were named after a steel company which in turn provided sponsorship. Far more than just a group of singers and dancers, they have been an integral part of Košice's culture for half a century:

A JA TAKE ĎIVČA ĽUBĽU
HEJ, POMALY OVEČKY

FS Železiar

Fujaristi z Kokavy

"Currently, the ensemble functions under the patronage
of the Košice Self-governing District, through its District
Educational Centre. People involved in Železiar´s activities
have greatly contributed to the fact that numerous folklore
groups in Košice and the whole region live as an open
community. They co-organize the Košice Folklore Days and
an international folklore festival, Cassovia Folkfest. They
create a ground for various activities at the House of the
Folklore Dance at Starozagorská Street in Košice. A new
generation of folklorists is being brought up at the Private
Elementary Art School and motivated by membership in the
Youth Folklore Ensemble Železiarik. Activities in folklore
workshops and the Archive of Traditional Culture are being
supported. Hundreds of children are made familiar with
the traditional art thanks to educational concerts." [2]

This is why the life of a súbor, a folk ensemble, can continue for
decade after decade: it's the property of a whole community, not
just one or two individuals. As I understand it, súbors took root
during the Soviet era, borrowing and developing traditions as they
did so, and cladding performers in modern versions of traditional

dress. These town-based ensembles enriched themselves by drawing on folk traditions that were still practised in many rural areas by smaller musical groups (skupiny). Železiar took a particular interest in the music and culture of eastern Slovakia. The delightful dance track **A JA TAKE DIVČA ĽUBLU** is taken from an album of Rusyn song. The Rusyns are a people whose home is in the Carpathian Mountains: in Slovakia they are concentrated in the Prešov region in the shadow of the spectacular Tatra Mountains. After Slovakia gained independence in 1993, the Rusyn language was recognised and from a very weak position Rusyn culture has enjoyed something of a revival.

Outside the towns, a picture emerges of a remarkably diverse folk culture. Ondrej Demo is a Slovak ethnomusicologist who has witnessed this at first hand. Each region of the country, he says, "has different dialect, different habits, different costumes, different songs". This can often be seen just by going from one village to the next. "This is what makes Slovak folklore so unique and distinctive and I will dare to say the richest in central Europe. And this is not the case only in vocal song creation, but also in instrumental creation. None of the neighboring countries can boast such a big number of musical instruments. For example the ethnomusicologists from the Slovak Academy of Sciencies state that we have around 120 different types of shepherds' blows." [3]

The mountain village of Terchová is a remarkable example of the strength of regional folk tradition. In 2013, Unesco recognised Terchová's music for its heritage value. The village is "renowned" they said "for its collective vocal and instrumental music, performed by three-, four- or five-member string ensembles with a small two-string bass or diatonic button accordion... There are over twenty professional musical ensembles in Terchová, while amateur ensembles perform at family, traditional and other events." [4] For a population of just over 4,000 that's a lot of musical ensembles! But Ondrej Demo, who's frequently visited Terchová to make recordings, can verify: "Every year they organize in their village a three-day folklore festival called Jánošík Days, where they present themselves in various forms and appearances... it is a culture through blows, drumblas, accordions, stringed instruments, from the youngest people to the oldest. It is four generations. If I tell you that there are four unique children's music ensembles and their members do not have to attend music schools, but they learn everything from the older ones, then I can only take my hat off to them."

Jánošík Days is so named in honour of Juraj Jánošík, Slovakia's own outlaw folk hero who came from Terchová. He was a member of the rebel army, made up largely of peasants, who rose up against the Habsburg Empire at the turn of the 18th century. After the rebels were routed at the battle of Trenčín, Jánošík was either recruited or coerced into the imperial army. Then, while working as a prison guard, he assisted the escape of brigand leader Tomáš Uhorčík. The two men teamed up to form a group of bandits who went around pulling off daring robberies. Jánošík succeeded Uhorčík as the band's leader. The legends all say that he robbed the rich to give to the poor: there's no documentary evidence of this, but then I don't suppose that illiterate Carpathian peasants were in the habit of leaving document trails. What we do know is that he was captured, put on trial for highway robbery and executed in March 1713, shortly after his 25th birthday.

Another folk festival worthy of mention is the Folklore Festival Poľana, held every July in Detva. Folk ensembles from far and wide congregate in the small town, located in the heavily forested Podpoľania region in central Slovakia. As well as watching the performances, you can learn more about some of these 120 types of shepherds' blows, or take classes in playing the fujara. The fujara is unique to Podpoľania. It's a flute four to seven feet in length with three finger holes and an attached windpipe which is played standing upright. Other instruments include the koncovka, an overtone flute with no side holes; and a six-hole whistle.

Pavel Bielčik (born 1939) lives in Hriňová, which is close to Detva. He's a master instrument maker who's produced hundreds of fujaras, flutes and whistles using only traditional tools and methods, decorating them all with natural motifs. He can play a bit too. For over four decades he's performed with the local ensemble FS Kokavan, who specialise in the dance and music of the region. There is a Kokavan CD, Z Kokavských Kolešní, with both archive and more recent recordings, which is available on iTunes. The album surprised me – I had expected to hear something more dance oriented – but its slow graceful numbers are most enjoyable. I wanted, though, to let you hear what Slovakia's most iconic instrument sounds like. So I've gone for a track from Fujaristi z Kokavy, an album that Pavel Bielčik recorded with a group of friends. Although there are five of them, they all do solos on different tracks. **HEJ, POMALY OVEČKY** is one of Pavel's tracks, and on this one he's supported by a second fujara player, John Kroták. The two great pipes combine to make an unearthly sound.

NOTES

1. http://www.rawstory.com/rs/2013/01/19/slovakian-steel-hub-remaking-itself-as-european-capital-of-culture/
2. http://zeleziar.sk/people/?id=100, retrieved March, 2014
3. http://www.panorama.sk/en/guide/interview-with-slovak-ethnomusicologist-ondrej-demo/1138
4. http://www.unesco.org/culture/ich/RL/00877

SLOVENIA

In my musical odyssey, Wikipedia has often been my friend, pointing me in the right direction. The Slovenian music entry though is distinctly unencouraging. "Slavko [Avsenik] and his brother, Vilko, are usually credited as the pioneers of Slovenian folk music," it tells us. The Avsenik brothers were great professionals who certainly contributed a lot; but to my way of thinking the Alpine orchestra music style which they made popular was rooted in nostalgia rather than any real curiosity about the past. In short, it was neo-traditional and kitsch.

There is another Slovenia though – a darker Slovenia, with a fondness for danger and unpredictability. It's epitomised in the music of the band Laibach: an industrial avant-garde sound that challenges you to rethink your preconceptions of what music is all about. The band have long had a genius for being provocative. Laibach is the German name for the Slovenian capital, Ljubljana. In 1988, the band released a cover album of Beatles songs, Let It Be. And in 2015 they claimed the dubious honour of becoming the first western rock band to play in North Korea.

Katalena are a band with the same kind of anarchic spirit: a band who defy musical rules and easy categorisation. They would take old forgotten folk songs and reinterpret them in an art rock

KEME MERAV
Sukar

RASTI MI, RASTI, TRAVCA ZELENA
Bistrške Škvorke

style, playfully exploring different sound effects and genres. This degree of experimentation was unusual, but the point to note is that the two and a half decades since Slovenian independence have seen a lot of diversity and creativity, with more and more bands choosing to follow their own path. Katarina Juvančič writes of a new generation of folk artists with a more global outlook:

> "These musicians create an individual vision of folk music built on the foundation of multi-faceted, multigenre and technological possibilities and collaborations... pairing folk music with jazz (Maja Osojnik, Vasko Atanasovski), rock (Orlek, also Katarina Juvančič and Dejan Lapanja), rap (Boštjan Gorenc – Pižama with the group Tolovaj Mataj), chanson (Same babe), electronic music (Arsov), bossa nova (Bossa de Novo), tango (Vesna Zornik), Balkan music (Carmina Slovenica), Arabian music (Essaouira Project), Indian music (Igor Bezget) or Touareg music (Chris Eckman – Dirtmusic)." [1]

The list could easily be extended. And while Slovenian artists make an impression on the world music scene, Slovenia has been claiming its own slice of that scene, with a couple of big world music festivals (Okarina, Etnika).

Back in 1999, The Rough Guide to World Music reported that the Avsenik style of folk music had "swept aside other, older styles of music, although there are some remnants..." [2] There are many signs though that things have shifted since then. There is a creative space that's been unlocked by these world music festivals, and opening up to other cultures and other possibilities. This gives artists more confidence to explore unfashionable genres, and as far as traditional folk music is concerned, artists now have access to much improved resources, such as the Celinka record label, and Sigic, the Slovene music information centre, which has also participated in a number of projects.

Singer Jani Kutin and accordion player Renata Lapanja, collectively known as Duo Bakalina, are from the provincial Alpine town of Tolmin and sing in a heavy local dialect. It's very lyric-driven music, difficult for English-language speakers to appreciate, but reports tell of songs rooted in rural life, which although self-written have something of the traditional about them, and which are beguiling in their straightforwardness, their sincerity and their humour. Their own background lends them a certain authenticity, as does the humour and the wisdom with which Jani introduces the songs. Since 2009 the duo have released four albums.

When Sukar were starting out in the early 1990s there were no other bands playing Roma music, so what inspired them? There was no agenda, says Igor Misdaris, what brought them together was "the result of some strange coincidences which have happened to us throughout our career". [3] The band members had diverse backgrounds, they'd come by different routes to tamburica music and somehow they worked their way around to playing gypsy music where they found a common bond.

There's a tradition of tamburica bands in the Balkans which goes back a long way. Sukar can adapt depending on the occasion from performing as a traditional quintet to a 12-piece band. They're musical adventurers with a particular interest in exploring all things Romany. They do this in a very serious way, not just performing dances which may have originated anywhere from Russia to Hungary or Italy, but which are also sung in the different languages and dialects of the various Eastern and Central European Romany peoples. **KEME MERAV** starts out as a nostalgic-sounding waltz, but as the vocals kick in, first the male voice then the female, the gentle melody becomes more and more emotionally charged – it sounds simple, but it's remarkably effective.

The song was released in the mid-90s on an album called Amaro Dive (Our Day). Sukar had recently established themselves on the national scene, appearing at the Okarina Festival in 1994 where, along with the Hungarian group Ando drom, they produced the programme of the gypsy evening. Over the following few years they would be much in demand as a festival band. They were playing music they loved, there was no other agenda, yet this was also the culture of Slovenia's most vilified minority. In the 21st century the Roma population has continued to be the target of hatred and violence. But there is also hope. In 2009, the first Roma Culture Month was organised in the cities of Ljubljana and Maribor: over 50 events, including round tables, talks, exhibitions and lots of music, with Sukar and another leading Slovenian group, Kontrabant, performing along with Roma bands from across Europe.

Ljubljana's Institute of Ethnomusicology (GNI) has surprisingly been going since 1934, though at that time it was run by "a single man with almost no equipment". [4] Since independence it has grown in status and seems to have found a renewed sense of purpose. They now have a digital sound archive that houses their vast collection of song recordings, and they've stepped up production of books, CDs, radio programmes, etc. The list of publications on their website includes many CDs which can be purchased there (but nowhere else), and which sound very interesting from the descriptions given, though in the absence of any sound clips I've not taken a chance on any of them.

Celinka Records was founded in 2006 by accordionist Janez Dovč (formerly of Terrafolk, latterly of Jararaja), who for the last decade has also been its artistic director. In this time Celinka has released over 100 albums – folk, rock, jazz, and no shortage of genre-bending fusion and world music, and its catalogue reads like a who's who of what's exciting in Slovenian music today.

Celinka's most important initiative is called Sounds of Slovenia. Sounds of Slovenia is a collective of top musicians and vocalists who interpret folk songs from the Celinka back catalogue under Dovč's direction. It is also a series of albums of traditional Slovenian music which reveal a much greater diversity than many may have expected. It's also a double CD of songs released in 2011 compiled from all parts of the country in a variety of dialects, Sozvocja Slovenije (Sounds of Slovenia). The album comes with a 70-page booklet. The 63 songs on it were selected from over 300 that were recorded in different locations over a three-month period. The recordings are clean, they're good quality, but there's no attempt to add extra elements: Dovč wants us to hear the echo of how the songs would have sounded long ago.

Of special note are the many examples on the album of rural multipart singing which, despite at least one notable absentee (the female harmony group Katice who've represented Slovenian music many times on the European stage), show that older styles of music still have plenty of life left in them. The group I've chosen to focus on are four young women from southern Slovenia who call themselves Bistrške škuorke. The minute that they come on stage it's clear that this is a folk group with a very different attitude to that of the Avsenik brothers: instead of colourful design-heavy show costumes, they're garbed in simple monochrome dresses such as working women may actually have worn in the late 19th century. The quartet include an athlete, professor, economist and lawyer. They've been singing together since 1994, and they've formed their own cultural association for research, collection, preservation and singing of folk songs from the region where they live.

RASTI MI, RASTI, TRAVCA ZELENA is an old folk song about heartache. The women sing in the style they've learned from the elderly singers they've met in the course of their research, and their voices are strong and clear.

Finally, I must mention one more compilation album also released in 2011, this one by the Sigic organisation, Etno: Music Routes – Highways and Byways. The accompanying booklet describes it as "an excellent supplement to the material presented on Sozvocja Slovenije. Here, traditional music is not the goal, nor is it an artefact that the musicians are supposed to preserve in its purist form; instead, traditional music provides a point of departure for creative development..." [5] The two CDs include songs from an impressive range of artists, including Terrafolk, Marko banda, Katalena, Katice, Sukar, Kontrabant, Vruja, Brencl Banda, Duo Bakalina, Jararaja and Same babe.

NOTES

1. Katarina Juvančič – Between Local Music and the Music of the World – the Folk, Ethno and World Sounds of Slovenia http://www.sigic.si/upload/custom/articles/files/Knjizica%20Etno%20spread%20za%20net.pdf
2. Simon Broughton, Mark Ellingham and Richard Trillo (eds) – Rough Guide to World Music Volume One: Africa, Europe & The Middle East (Rough Guides, 1999), p278
3. https://www.rtvslo.si/zabava/glasba/sukar-vodi-nas-resnicna-ljubezen-do-romske-glasbe/240559
4. http://www.dismarc.org/info/gni.html
5. http://www.sigic.si/upload/custom/articles/files/Knjizica%20Etno%20spread%20za%20net.pdf

SPAIN

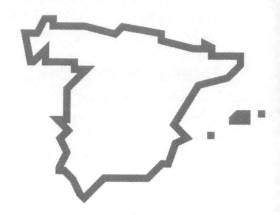

Having flamenco music at the heart of this chapter may seem to some like the easiest of decisions to make, but to me it wasn't so obvious. Sure, flamenco had to be in there, but I was aware that there was quite a bit of competition. Since Franco's death in 1975, there's been a huge growth of interest in all kinds of regional music. And there are so many kinds to talk about! Look at all the musical instruments that are strongly associated with particular regions – the gaita (bagpipe), popular in the northwest, in Asturias and the four provinces of Galicia; the txistu, the Basque flute; the Catalan gralla. Castanets are a vital part of jota dance and music which, although it has regional roots, is now widely performed up and down the country. The use of such diverse instruments, and the labours of musicologists in uncovering a rich heritage of vocal music, together with the many old dances that have survived, all helped to ensure that folk music followed different lines of development in each region.

So, following a vaguely formed plan, I started out exploring what some of these regions had to offer. I was listening to a lot of music, I was learning plenty, but I felt a growing sense of frustration. I wanted Spanish music to inspire me more than this. And then, very late one evening, I came across a singer whose

SOLEARES	*Agujetas*
BULERIAS DE LA PERLA	*Camaron De La Isla*
QUE LLEGUE EL DOMINGO	*Estrella Morente*
TXORIA TXORI	*Mikel Laboa*
NO RECONCO	*Banda De Gaitas Ledicia*
ROMANC DE LA PORQUEROLA	*Mara Aranda & Solatge*

songs made my hair stand on end and transformed the whole way that I thought about Spanish music. His name was Manuel Agujetas.

On **SOLEARES** there are no trappings, no big production. Just one voice and one guitar. And it has all the intimacy of a private conversation. The singer isn't trying to impress you, to show off his vocal range: it's all about expression of emotion. And everything about it feels as authentic as if you were learning his innermost secrets. Of course it takes a great deal of skill to achieve this kind of effect. The arrangement is carefully calibrated, the darts and sallies of guitar work put you on edge, building up the tension in the song. Nowadays we hear the Spanish guitar sound in so many places, but it's in flamenco music that it really comes into its own, that the virtuosity of the guitar players receives its reward. The greater the skill of the singer, the greater the reward. As with any flamenco, there is much mental and vocal discipline required, but there are also qualities in the singing that can't be taught, qualities that only the truly gifted can find.

We may hear much the same emotion being expressed in many other flamenco songs. It's a cry of pain deep from the soul, the anger of a person wronged. The Spanish have a word for communion of art with the human condition: Duende. For those who've experienced Duende it's a very intense, almost spiritual moment. Among connoisseurs of flamenco music, Duende is highly prized: for them, flamenco is far more than just a skill to be mastered; the true genius is one like Agujetas who lives and breathes the music.

> *"Those who haven't suffered can't sing flamenco. One must suffer, and often go hungry, and have lice. If you've been well brought up, in good circumstances, then you can't sing worth a damn. Understand? You must have a cause, a reason, within yourself."* [1]
> *"A person that knows how to read and write can't sing flamenco because his pronunciation isn't right."* [2]

There's more than a bit of myth-making going on here in these quotes from Agujetas, but I can't resist sharing them. Part of me must be buying into the myth, because to me his origins do matter. It matters that he was born a gypsy (gitano), partly because he understands what it means to be despised and oppressed, but also because in his country he is one of the last carriers of oral tradition. His grandfather and his parents were all accomplished flamenco singers. His musical education wasn't acquired in music school, but in the family blacksmith's forge where he worked as a child. It stood him in good stead: still a youth, he left home and started singing in the nightclubs of Madrid, where his talent quickly shone out.

A few years later, in the 1970s, following his first major label release, he established himself as an important figure on the international scene. Many were fascinated by this gypsy singer who sang flamenco that was darker than anything they were used to, and evocative of an earlier age. Agujetas had no intention though of becoming some kind of celebrity. He gave few interviews, and those he did revealed a character that was difficult, truculent, straight-talking and playfully provocative. He wasn't going to soften his image for anyone. Passionate about the integrity of his music, he was often quite rude about his fellow artists. Was he happy, in his later days, to see flamenco becoming more popular than ever around the world, to see younger singers coming through and taking up the art? Not a bit of it. He was dismissive of almost all modern singers, declaring, "All this modern stuff is a bad copy of flamenco." [3] Real flamenco for him was singers steeped in gitano tradition like the great Antonio Mairena (1909–83), or his protégé, Juan Talega (1891–1971), a cattle trader who only started singing professionally when he was in his late 60s.

Despite his iconic status, Agujetas never achieved the level of fame and adulation enjoyed by three of his contemporaries, all giants of Spanish music: Enrique Morente (1942–2010), Paco de Lucia (1947–2014) and Camarón (1950–92). Of this trio, both older men were in awe of the talent of the young Camarón.

Camarón was of gypsy blood, and just like Agujetas his father was a blacksmith. At the age of seven his father died and he gave up his schooling in order to work. Meanwhile, even as a child, he sang so well that everyone said he was born to sing. After reaching 12 he turned professional and got the chance to sing for Antonio Mairena, who was mightily impressed. The life-changing moment, though, was to be his first encounter with Paco. Here's how Paco remembered it: "We were at a fiesta, all night long and the next morning and until four or five in the afternoon. That day I knew that Camarón was the best artist ever born into flamenco." [4] At that point Camarón was just 16 years old. The two boys soon became inseparable, closer than brothers. They drank together, they rehearsed together, they exchanged thoughts about their future. And over the next decade they would record 11 albums together.

In the late 1970s, a change of direction: Camarón teamed

up with a new young guitarist, Tomatito, and a new producer, and made an experimental album, flirting with jazz and rock, La Leyenda del Tiempo. Purists were horrified, they couldn't believe that Camarón could make such a record, and it was a commercial flop; but the album would become an important reference point to artists interested in taking flamenco in new directions. Was this a purely artistic decision, or were there also some personal difficulties between Camarón and Paco at the time? If that was the case then any problems were soon mended, as before many years had passed they were recording together again.

On Calle Real (1983) both Tomatito and Paco lend their guitars. I remember that time well: Michael Jackson's Thriller and Prince's Purple Rain were taking the music world by storm, selling in their millions, hauling in Grammies and receiving acclaim from all quarters. I don't remember hearing any songs by Camarón at the time. Now I feel I've been sold a lie: Camarón's album has far more to offer. The music is rich in hot, steamy rhythms, but it also soars majestically thanks to Camarón's impassioned vocals. The rhythm on **BULERIAS DE LA PERLA** is fast and fiery, while the vocals are like a dark howl coming out of a bottomless pit: again and again the singer pleads his case, with such heartrending emotion that you can't wrench yourself away.

What inner demons was he trying to escape? By the 1980s he was taking a lot of heroin, having moved on from cocaine. He managed to come off the heroin, but continued smoking several packs of cigarettes a day for the rest of his life – he died of lung cancer at the age of 41. On his death there were many scenes of collective grief. To some in the gypsy community the tragic life of their greatest singer played to a deep-rooted sense of injustice. Rumours spread that the illiterate Camarón had been cheated by Paco from monies that he'd earned throughout his career. It was nonsense: Camarón's record sales had consistently been disappointing, that was why he'd earned less money. For Paco, consumed by grief at his friend's death, the allegation felt like a flesh wound. Though not a gitano himself, he'd always had a strong rapport with gypsies. "The truth is there for those who want to discover it," he fired back, "because I've never taken anything from him. I gave all my ability, my inspiration and my love. Camarón was one of those three immovable objects in my life." [5]

The notion that flamenco can be conquered through diligent study alone runs against the gitano myth that it's in the blood and in the soul. Yet that was precisely the route that Enrique Morente took to greatness. The home where he grew up was a house without any real musical tradition. To find inspiration he had to visit the tavernas in his Granada neighbourhood. Pepe de la Matrona, a veteran from the golden age of flamenco, became his teacher after he moved to Madrid. Tellingly though, according to Enrique's own website, what initially impressed the master wasn't so much Enrique's natural talent as "his attitude towards things, his respect and his learning capacity". [6]

Enrique married a gypsy dancer from Madrid, Aurora Carbonell. Her parents thought they were both too young to marry:

> "So we escaped to Granada. We spent the first night on a stone bench, next to the Alhambra. He fell asleep with his head on my lap and I watched the sun rise… Then, as he was a very honest man, we returned to Madrid, we got permission from my parents and we were married by the Church." [7]

So it was that their daughter, Estrella (born 1980), unlike her father, grew up surrounded by music and dance. Her father was then at the height of his fame, but there were also many flamenco singers, musicians and dancers on her mother's side. Enrique was no traditionalist, though, and she never felt constricted by tradition: "My household is a flamenco household, but it's an open household and any genre of music that enriches me is part of life. Jazz, blues, Caribbean and Cuban son, rancheras, Colombian song, Portuguese fado and classical music have been great sources of inspiration." [8]

Like her father, she married young and in romantic fashion. The groom was a matador, and the wedding at La Basílica Nuestra Señora in Granada was a big society occasion, complete with coach and horses.

She already knew then that singing was her vocation. On her debut album, Mi Cante y un Poema (2001), she enlisted the help of several cousins and uncles, but the real guiding light was her father who produced the album and composed or adapted much of the music. **QUE LLEGUE EL DOMINGO** is another buleria full of drama, pained emotion and an invitation to dance. The music on this album is more traditional than on later albums where we see more originality, more borrowing from other genres; which is largely why I chose to feature it. All her work though is rooted in and respectful toward classic flamenco. The album Autorretrato (2012) was released some time after her father died, but he had been very much involved in the album's conception, and until a few days before his death had been busy producing some of the songs. "Autorretrato makes me fall in love with the ancient cantes, with the history of the purest flamenco all over again, in order to set it free," Estrella tells us. [9]

The ancient Basque language, Euskara, is one of the most unique in the world. Of the three million people who live in the Basque country, 700,000 speak Euskara. Apart from the language, I'm not sure how much of the pre-Roman culture survives, but modern-day Basques can lay claim to a distinctive cuisine, a wide array of Basque folk dances and, last but not least, Basque musical instruments. The txistu (three-holed flute) could be played with one hand, leaving the other hand free to play a percussion instrument, so traditional txistu music will always be accompanied by drums. There is a txistulari association that's been going since 1928: the Euskal Herriko Txistularien Elkartea. Disappointingly, though, virtually the only modern recordings of the txistu that I could find were in orchestral settings: there are (from the evidence of YouTube clips) folklore groups who play the instrument, but no one seems to be trying to revive it. The trikiti is a Basque diatonic accordion, traditionally part of a duo with a pandero, a frame drum similar to a tambourine. In recent years trikitixa music has been modernised and given a new lease of life by the Bilbao-born musician Kepa Junkera.

To a large extent then, it's singing in Euskara that's the hallmark of Basque music. For years the Basque language was suppressed under Franco, and singers such as Mikel Laboa were central to a cultural revival that took off in the 1960s and which quickly led to publications in Basque, Basque radio stations and Basque language schools. Inspired by the Catalan singing group Els Setze Jutges, Mikel approached other Basque singers and invited them to join his project. They needed new material, so he wrote songs. One of these was to become the most famous anthem of Basque nationalism: **TXORIA TXORI**.

What I wasn't prepared for was to find that Txoria Txori is such a good song. It's a 1960s-style folk song, it's got lovely guitar arrangements, and the lyrics with their simple metaphor of the bird's desire for freedom, while they can be taken as a commentary on the political situation in Francoist Spain, have a timeless quality. The words are those of Joxean Artze:

"So the story goes, the words came to Artze during dinner one night in a Donostia restaurant and he hurriedly wrote them down on a napkin in the form of a poem... Marisol Bastida, Laboa's wife, noticed Artze doing this, read the poem, liked it, and told her husband he should read it too. He liked it as well, took the napkin home with him that night, and composed the music there and then." [10]

It was around the same time that the Catalan singer Lluis Llach composed his famous Catalan freedom song, L'Estaca. Llach was a leading light of Nova Cançó, an artistic movement that aimed to normalise the Catalan language in popular music. But in the 1970s, as democracy was being restored to Catalonia and steps taken toward recognising Catalan as an official language in the region, Nova Cançó was petering out. The reasons of course may not have been entirely local ones: the folk music revival was by this time in rapid retreat in many countries. Nonetheless, the gradual death of Nova Cançó represented a real defeat which showed the limits of democratisation. Writing in 2014, Núria Borrull reports that Catalan language singers of all genres find it difficult to get airtime on mainstream media. She cites a couple of telling examples. On one occasion, interviewed on Spanish TV, Llach is asked why he doesn't sing in Spanish as well as Catalan – a question that one can hardly imagine being put to someone of any other nationality. He's forced to explain his stance about normalising use of the Catalan language. Another Llach TV appearance a few years earlier prompted a viewer to write to the national newspaper El Pais, accusing Llach of intolerance because of his refusal, in a multicultural society, to sing in Spanish! [11]

Much has been written about Galicia's supposed Celtic heritage. As I soon found, trying to disentangle fact from myth is no easy task. I quickly discounted the notion that Galician is a Celtic language: it's actually related to Portuguese. The belief that Galicia has a Celtic culture is not a new one: it was promoted by nationalist Galician writers in the 19th century. In pre-Roman times the Gallaeci people who lived in the region had what can certainly be described as a Celtic religion and a Celtic culture. Since then many peoples have set up home in what is now Spain's northwestern corner. Is there any evidence that communities of Celtic origin passed on traditional beliefs and cultural practices for over 1,000 years? I'm sceptical. I'd want to see historical records showing that such communities existed, and that they practised religious rituals, traditional dances or singing methods that survived to recent times.

The greatest symbol of Galician culture, and of its Celtic heritage, is the gaita (bagpipe). But here too there's a problem: the origins of the gaita are unknown, or at least disputed. Gaita player Susana Seivane's website has this to say: "According to the experts, it is likely that the gaita, as a cultural element with a possible Celtic origin, was introduced in Galicia long before the Christian age. However, it was, the truth is that the gaita is as remote as our own history." [12] The word gaita, though, is of Germanic origin, and other experts suggest that the instrument may have been introduced at a later date by the Germanic Suebi people – so it may not be quite as Celtic as some people think.

The reason for selecting **NO RECONCO** here was very simple: I wanted you to hear the gaita in its full glory, and this is a lively, rousing piece. The Ledicia bagpipe band is from Pontevedra province and at the time this album was recorded comprised 30 members and 15 students. Why the students, you ask. The band's director, Hipólito Cabezas, has also for many years run a bagpipe school. During my research I found a newspaper article from 2015 which says that in this time of austerity provincial government funding, which had enabled Cabezas to train 700 students in centres in five local towns, had been withdrawn. Cabezas was desperately looking for a temporary solution that would at least buy him some time. [14]

At the very least, Galician music is deeply influenced by Celtic music and dance. British and Irish sailors who crossed the Bay of Biscay must have contributed to this over time, exchanging tunes with the gaita players they met. And recently this influence has been strengthened by the setting-up of Celtic music gatherings, cultural organisations, and so forth. The musician Carlos Núñez was invited at the age of 12 to perform at the Inter-Celtic Festival of Lorient in Brittany. From that moment, he says, he's felt a "feeling of brotherhood" with other Celtic nations. [13] He will argue with anyone who cares to listen that Galicia itself is a Celtic nation, but it's interesting that the root of this belief was his experience of the music, discovering for himself how much Galician folk music and Celtic music had in common.

For a couple of years Núñez was part of a group called Matto Congrio playing instrumental music. After the band split up in 1995, two new groups emerged: Berrogüetto and Carlos Núñez's band. Both groups were to become very popular, spearheading a volley of interest in Galician Celtic music. This interest didn't come from nowhere: the ground had been set already by work that had been going on since the 1970s. Even before Núñez began going to festivals, Fuxan os Ventos in the 1970s and Milladoiro from the early 1980s had blazed the way for the new Galician music. Schools of traditional music had been founded: one of these was the Escola de Gaitas de Ortigueira directed by Antón Corral. Corral was also to play a central role in establishing Ortigueira's Festival of the Celtic World, Galicia's most important folk festival, which has been running annually since 1978.

When I listen to these bands and the many who've followed them, I see a lot of diversity, a lot of creativity. What in general I don't see is any sense of continuity with a musical legacy that communities have kept alive over the centuries. There are often elements from the past: old musical instruments revived, old tunes and songs; these, however, are combined with other influences in a spirit of exploration. Each group does its own thing, has its own preferred instruments. It's not that the Celtic heritage doesn't exist, rather it exists as an invented tradition, a reimagining of what it means to be Galician.

It seems that just as Camarón's musical explorations gave 'permission' to other flamenco artists to follow their own path, to be more creative, so too has the unconventional approach of many of the groups involved in the folk revival helped to foster a diversity of style and approach. Spanish folk music is continually looking outwards, being open to other influences, and at its best marrying these influences to create something richer than what's gone before.

Valencia-born Mara Aranda's musical output is a perfect example of this. Along with Efrén López, she was a leading member of one of Spain's most interesting roots bands, L'Ham de Foc. Mara and Efrén travelled widely, collecting traditional instruments from Spain, Greece, Turkey and elsewhere – Mara even played a didgeridoo – and composed songs inspired by these instruments and traditional melodies. In the last decade, Mara's taken on quite a number of musical projects. Interviewed in 2014, she explained the thinking behind it all: Mara Aranda & Solatge focus on Mediterranean music; Mara Aranda Sephardic Legacy on the music of North Africa, Turkey and the Balkans; Al Andaluz Project on Sephardic music; and so on. [15] I've not covered everything, but you get the picture. She's hugely knowledgeable, and all her research and study of traditional cultures informs her music.

The first two minutes of ROMANC DE LA PORQUEROLA play out like a medieval chant. The vocals are haunting and captivating, the drone sound adding atmosphere. The song then goes into a completely new phase, lighter and more contemporary, before going into a slow finale. It's from the album Deria, an album of old traditional songs from her part of Spain, including dances, ballads, work songs and cant d'Estil, an old Valencian singing tradition. Mara of course rearranges the songs, putting her stamp, her interpretation on them. It's an intriguing concept: she's immersed herself in the cultures of other Mediterranean countries, and so when she returns to Spanish music, as no doubt she will again, she has something unique to add.

NOTES

1. 1998 Radio Interview, translated by Brook Zern, retrieved April, 2016 http://www.flamencoexperience.com/blog/?p=455
2. http://www.chicagoreader.com/chicago/agujetas-cantaor/ Film?oid=1053731
3. https://www.nytimes.com/2012/05/24/arts/music/manuel-agujetas-at-elebash-recital-hall.html
4. https://elpais.com/elpais/2014/02/26/eps/1393427808_114926.html
5. http://elpais.com/diario/1992/09/17/cultura/716680801_850215.html
6. http://www.enriquemorente.com/ingles/morente.htm
7. http://cultura.elpais.com/cultura/2013/12/23/ actualidad/1387828686_640713.html
8. http://www.sfgate.com/music/article/Estrella-Morente-s-flamenco-singing-inspired-by-5312007.php
9. Ibid.
10. https://basquebooks.blogs.unr.edu/whats-in-a-song-txoria-txori/
11. Núria Borrull – The Catalan Nova Cançó: Resistance and identity through song, in Barbara Geraghty, Jean Conacher (eds) – Intercultural Contact, Language Learning and Migration (Bloomsbury, 2014), pp 202–3
12. http://www.seivane.es/en/documentacion/index2.html
13. http://www.carlos-nunez.com/carlos/
14. http://www.lavozdegalicia.es/noticia/vigo/vigo/2015/09/22/270-alumnos-quedan-vigo-escola-gaitas-diputacion/0003_201509V22C6991.htm
15. http://www.b-ritmos.com/hablamos-con/mara-aranda-i-solatge-lo-testament

SWEDEN

The nyckelharpa is an elegant-looking instrument, about the size of a violin, but leaner shaped. Like a hurdy-gurdy, the instrument has keys, but instead of being played with a wheel, it is played with a bow. So, a nyckelharpa is a 'keyed fiddle'. The modern chromatic nyckelharpa has four strings that can be bowed and a dozen metallic 'sympathetic strings' which resonate as the other strings are played, creating a very special sound.

At the start of the 20th century the nyckelharpa was an obscure folk instrument, associated almost exclusively with the Uppsala region just north of Stockholm, where it was being kept alive by dwindling numbers of musicians. August Bohlin (1877–1949) grew up among nyckelharpa players, but his instrument of choice was the violin. As an instrument maker, though, he made both instruments, and in his 40s he took up playing nyckelharpa and entering competitions. At one of these he noticed that because of its limited range of keys the nyckelharpa couldn't play all of the tunes. So he designed and built, in 1929, the world's first chromatic nyckelharpa.

This was still a small beginning, but it paved the way for the man whose unstinting efforts were to transform the fortunes of the nyckelharpa and of Swedish folk music generally. Eric

GAMMAL LJUNGKVISTERVALS EFTER GÅS ANDERS

Sonia Sahlström & Håkan Larsson

S:T GÖRAN OCH DRAKEN

Lena Willemark, Ale Möller

LIMU LIMU LIMA/LILLE LASSE

Kraja

LILLADE ANNA

Triakel

PÅ VÅG

Ralsgård & Tullberg

Sahlström (1912–86) was born to another family of musicians in a tiny Uppsala village called Tobo. An instrument maker and musician, he too became interested in designing chromatic nyckelharpas, and there are very few things that a nyckelharpa player will treasure more today than an instrument made by the hands of Eric Sahlström. Sahlström performed many old tunes, but also composed new ones that fitted within the tradition. He was a great ambassador for the instrument, often appearing on TV. Besides working as a farmer he also found time to teach music, and demand for his services grew steadily – Andrew Cronshaw mentions that he "received a state artist's salary from 1977". [1]

How times have changed. Today the nyckelharpa is seen as an icon of Swedish culture and is more popular than ever, with players numbering in their thousands. And while there are many traditionalists, there are also many players experimenting with the instrument, testing its possibilities, incorporating it into the sound of different bands. A sign of the times, perhaps: Benny Andersson, formerly of the group ABBA, took delivery of his first nyckelharpa at Christmas 2009. A few years later, his teacher confided that progress hadn't met expectations – "at his age it is very difficult to learn the technique." [2]

The Eric Sahlström Institute, founded in 1998, claims to be Sweden's first national folk music centre. It's situated not in Stockholm, but in the Sahlström home village, Tobo. Among its highly qualified music teachers is Eric's daughter, Sonia Sahlström. Her only release to date is the somewhat underappreciated album Glädjen in which her husband, Håkan Larsson, plays harmonica and other instruments. Her own instrument is an old-style nyckelharpa called a silverbasharpa. It's an enjoyable collection of traditional Uppsala tunes. Many are described as 'efter Eric Sahlström', 'efter August Bohlin', etc. This means that the tune comes from the playing of the artist in question, not that they composed it. Back in the day there were few people who could read music, and what you were first taught would be someone's interpretation of a song. I have to admit, my first thought was to pick out a tune in which Sonia paid tribute to her father, but that all changed when I heard GAMMAL LJUNGKVISTERVALS EFTER GÅS ANDERS. The song's so fresh, so joyful, so full of life. But who was Gås-Anders? It turns out that he was a zesty nyckelharpa player from Uppsala born 200 years ago, who, when he played, was always in motion, dancing and jumping over chairs and benches.

Until the latter part of the 20th century a lot of Swedish folk music was rooted in localities. A spelmän (folk musician) would generally play in a local style and include a number of tunes from his home region in his repertoire. Now much has changed. For one thing, as we shall see, a great many folk musicians are now women. But also for the most part they've studied music in schools and they no longer feel hidebound by a particular set of traditions.

Ale Möller was one of those who made a career out of challenging conventional thinking and ways of doing things. Having spent a few years in Greece where he learned to play the bouzouki he came back to Sweden wanting to deepen his own knowledge of what Swedish music was and where it had come from.

> "Möller moved to Darlana, a region particularly strong in the fiddling traditions of Sweden. He started what was to be a ten-year journey, studying the music, learning not only the tunes, but the people behind the tunes, and fighting all along the way against one small prejudice. 'I was told I had to play the fiddle, the instrument of that tradition. But I refused. I knew from all the other kinds of music I played that the instrument is just a voice. The music, the style, is the language. I tried to translate it into my instrument, the bouzouki. I found that it could be done.'" [3]

He was moving in two directions at the same time: on the one hand, familiarising himself with tradition and learning old tunes; and on the other, pushing against the boundaries. He takes delight in working with musicians whose background and ideas differ from his own. Though best known for his work with the bands Filarfolket and Frifot, he's appeared on at least 60 albums, including many collaborations with other artists. From Filarfolket onwards he was known for his use of a wide array of instruments, but there was always method to it. He would adapt his bouzoukis and mandolins, changing the positions of the frets so that the sound they made was more compatible with fiddle-based Swedish folk music. It all seemed to work, because he was creating a product that people liked, and because other artists were soon asking the same kinds of questions: Why do Swedish songs have to be played only with certain instruments? What can modern studio techniques and access to big festival stages add to Swedish folk tradition?

Lena Willemark and Ale Möller were kindred spirits: musicians grounded in Swedish folk tradition but with a love of other genres and a yen for musical exploration. Willemark has the unusual distinction of coming from a small village which boasts its own language. Älvdalen in Dalarna County is just about the only place in the world where Elfdalian is widely spoken. Though not recognised as a language by the Swedish government, its backers will quote linguists who are fascinated by this old tongue that goes back to the time of the Vikings and contains several features unknown in modern Nordic languages.

Willemark and Möller were both part of Frifot when they took leave from the group to record a joint album, Nordan. The sleeve notes describe this as, "music based on medieval ballads and folk songs, performed by musicians from the living Swedish tradition and from the world of improvisation." S:T GÖRAN OCH DRAKEN translates as 'St George and the Dragon' and it's one of the oldest known Swedish ballads. I've no doubt that the musical arrangement has been entirely reimagined, but it feels right: the slow-paced atmospheric music allows Willemark to command attention as she sings.

In the wake of the folk revival, folk singing is now flourishing in Sweden again. But instead of learning the words to long ballads, Swedish folk singers today are training their voices and looking to use their voice almost as a musical instrument. The singing itself is an art form, encompassing a range of techniques and styles. The fact that so many folk singers have the knowledge and ability to switch between singing techniques helps to give Swedish vocal music a real vitality: there's a lot of ideas, a lot of creativity; you get a sense of a music which, while it has solid historical roots, can take you to some new undiscovered places.

Sweden's lively folk music scene gives these new ideas many opportunities to take root. Lisa Lestander (Kraja) tells me that she's an admirer of Lena Willemark; she also remembers clearly what first inspired her to take up folk singing:

> *"My sister (who also sings in Kraja) visited the Folkmusik festival in our hometown, Umeå. This was around year*

2000. She brought home a CD with the group Rosenbergs 7
with folk songs from Sweden in four parts, and we both fell
completely in love with the songs and the harmonies and
wanted to sing this kind of music ourselves." [4]

Rosenbergs 7, also known as Rosenbergs Sjua, or just R7, were
four female vocalists and three string players. The genius behind
the ensemble was Susanne Rosenberg, now head of the folk music
department and professor of folk singing at the Royal College of
Music in Stockholm. "The style of arranging for vocals in this
way," she says, "was then never tried in Swedish tradition and is
more related to the bulgaric voice settings but also to old vocal
singing style and the polyphony of old choral singing and some
archaic old Scandinavian style." [5]

Both Willemark and Rosenberg have collaborated with the
classical composer Karin Rehnqvist. Rehnqvist has a particular
interest in kulning, the traditional high-pitched herding call used
by women to gather herds of goats or cows. I can only suppose that
those farm girls spent many lonely hours training their voices,
because kulning, as it's performed today, is a highly technical
skill requiring great vocal flexibility. Kulning is taught today in
music schools and workshops, but the fact that there is so much
genuine interest in it is because people have heard the wonderful
sound that trained singers can produce, and because Willemark
and Rosenberg have shown that the sound can be adapted to fit
modern compositions.

LIMU LIMU LIMA/LILLE LASSE is actually two songs. Here's how Lisa
Lestander describes it:

"Limu limu lima is a traditional herding song and also a
prayer for the sun to shine over the little herding children
who walk the great forests during the summer, watching
over the cows. This could be a very lonely job and the
children started working at an early age. Lille Lasse is a

*lullaby about a little boy... He is sad because he has lost his
boat and all the fish in it but in the end he finds it and it is
full of fish."*

Kraja are an a cappella group, just the four female vocalists.
Their harmonies are graceful and easeful. This was from their
second album in 2008: since then, they've been writing most of
their own material. Lisa, though, released a solo album in 2014
called Sånger från norr, which was a collection of old songs
from Sweden's northernmost provinces, which she'd found while
digging through music archives.

In the late 1990s two of the singers from R7, Sofia Sandén
and Ulrika Bodén, formed the group Ranarim, in which they're
accompanied by two men on guitar and nyckelharpa. The four
of them met up while studying folk music at Stockholm's Royal
Academy of Music. Ulrika Bodén, who grew up on a goat farm,
didn't develop a serious interest in folk singing until she was in her
late teens. Some purists, she says, don't like the idea of studying
folk music at an academy – "they think folk music has to be as it
always has been, passed on just like a tradition." [6] It's that debate
again about 'authenticity' – the music is changing, but does that
mean that it can't be natural and authentic? Ulrika welcomes the
new academy courses: they "give a new status to the music".

Ulrika specialises in songs from her home region of
Ångermanland in northern Sweden. In 2016, she released an
album, Te berga blå, which she says is "a tribute to the herding
music and its tradition bearers".

The vocal trio Irmelin were formed in a very similar way,
by three women studying together at the Royal Academy of
Music. All three are adept kulning singers; all are experienced
teachers who give workshops, so we're told, "in folk singing,
kulning and diddling/mouth music". But there's nothing arcane
or overly technical about their music – it's all beautifully arranged
harmonies and polyphonies. North Sea Stories (2013) is a

collection of songs from Sweden, Norway, the Faroes, Shetland, Scotland and England.

Kongero are a female vocal quartet, and by now it should come as no surprise that all four studied at the Royal Academy of Music, though this wasn't how they first got together. Between them they have a range of experience and interests. Emma Björling has toured with Ranarim, and is also in the groups BaraVox and Lyy. Lovisa Liljeberg makes bluegrassy music with the Lily Mountain Band. As Kongero, though, their music has a lightness and playfulness which sets them apart from other groups – they call their style 'Folk'apella'.

Triakel (Emma Härdelin, vocals and violin, Kjell-Erik Eriksson, violin, and Janne Strömstedt, harmonium) are from Jamtland. Jamtland is as different from metropolitan Sweden as Scotland is from England. A thousand years ago Jamtland was a self-governing statelet with its own 'parliament', the Jamtamót, which assembled once a year to make important decisions and to decide legal matters. All were allowed to participate. In the 12th century Jamtland was conquered by Norway, and it remained part of the Norwegian kingdom for over 450 years. It's a rugged, sparsely populated upland area of lakes, rivers and forests. It's also home to some of the Sami people, the indigenous people of Scandinavia. On its coat of arms is a silver moose.

I love the title of Triakel's third album: Sånger från 63° N (Songs from the 63rd Latitude). It was a neat way of declaring the music's identity, and they have followed this up with two tributes to Jamtland musical figures – Ulrikas minne – visor från Frostviken (2011) and Thyra (2014). The first of these is dedicated to Ulrika Lindholm (1886–1977) who hailed from a particularly remote and beautiful spot delightfully named Frostviken. Checking out the tourism websites for the area, one of them recklessly informs us that, "no other area in the world contains the same amount of brown bears!" It seems that Ulrika knew a vast repertoire of old songs, and late in life she recorded some 300 of them for Swedish radio. Triakel spent many hours listening to this archive and making selections from it for them to sing on the CD.

Thyra is a collection of songs taken from recordings by Thyra Karlsson (1912–2001). Thyra was a great collector of folk songs, ballads, children's songs and popular tunes who used to accompany herself on the cittra (a type of zither). So presumably her rendition of **LILLADE ANNA** wouldn't have had the cheerful violin dance music of Triakel's version. I singled out this song for inclusion here because of its strong melody and hook line.

Thyra would have been deeply touched by the Triakel tribute, but what she had wanted above all else was to make a CD of her own. And in 2016, 15 years after her death, she got this too. Sångarporträtt is a collection of recordings compiled by Thyra's daughter, and what it shows is that Thyra was some singer. She attacks every song with gusto, her voice is strong and clear, and through each change of musical style she remains perfectly in control. The CD also contains a couple of Triakel's interpretations of songs from the album for good measure.

It's a return to instrumental music with my final track from Sweden. Flute playing was very popular in southern Sweden back in the 19th century, but the flute had not played a major part in Sweden's folk revival. So a couple of flautists, Andreas Ralsgård and Markus Tullberg, decided to see what they could do about this. In 2010 they released a CD of flute duets. A follow-up album, simply called '+1', came out in 2014. On this release the music was fleshed out by the addition of nyckelharpa, cello and harpsichord, but the flutes remain very much the stars of the show. **PÅ VÄG** means 'On the Road': it's certainly a tune full of movement, it's like the flutes are dancing around one another. It's also one more illustration that Swedish folk music today is a music that's full of possibilities.

NOTES

1. Simon Broughton, Mark Ellingham & Richard Trillo (eds), World Music: The Rough Guide Volume 1 (Rough Guides, 1999), p299
2. http://www.uppsalatidningen.se/helg/spelman-i-modern-morkare-tappning-3894639.aspx
3. http://www.rootsworld.com/rw/feature/moller2.html
4. Email 22/10/14
5. http://www.susannerosenberg.com/andmore/r7/r7.html, retrieved August, 2016
6. http://www.folkworld.eu/18/e/ranarim.html

SWITZERLAND

For many young people in cities like Zurich and Berne, Swiss folk culture is unappealing. It's conservative, rooted in an unfashionable past, resistant to change and creatively stifling. It's associated with dressing in 'traditional' costume, with yodelling about Alpine flowers, with instrumental folk dance music, and the alphorn. From a cynical viewpoint, the prominence of the alphorn seems to owe little to the capabilities of the instrument itself with its limited tonal range, and more with a desire to create a Swiss culture brand that is attractive to tourists.

It's a valid question: who is the music for? As we've seen, in many countries folk and traditional music is used as a vehicle by artists wishing to explore current social or political issues. Swiss folk music provides little scope to do this.

So what's the case for the defence?

There are many hundreds of clubs in Switzerland where people can learn and practise yodelling (or alphorn playing, or flag tossing – and yes, flag tossing is regarded as a skilled activity). The clubs belong to the Swiss yodelling association which claims over 21,000 members. Membership and levels of interest appear to be growing. In August 2013, on a Swiss mountainside, a new world record was set for the largest ever alphorn group performance –

ALPHORN-JODEL   Franz Stadelmann & Vreny Stadelmann

by 508 alphorn players dressed in traditional Swiss costume. The pictures of the alphorn world record went all round the world; they were fantastic publicity for Switzerland. But they are also evidence that there is a real living culture, albeit concentrated in the Alpine regions of the country; and one that is in robust health.

The traditions within Swiss folk culture are relatively new in historical terms. The Swiss National Costume Association was formed in 1926 and heritage enthusiasts effectively redesigned traditional costume, abandoning the rich variety of materials, shapes and colours in favour of a much more uniform design and a rigid set of rules. Folk music followed a similar trajectory. In the 19th century it was not uncommon for string instruments and brass instruments to be used. Alphorns on the other hand were rarely seen in the early years of the 20th century. In the decades from 1930 onwards, Swiss folk traditions were solidified in the forms familiar today. According to museum curator Thomas Antonetti, "folk music has always been lively, but the desire to defend a Swiss identity in the 1920s and 30s led to its development being frozen. Some associations wanted to define exactly what was authentic and what wasn't." [1] Accordion-led bands played ländlermusik (country dance music): simple melodies in 3/4 time including polkas and waltzes. And under the auspices of the yodelling association, yodelling and alphorn playing became integral to the sense of national identity. The dates are significant. The 1930s to the 1960s were the period of Geistige Landesverteidigung: a conservative political and cultural movement that aimed to strengthen national identity as a bulwark against Nazism, and to promote Swiss values and customs.

The argument then goes like this. The slowness of folk music to change or evolve in the decades after the Second World War can be largely attributed to the particular set of circumstances that existed at the time. However, in recent years folk music organisations have begun to change to fit the changing times, and the music itself is changing and becoming more diverse.

I take this on board, but I've yet to be convinced. Some rules may have been relaxed, but the yodelling association still dictates what alphorn players can wear to festivals and restricts what they can play. The great majority of folk groups play the same instruments and wear traditional dress when performing. There is no singing at all except in the yodel groups.

Although the alphorn will forever remain the symbol of Swiss music, I believe that yodelling is of much greater interest and importance. It has deep roots: in the past, mountain shepherds are said to have yodelled to their flocks. It requires great skill and technique to change the pitch of a note in a controlled way. And improvisation is often involved – which sits uneasily with the idea of a fixed tradition! There are two types of Swiss yodel: the natural yodel and the yodel song. The natural yodel has no words and is usually improvised. Yodel songs are songs which incorporate an element of yodelling. Franz Stadelmann's yodel is a natural yodel. And indeed it sounds natural and organic, and the harmony on **ALPHORN-JODEL** is exquisite. Stadelmann, who comes from a farming family, is today in his 70s, having yodelled for all his adult life. He's composed many tunes and yodels.

Another fact about Franz Stadelmann: he's essentially an

amateur musician, whose day jobs have included farming and driving instruction. He's not unusual in this. These folk groups and alphorn players are pretty much all amateur enthusiasts. If you imagined that the Swiss government is ploughing money into alphorn festivals and yodelling schools that's not the case. Government money goes to opera and jazz : music that is deemed to be 'High Art', whereas Swiss folk music is not held in the same esteem. "As far as academically sound research goes," claims musicologist Franz-Xaver Nager, "I am afraid to say that the field is a disgrace. Internationally, Switzerland comes dead last in this regard, which is odd considering that Swiss officialdom otherwise misses no opportunity to trot out our folk culture... For its part, the University of Zurich has evidently thrown in the towel, eliminating the only remaining study programme in Swiss-German ethnomusicology as of mid-2008." He sees funding and practical support as vital to creating a climate where musicians will develop the music and take it in new directions. "We've got the seedlings – it's time to start cultivating our garden." [2]

NOTES

1. http://www.swissinfo.ch/eng/culture/Yodelling_reinvents_itself_for_the_modern_day.html?cid=8836636
2. https://prohelvetia.ch/app/uploads/2017/03/passagen_e47.pdf

UKRAINE

Ukraine is a bilingual country. According to a 2012 opinion poll, 50% of respondents named Ukrainian as their native language, 29% said Russian and another 20% told the pollsters that they had two native languages. [1] And in their daily life people are just as likely to converse in Russian as they are in Ukrainian. Inside most of the big cities, including Kiev, the Russian language still dominates.

When Ukraine gained independence in 1991, Ukrainian became the only official state language, and the state tried to promote its use, but it ran into problems. Businesses and the media had little incentive to change. Twenty years later, over 60% of newspapers, 72% of TV programmes and 87% of books were in Russian, which was also the preferred language on 80% of Ukrainian websites. [2] Worse than this, a backlash was underway. Russian-speaking regions sought to have Russian recognised as a regional tongue, and this led to courtroom battles – an early warning of the real life battles which a few years later would bring bloodshed to the same city streets.

The vision of a unitary state with its own unique language in which the rights of ethnic minorities were protected had begun to founder. And part of the reason for the catastrophic events of

MITZVE TANTZ	The Kharkov Klezmer Band
THE SKY COVERED THE BRIGHT STARS (НЕБО ЯСНЕ ЗІРКИ ВКРИЛИ)	Buttya
ÖKÖRMEZŐI RUSZIN KOLOMEJKA	Técsői Banda
VASYL CRIES	Hudaki Village Band
PYIEMO, PYIEMO	Mariana Sadovska

2014 lay in a collective failure to resolve questions of national identity. Ukraine is a territory where people of different origin had lived side by side for centuries, and each ethnic group had its own unique history, and its own attitude to the national question and to its relationship with the national state. A more inclusive approach by the state, whether or not it could have prevented conflict entirely, may have brought better rewards.

The more I explore 'Ukrainian' traditional music, the more I'm drawn to the conclusion that Ukrainian culture is a mosaic of different cultural identities. As we shall see, these cultures are not exclusionary. Borrowing from the dances and songs of other regions and other groups has long been commonplace. The musicians who enhanced their repertoire in this way didn't burden themselves with questions about cultural identity: they just rejoiced in the richness of the region's music.

The Pale of Settlement was the term given to a vast region of the old Russian Empire, which included most of present-day Ukraine, in which Jews had rights of permanent residency. The Jewish folk musicians of the region, known as klezmorim, would perform at events such as weddings. They took on influences from all around them as they performed gypsy, Hungarian and Polish tunes, Russian dances and Middle Eastern rhythms. From this a very special type of music was born.

A memorable scene in the film Fiddler on the Roof is a Jewish wedding where for a brief time fears and personal differences are put aside in the joyful dancing to the tune of the fiddle. The dance is brought to an abrupt end by the arrival of policemen who start a pogrom, causing the hero, Tevye, to ask why God has allowed this to happen. The film is set in a Jewish shtetl (village) somewhere in the Pale at the turn of the 20th century, when pogroms would have been all too familiar. Pogroms and other forms of repression would account for the emigration of vast numbers of Jews from Eastern Europe at that time, with over two million going to the United States alone. But far from killing the music, the emigration ultimately gave it a new lease of life. Naftule Brandwein (1884–1963), Shloimke Beckerman (1883–1974) and Dave Tarras (1897–1989) were all born within the borders of present-day Ukraine, but it was as Americans that they became great musicians. The bands which they formed there and the music they recorded came to define what we now know as klezmer music.

In **MITZVE TANTZ** we start with the sound of the violin, then gradually other instruments (accordion, clarinet) are introduced as the music becomes faster. The violinist is bandleader Stanislav Raiko who formed the Kharkov Klezmer Band with a small group of musicians who'd all studied at the Tchaikovsky National Music Academy in Kiev. They are revivalists in the truest sense: they want to recapture the soul of early 20th-century klezmer music. Several of the tunes on the album Ticking, again are songs collected by Moisei Beregovsky, a folklorist who made hundreds of field recordings of Ukrainian Jewish music in the first half of the 20th century.

While it's good to know that there are now klezmer bands of

such high quality performing in Ukraine, the outlook for Ukraine's Jews is uncertain. During the 1960s and '70s discrimination within the Soviet Union forced many thousands of Ukraine's Jews to emigrate to Israel. For all the hopes that 1991 would prove to be a watershed moment, since then net emigration has remained stubbornly high, leaving behind a Jewish population many of whom are pensioners. What can be said, though, is that there is little support for attempts by extremists to stir up antisemitism. The elected mayor of Kharkov, Hennady Kernes, is a Jew. And although Kharkov is a predominantly Russian-speaking city close to the eastern border with Russia, he wasn't afraid to assert that "I am confident that the vast majority here, including Ukrainians, will advocate for Ukrainian statehood." [3] A few weeks after this interview, he was shot in the back; but the motive for the attack – which he survived – is understood to have been political rather than antisemitic. The governor of Dnipropetrovsk Oblast (an appointed position) is Ihor Kolomoyskyi, who is president of the United Jewish Community of Ukraine. Dnipropetrovsk has a dark history: in 1941 Nazi occupiers rounded up 11,000 Jews and took them away to be shot. Then during the Soviet years all but one of the city's synagogues were closed down. But since 1991 Jewish organisations in the city have flourished and collaborated on several successful projects, culminating in the opening in 2012 of what's been described as the world's largest Jewish centre. Built around the Golden Rose Synagogue – itself reclaimed from life as a coat factory during the Soviet years – it houses banqueting halls, hotel, office space, an Institute for Jewish Culture and a Holocaust museum.

In trying to identify music that somehow defines Ukrainian culture, Ukraine's folk ensembles demand our attention. They see themselves as proud defenders of a musical heritage, usually specialising in the culture of a particular region. Buttya, who are from Kiev, tell us that they surveyed 300 Transcarpathian villages to build up their repertoire of songs and dances. Halychyna (from

Lviv) perform songs from many regions of western Ukraine – Bukovina, Transcarpathia, Galicia, Pokuttya, Hutsul. Bukovyna (based in Chernivtsi) have a particular interest in Bukovina music and dance. In some of the eastern towns, ensembles perform Cossack songs. For these groups, there's no conflict between Ukrainian and Russian identities, any more than there is between Ukrainian and Ruthenian identities in Galicia. They use their mixed heritage to their advantage. Each ensemble has very experienced musicians and a wide range of traditional instruments, so they can and they do play songs from other regions.

Buttya is essentially a family group, formed by multi-instrumentalist Vasily, son Oleg (first violin) and daughter Oksana (cymbals, tambourine). Asya learned to play the basolia (Ukrainian instrument like a cello) under Oleg's direction: one thing led to another, they married, and Asya is now part of the family. As the group established itself, other musicians joined, inspired by Buttya's knowledge and love of Ukrainian folk music. Since 2000, they've made a series of home-recorded audio albums and DVDs, and detailed notes on each of these are on their website. [4] Of particular interest are the albums exploring Ukraine's vocal traditions: polyphonic singing, wedding songs and Christmas carols. The featured song (which for want of a better translation I'm calling THE SKY COVERED THE BRIGHT STARS is an example of polyphonic singing with male and female vocalists providing the contrasting melodies. It's from an album of 'rural music from all over Ukraine', this one being from the western Ternopil Oblast.

Like other Ukrainian folk groups, dance is also an important part of what they do. They've collected, performed and recorded many dance tunes, and since 2005 Buttya have co-sponsored free weekly classes in traditional Ukrainian dance at the Ivan Goncharov Museum in Kiev. Ukrainian dance was not always accompanied by music: a number of ritual folk dances are performed to the sound of chanting voices. But at a Ukrainian dance today you'd be right to expect lively string music and equally vigorous dancing. Male Cossack (kozak) dancers typically wear loose shirts, a sash tied round the waist, billowy trousers, tall boots, and often hats and swords, and often the men will seek to impress the ladies with acrobatics, kicks and spins. Ukraine's most famous dance, the Hopak, is a Cossack dance. Originally a Hopak would be highly improvised, but that has changed: "Today, the Hopak has changed its values to fit a more modern-day perception of dance performance, being that it only appears improvisational. Most of the dance is performed in unison, as the women spin and the men squat repeatedly. The acrobatic aspect of the Hopak has been amped up and performed by male soloists, executing high leaps, turns and split jumps as the climax of the performance." [5] Hutsul dances are also much celebrated. The Arkan dance is performed by men standing in a circle (traditionally around a bonfire) with their arms on each other's shoulders, side stepping in unison, then stamping as the dance gains momentum. The Hutsul kolomyika is another circle dance: a highlight of many a Ukrainian wedding, it's become popular throughout western Ukraine, and indeed among Ukrainian communities overseas.

Técsői Banda treat us to a kolomyika on the featured track **ÖKÖRMEZŐI RUSZIN KOLOMEJKA**. Kolomyika dance tunes often come with humorous lyrics, but this one is from an almost exclusively instrumental album, Vertek Engen, Vertek. The four musicians include three brothers: Jóska on the bayan accordion, Misha on the hammered dulcimer (cimbalom) and Júra on drums, jew's harp and something they call a 'plonka' – "a small plastic piece inserted in the mouth and played by pressing it between the lower teeth and gums". Violinist Iván completes the quartet. The band are named after their home town: Técső is the Hungarian name for Tyachiv, a small Transcarpathian town on the banks of the Tisza river on the border with Romania and also close to Hungary. In 2007, a couple of years after this album was released, the band suffered a tragedy when Misha died at the age of 60. At the time a film crew were shooting a fly on the wall documentary about the band, and the resulting film, The Last Kolomeyka, follows the story as the band resolve to carry on without Misha.

Again, the question of identity arises. Bob Cohen, an American-born fiddler who knows the band well and has written about them several times on his Dumneazu blog, says that "the Técsői Banda identify themselves as Hutsul or Ruthenian more strongly than as Ukrainian." [6] Even this doesn't begin to do justice to the complexity of their musical roots. The three brothers and Iván the fiddler all came from gypsy musical dynasties. They still play a lot of the Jewish klezmer music that their father used to play for the local Jewish communities. Although the majority of their income comes from performing at weddings, they're signed to a Hungarian record label who frequently book them to appear at Hungarian festivals. They live adjacent to the Muramures region in the north of Transylvania and are influenced by its culture. Most of the band speak Hungarian, Ruthenian, Ukrainian, Russian and Romani.

From Tyachiv it's just a few miles along the Tisza river to the town of Khust. Between the two there's a tiny village nestled in the hills called Nyzhnye Selysche. It's known for two things: cheese making and the Hudaki Village Band. The band's founder, Jürgen Kräftner, is an Austrian who moved to the Khust district 20 years ago to make cheese but quickly developed a passion for Carpathian music. Formed in 2001, Hudaki have become a familiar name on the European festival circuit. Their repertoire includes songs and dances from the many communities of the local region, but while they remain true to the spirit of the music, theirs is a more modern focus. Cimbalom player Volodymyr Korolenko says that Hudaki are a band rather than a traditional folklore ensemble: "we don't play music as it was played traditionally in the region. An authentic group from Khust would have a cello, two violins and a small cimbalom." [7] Hudaki have seven musicians and make great festival music: **VASYL CRIES**, with its rapid beat and breathless fiddle playing is a real footstomper. Listen out for the sparkling vocals of Kateryna Yarynych and Olga Senynets which enliven the last couple of minutes of the song.

For centuries the Transcarpathia region was under the administration of the Habsburg Empire, then becoming part of Austria-Hungary in the 1860s. In 1919 it was incorporated into Czechoslovakia before it fell under Hungarian occupation in 1939. So it has had a chequered past, but today its different communities seem largely united in asserting their wish to be part of a westward-looking democratic Ukraine. And certainly Hudaki, who were filmed performing at the Maidan protests in Kiev in 2013, have not been slow in nailing their political colours to the mast.

Mariana Sadovska grew up in Lviv in western Ukraine. After training at the Lviv National Musical Academy, she joined first the Les Kurbas Theatre in Lviv and then the experimental Gardzienice theatre group. Gardzienice carry out anthropological fieldwork in rural communities, which they bring to the stage, and as its musical director, Sadovska was involved in many such expeditions. She brought to these her own approach, building up strong relationships with the women who taught her the songs: "Each song I sing was given to me by a specific woman. I heard the story of the song, learned the way it should be sung, and understood that a song can be the map which leads you to your life." [8] In her role with the theatre she also had to find ways to interpret the songs that would connect with a theatre audience. The quietly effective **PYIEMO, PYIEMO** (We drink, and drink) is taken from Songs I Learned in Ukraine, a collection of songs gathered in her village expeditions and performed with a harmonium.

Since parting company with Gardzienice in 2001, Sadovska's been involved in a remarkable range of projects, working with theatre and music ensembles in Germany, Poland, Czech Republic and the USA, doing fieldwork in Afghanistan, and securing a coveted guest artist fellowship at Princeton University in 2005. Throughout this time she's continued to expand her knowledge of Ukrainian music, but she's had to call time on the field research as she's been living for the last few years in Germany.

As an artist, Sadovska sees both the benefits and the dangers of living abroad at a distance from the culture that she knows and loves. From a personal point of view, exile has been almost unbearably hard since the Euromaidan uprising that began in November 2013, and the subsequent conflict. In an interview for the BBC in May 2014 she said, "My country now in this moment is in a war. My country is now under occupation... and it's not easy on myself, because I want the most to be now in Ukraine and basically to serve with my hands, but I have voice, and all my family and all my friends tell me, no no, you have to sing. We have to be heard through you." [9]

But the compulsion to be in Ukraine was too strong. On 14th September she posted this on her Facebook page:

"I am back to Kiev after a few days in Mariupol, city surrounded by Russian army... I cannot describe everything I saw and heard, every meeting, every conversation, each story made me, for sure, stronger, and in the same time I feel now, like most of the people over there – calm and ready to face the worst. Everybody is getting prepared for a long, dark, cold winter. For the war. Nobody has doubts, not in the West of Ukraine, not in the East: this is the Russian army and Putin who are now bringing death, destruction and suffering into Ukraine.

I was not alone in Mariupol – I was there with my dearest friends and teachers. We were performing twice a day in front of the soldiers of the Battalion Azov, who now are protecting the city – all young, all beautiful, some of them – doctors, teachers, artists, musician, theater and film directors. In front of the Students of University of Mariupol

– wise, attentive, full of energy. In the city theater – full of people – beautifully dressed kids, flowers, standing ovations everywhere. And, when we were singing the Ukrainian National Anthem – I thought, that, maybe, this is only in Ukraine, when people are singing the Anthem with such energy, trust and love.

In every city everything is painted with blue and yellow – each bridge, each sign, everywhere flags, it seems people are trying to believe that these colors will keep away the evil... lots of tears, and lots of jokes, the sound of the Azov sea, sunshine and joy, hope and fear."

NOTES

1. http://ratinggroup.com.ua/en/products/politic/data/entry/14004/
2. http://nationalinterest.org/commentary/ukraines-culture-war-9838
3. http://euromaidanpress.com/2014/03/03/kernes-convinced-kharkiv-will-support-ukrainian-statehood/
4. http://www.buttia.kiev.ua/disco1.html#2005
5. http://dancehistorydevelopment.wordpress.com/2013/05/17/hopak-the-national-dance-of-the-ukraine-2/
6. http://horinca.blogspot.co.uk/2007_02_01_archive.html
7. http://beyondkarpaty.mutiny.net/2010/12/interview-with-cimbalom-player-volodymyr-korolenko-of-hudaki/
8. http://www.marianasadovska.de/ukrainian-callings.html
9. http://www.bbc.co.uk/news/world-europe-27496599

UNITED KINGDOM

In every folk revival there is a search for the authentic. Within British folk music there were few touchstones – living breathing musicians whose music spoke to people as directly as that of Bob Dylan or the great American blues singers. In 1963, an English teenager, Anne Briggs, released a four-track EP of traditional songs (The Hazards of Love) on which she sang with no accompaniment whatsoever. One of those four songs was **POLLY VAUGHAN**: a haunting ballad from a long-lost pagan past of mystery and magic. A.L. Lloyd wrote in the sleeve notes, "Polly Vaughan is a fine relic of a very ancient ballad concerning one of those magic maidens, familiar in folklore, who are girls by daylight but swans (or white does) after sunset, and are tragically hunted and killed by brother or lover." Anne's singing voice is pure, natural and unaffected: it weaves its own spell, and for four and a half minutes you're transfixed as she tells her sad tale.

The folk singer June Tabor once told how "I went and locked myself in the bathroom for a fortnight and drove my mother mad. I learned the songs on that EP note for note, twiddle for twiddle. That's how I started singing. If I hadn't heard her I'd have probably done something entirely different." [1] Other budding folk singers of the late 1960s have also acknowledged a big debt to

POLLY VAUGHAN	Anne Briggs
JAMIE'S TUNE/UP SOUTH	Fred Morrison & Jamie McMenemy
LAMENT FOR LIMERICK	Conor Lamb, Brendan Mulholland & Deirdre Galway
LEVI STUBBS' TEARS	Billy Bragg
MACCRIMMON'S LAMENT	Fiona Hunter
AMBELL HIRAETH	9Bach
BONNY BUNCH OF ROSES	Sam Lee and Friends

Anne Briggs for this little recording – Sandy Denny and Richard Thompson both wrote songs about her, while Christy Moore called her "the most influential person for me on the British folk scene". [2]

Yet just a few short years later Anne Briggs disappeared from this scene, breaking her ties with the music industry so completely that she raised her two kids in ignorance of the fact that she'd ever been a singer.

In fact Anne Briggs never had much love for the music industry. She lived in the 1960s as a free spirit, and for her, singing was just like a way of being. She was still a schoolkid in 1959, when she hitchhiked to Edinburgh with a friend from her home in Nottinghamshire, so that she could check out the city's folk scene. Here she met another teenager, Bert Jansch, whose path was to be closely intertwined with hers in the coming years. In 1962, Ewan McColl's Centre 42 tour passed through Nottingham, and Anne got to perform on stage and to join the tour. She moved to London where she lived for a time with Jansch in a squat in Earl's Court. Her life was just entering its wildest phase:

> "Many summers were spent in Ireland with her lover, the traditional singer Johnny Moynihan... They travelled around the country in a horse and cart or a VW van, meeting new people and playing for anyone who would listen. Briggs learned the bouzouki and loved busking, relishing the excitement of singing for her supper away from the formal atmosphere of a concert. 'The travelling I did and the singing was a more valuable experience to me personally than the gigs and the recording,' she says. 'It was always difficult for me. Occasionally I did gigs... where I really got through to the people that I was singing to – that was great, when I could do that, amazingly, within the structure of a club. But it was always much easier to do informal sessions in the Irish countryside with traditional musicians or busking in the street.'" [3]

Actual concerts were always a challenge for her: she would drink large amounts of alcohol to get the courage to go on stage, and often she wouldn't show up at all. In 1971, she got round to releasing a couple of full-length albums, and on The Time Has Come fans got to hear her sing a number of her own songs. Early in 1973 she recorded a third solo album, Sing a Song For You. Studio time was kept to a minimum – there was just one day of rehearsal with Steve Ashley's backing band and one day of recording. Anne, ever her own severest critic, didn't like the sound of her recorded voice. The album was blocked from release and the record company dropped her. Anne retreated with her young family to a remote village in the north of Scotland. She seems to have had a rewarding life, though her restless spirit has seen her move home and pursue different projects several times over the decades.

Anne's music, though, continued to attract new followers. Sing a Song For You was finally released in 1996 to a joyous reception. Lal and Norma Waterson loved its spontaneity, the 'element of risk' in the way that she sang. [4] Many voices were raised entreating Anne to sing again. In 2007, she revealed to the Guardian that she had been doing some writing and singing, but she didn't feel that she had anything yet worth recording. [5] But maybe someday...

The term 'folk music' is of modern coinage, and the images it conjures up do scant justice to the United Kingdom's vast treasury of traditional music that includes ancient ballads whose origins may go back many hundreds of years; broadside ballads, very popular in the 17th and 18th centuries, which were printed on cheap paper and were often very topical (Robert Burns was a famous and provocative balladeer); sea shanties; work songs; drinking songs; lullabies and carols.

Since the 1950s, British people's perception of folk music has been largely shaped by folk clubs. Throughout this time folk clubs have been one of the greatest strengths, but also one of the greatest weaknesses of the British folk movement.

By the late 1960s the number of folk clubs across Britain ran into the thousands. Any numbers can only be an estimate because they were and are very informal, and were starting up and shutting down all the time, but the number of folk clubs today has held up remarkably well, several hundred are still going, and they've retained their essential character of being open, democratic places where anyone can walk in and sing a song.

The 1960s, though, was undeniably the heyday of the folk club. It was here that many artists whose names would later resonate far beyond the folk scene first cut their musical teeth:

David Bowie, Marc Bolan, Rod Stewart, Steve Harley. When Sting revisited his northeastern roots with The Last Ship in 2013, he recalled in an interview that, "my early experience as a musician was in folk clubs and I have a great affection for it." [6] One might ask the question though, what was it that caused them all to move on? What was it that was missing for them in the folk scene?

The focus of the folk clubs was on singing. Singers generally accompany themselves, most often on the guitar. There's none of the emphasis on musicianship that you can find in a Scottish Highland jamming session, and you won't find a lot of dancing going on. At folk clubs the audience sits in hushed attention. Much as I enjoy folk clubs, I can see the weakness in this model. They're defined by their amateurishness: for every good performer there will be one or more poor ones. They can't compete with the thrill and energy of a good rock concert.

Of course content is important. But Shirley Collins, one of the most trenchant critics of the folk club movement, argues that Ewan MacColl and others steered the folk clubs away from an orientation on traditional working-class song. She liked the rule that you should sing a song from your own region, if you had one. However, it didn't stop there:

> "MacColl and Seeger and Peggy Seeger, they're such proselytizers. They've got an agenda and everything is going to fit that, and I mind that terribly. They're usurping all these songs to make their own point and that's not what these songs are about. What you're doing is representing generations back. The minds and the hearts and the work of all those people, and you haven't got the right to take it over and make it a political statement." [7]

There was a thirst in the 1960s for political songs, and the folk clubs catered for that. But the way Shirley Collins saw it, they were losing their soul, their reason for being. Having travelled round America with Alan Lomax in 1959 collecting traditional songs, she was becoming increasingly uncomfortable with what she found back in Britain:

> *"I quite despised a lot of the singers because they were singing a lot of the same old songs night after night. Half of it was American, half of it was the most commonplace stuff; they just weren't looking for material, they just seemed content to just thrash it out night after night. And a lot of it was American, but not good American. It was ersatz American. And once you've seen and heard the real thing, again, there's no interest in stuff that's not the genuine thing."* [8]

Here was the nub of the problem, the reason why the folk club movement was unable to sustain itself beyond a certain point. All too often the folk clubs weren't the bearers of tradition: they were simply places where people went to sing songs that they were familiar with and enjoyed. Folk music was being redefined as anything sung by 'folk singers', so the lines between folk and other genres became blurred.

Folk singers weren't to blame. The British folk revival of the 1960s was very strong and healthy compared to most other countries. But the Britain of the 1960s was a place where TV and radio presenters spoke in clipped accents: regionalism was thought to be a thing of the past. In the real world people still spoke in accents, but the sense of what it meant to be from Lancashire, Northumberland or Devon had declined. In most places, the task of resurrecting a regional cultural identity through song was to prove too great.

"The most traditional thing about traditional English music," writes John Kirkpatrick, "is that most people in England, in the British Isles, and in the world at large neither know nor care what it is." [9] There's no English national instrument (Wikipedia suggests church bells, perhaps not very helpful if you're a musician!). The nearest thing to English national folk dance tradition is the widely derided Morris dancing (apparently enjoying a modest upturn in popularity in the 2010s after attempts to modernise). English national song is another touchy subject. Hymns and carols aside, how many traditional songs have become so loved that they're part of the national psyche? People are more likely to identify with American or Irish folk songs than with English ones. One example among many is the anthem of English rugby fans: Swing Low, Sweet Chariot, an American negro spiritual.

Scottish music today, by contrast, is very well integrated with national culture. Yet as recently as 50 years ago the situation looked very different. Several fortuitous turnings in its musical development contributed to this success story, but the story also has a political side to it: there was a natural link between the musical revival and the inexorable rise in Scottish nationalism during the same period.

As in England, one of the foci of the Scottish folk music revival was industrial song. An influential figure was the traveller Jeannie Robertson (1908–75): Ray Fisher never forgot the songs she learned from Robertson at her home in Aberdeen – "'I literally sat at her knee,' Fisher recalled, hearing the legendary Robertson sing muckle sangs – traditional narrative ballads – about tinkers or other, usually-downtrodden Scots. Robertson taught the young Glasgow lassie songs such as McCrimmon's Lament and the Jute Mill Song – 'they fairly mak ye work fir yer ten n' nine.'" [10] Ray's brother, Archie Fisher, and Hamish Imlach were in the same tradition. In the 1960s though, the more visible face of Scottish music was a very conservative one, represented by the TV series The White Heather Club hosted by Andy Stewart. A third strand just starting to emerge comprised more freewheeling, independent artists such as Donovan and The Incredible String Band.

The folk song – performed by solo artists or small groups –

was the dominant medium. This was part of the folk club legacy, but by the 1970s it had started to change. The music evolved from being primarily vocal to being instrument led. As the sounds got bigger, faster and more exciting there was an explosion of interest in dance.

Karen Matheson probably speaks for most when she says, "We never set out on any mission. We were just doing the stuff we loved doing and the music we grew up with." [11] The emergence of larger bands north of the border in the 1970s reflected the kind of changes in the music scene that had also seen the rise of electric folk and folk rock: commercially it made more sense if you wanted to play larger venues and play more festivals; it also gave more scope for creativity. Each band had its own mix of instruments, its own sound – Ossian, Boys of the Lough, Silly Wizard, the Tannahill Weavers, the Battlefield Band, Runrig, Capercaillie. What anchored them all to a uniquely Scottish music tradition was a strong sense of identity, a bond with the music, and the growing importance of the ceilidh in Scottish culture.

If Karen Matheson did have a mission, it was surely to make the world aware of Scots Gaelic. Karen's mother spoke Gaelic as a first language, but it had been a rough ride for her, so she brought Karen up to speak only English. So when she joined the band Capercaillie and became a pioneer of Gaelic singing, she was reclaiming in a very real sense a dying heritage. The number of Gaelic speakers today remains very small, but music has undoubtedly helped to keep the language alive.

The fiddle was vital to all these new bands: the instrument of choice at any self-respecting ceilidh, it brought Celtic dance tunes to life. It was here too, back in the 1970s, that the clarsach (Celtic harp) began to make a comeback. The results have surpassed all expectations, according to Alison Kinnaird – "The explosion of numbers of players is quite amazing, with more people playing harps than at any time in their history. I think their future is quite safe." [12] Perhaps the biggest story of all though has been the revival of the bagpipe. Until the early 1970s, Scottish folk bands found little use for the instrument. The Clutha and the Whistlebinkies were the first to start experimenting with different types of smallpipe. By the early 1980s, leading bands such as the Battlefield Band, Ossian and the Tannahill Weavers featured bagpipe music as a prominent part of their set. It was perfect: a dramatic sound that could conquer the largest of arenas, and was instantly identifiable as Scottish. In the 21st century, not only folk bands but also an increasing number of Scottish rock bands have at least one piper in their lineup, and thousands of young people have come to see this as their culture – a big turnaround from the days when the bagpipe was associated almost exclusively with pipe bands and formal occasions.

On **JAMIE'S TUNE/UP SOUTH** we hear the Highland bagpipe in all its glory, by a man who many have acclaimed to be one of the greatest of modern-day pipers, Fred Morrison. The joyous, exhilarating noise comes from the freedom with which Morrison expresses himself. On the album Morrison plays Highland, uilleann and Border pipes and a low whistle, are aided and abetted by Jamie McMenemy's bouzouki. This tune's a real standout though. The Highland bagpipe is like a wild beast: give it its freedom and you find its soul.

I learn about Ceòl Mòr (or pibroch): a musical form unique to the Highland bagpipe. Morrison learned his skills from his father, Fred Snr, a native of South Uist – an island with a tradition to be revered. In Morrison's words: "South Uist and piping is a bit like Brazil and football. Or Shetland and fiddling. The sheer quantity and quality of pipers who've come from such a small island is just colossal." [13]

South Uist's population in 2011 was a modest 1,754! Despite this, winning the Ceòl Mòr competition at the South Uist games is highly prized among pipers, and Morrison tells us that they bring their own special magic to the pipes, with an emphasis on individual expression: "The Uist style I grew up with was all based on musicality and life and rhythm, and even with the Pibroch and the slow airs it was always full of passion, never just down to technicalities." [14]

On **LAMENT FOR LIMERICK** the pipe is again the star attraction, but this tune could hardly be more different. This is a slow air in which the pipe lingers on every note. We're informed that this much-loved melody was one of a number of tunes gathered by Edward Bunting at the Belfast Harp Festival in 1792.

Back in 2013 I sat down with Conor Lamb, who began by telling me how he started out:

> "I used to play classical music when I was younger, and then I was introduced to the Irish tin whistle by my uncle, and that was the start of the path then, so I learned some music on the tin myself, and then I heard Liam O'Flynn playing the uilleann pipes at a festival in Brittany and after I heard that sound I thought I want to be able to make that sound and play the uilleann pipes." [15]

(The sad news of Liam O'Flynn's death reached me just as this book was going to press. At his funeral Paddy Glackin paid a lovely tribute; he said, "Two musicians that Liam knew and loved, Seamus Ennis and John Kelly, they had a great word they used to use in relation to people who were special – 'magic'. Liam was a magic person." [16])

As we chatted I realised that I was going to have to rid myself of a few preconceptions about Northern Ireland. They love their trad – and it doesn't matter where you come from. In Conor's words, "music is music", it crosses divides, and there are those in the Protestant community who play Irish traditional music. It's not an alien culture: uilleann pipes have been enjoyed in the North for many decades, and there is a much older tradition as well from before the 20th-century revival. Conor Lamb is one of two uilleann pipers in Réalta, one of the most exciting trad bands north of the border, and I had planned to feature a Réalta song here. But with production of the book well under way, I was to get a rude awakening: members of the band had "extremely strong views" on Réalta being associated in any way with the UK. For all their pride in their Belfast roots, they identified as Irish, not British, and wanted out of this chapter! I'm grateful to Conor for offering his recently recorded track as an alternative.

John McSherry is one of the most respected uilleann pipers either side of the border. Like Conor, he was inspired to take up the pipes after listening to the Irish uilleann piper Liam O'Flynn playing with the band Planxty. This is he on Belfast's piping tradition:

"I'm also blessed with having the pipe and reed-making expertise of good friend and fellow piper Paddy O'Hare at my convenience. Paddy can whip up a good reed within minutes and has done so for manys the needy piper over the years. In 2008 myself and Paddy started up the Belfast Pipers Club. Belfast has always been known for its great piping tradition, stretching back over decades with the likes of O'Mealy, The McPeakes, McFadden and McAloon. The club encompasses everything from weekly lessons (beginners to advanced) to pipe maintainance and reed-making workshops." [17]

Paddy O'Hare plays in the band Craobh Rua: he was one of Aaron O'Hagan's teachers. Armagh also has a strong tradition: Conor mentioned to me about the Armagh Pipers' Club, which in 2016 entered its 50th anniversary year, running more classes and events than ever before.

For all these efforts, traditional music in Northern Ireland still faces an uphill struggle as it competes for space and attention with many other genres which command more airplay, more sales, and in the eyes of many, more credibility. The script hasn't changed that much since a young Van Morrison was playing the

Belfast clubs back in the early 1960s. Van the Man was no stranger to folk music: his very first band had been a skiffle group. Yet it was black American music that was to provide the inspiration for the songs with which he made his name.

Does folk music need airplay, sales and recognition? After all, there are hundreds of folk music festivals across Britain every year, and even though the majority of festival-goers may be 40 plus, the music clearly has a big following which is in no danger of disappearing. Maybe the truth is that Britain needs to come to terms with its own folk heritage more than folk music needs the recognition. The Scots seem to have benefited from having a stronger relationship with their own culture; perhaps this would be a healthy thing for other parts of Britain too.

Billy Bragg is important to this debate in several ways. Often identified as a folk singer, his main audiences have always been people who have never been to a traditional folk festival in their lives. He sings in a vernacular that seems natural and unpretentious, his songs are often topical and he's certainly not afraid to speak his mind. Yet he also wrote lyrics so poignant that they still chill the flesh 30 years later. Despite recent incursions into American music (the Mermaid Avenue project, Tooth and Nail), the bulk of his work comes from a place that's very English. Bragg himself has long tried to reclaim an English cultural identity – he's even written a book on the subject: The Progressive Patriot – A search for belonging.

Bragg's route to songwriting was not through the folk club, but through punk music. It was punk that made him realise that he didn't have to have been to music school, he could just pick up a guitar and start singing. Later he himself would make the connection between this and the folk music ethos:

"All through the history of popular culture, there have been two dominant strains that have continually struggled with each other: do-it-yourself culture and commercial

culture… the first one would be rural music, music people made for themselves, whether it was blues or country or folk or whatever. Where people would hear a song on the radio, learn how to play it, and then not bother listening to that song or buying the record. They'd just learn to play it on their porch… And that struggle has always gone on. At the moment, you would think the commercial aspect is completely overwhelming the DIY, but we're on the cusp of a time when people are going to be able to make music in their bedrooms and send it to you straight down the line without a record contract, without a record shop, without a radio, you know? And we're going to be back on a DIY trip again." [18]

That was in 1998, and Bragg's prediction has proven very prescient as the internet has since opened up new ways for artists to reach their fans without the involvement of record labels.

Like the original punks, Bragg trusted only himself: he wasn't going to buy into any off-the-shelf formula which told him what rules to follow. The Billy Bragg who came to prominence during the miners' strike of 1984/85 was a songwriter with an attitude: he'd get up on stage with no band, just an electric guitar which he played in his own inimitable rough and ready style, singing insightful songs about working class life which could be serious but also whimsical and fanciful. That's remained pretty much the cornerstone of his approach, though he's recorded with a great range of musicians over the years.

As a consequence of Mermaid Avenue, Bragg's name will always be linked to that of Woody Guthrie. And there's no doubt that he feels strong affinities with Guthrie. Guthrie's music was defiantly non-commercial; it too had that DIY ethos; it too was blunt and plain spoken; and it too was not always serious – it could be funny or sentimental at times. Nonetheless, when he agreed to take on the project, Bragg was no expert on Guthrie's music.

His more important influences were British: Dick Gaughan (from whom he took Think Again), Leon Rosselson (The World Turned Upside Down) and of course Joe Strummer. He once said, "the difference between me and Dick Gaughan is that Dick never saw The Clash – that's all it is. Apart from that, we're more or less the same." [19]

As a songwriter Bragg stands comparison with any of these names. On every album there are tracks that sparkle with wit or jangle with emotion, and there are many acutely observed lines. The lyrics from **LEVI STUBBS' TEARS** must rank among the finest of these. It's a superbly crafted mixture of wit and social observation, from the amusingly titled Talking with the Taxman About Poetry (1986). The song deals with the harsh reality of domestic violence with a deftness of touch. The woman is consoling herself, living in her mobile home, listening to old Motown records (Levi Stubbs was lead vocalist of the Four Tops). But as each verse piles on more grim information, the refrain carries less and less conviction: this is a desperately sad song.

While I don't wish to reduce Bragg to the status of 'protest singer', it's his songs of social commentary that connect him to the tradition of industrial song pioneered by A.L. Lloyd and Ewan MacColl, a tradition that he has enormously enriched. In his political songwriting Bragg has always followed a couple of important principles. First, he never romanticises the working class. And secondly he always promotes faith as opposed to cynicism. In this too, he takes his cue from Woody Guthrie:

"Our real enemy in trying to make a better world isn't conservatism, or capitalism or racism – they're manifestations of a deeper malaise, which is cynicism. And there's so much of that about, in our political and social discourse... as Woody Guthrie said, 'I never want to write a song that puts people down.'" [20]

On 23rd October, 2013, I was in Cardiff to see the Womex 13 opening concert, Land of Song, which was brilliantly directed by Cerys Matthews. This is from her introduction to the event programme:

> *"Until now Wales has largely kept her musical crafts and traditions to herself and despite being famous for our love of singing, little of our folk repertoire is known outside of our borders. Even as close as we are to mighty England few know about our crwth, triple harp, clogging, cerdd dant and marvellous songs."*

One might also ask how familiar many Welsh people are with these aspects of their culture. All of which raises a larger question: why is it that, unlike in Scotland, Welsh music has failed thus far to capitalise on the resurgence of interest in all things Celtic?

Lack of knowledge of the crwth is forgiveable: this box-shaped bowed instrument disappeared from Wales around the end of the 18th century, and it's only recently that the instrument has begun to be made once more. Musicians have had to work out from scratch how it should be played and what kind of tunes will work on it. Cass Meurig, who performed at Land of Song, is one of only a handful of active crwth players today. Her playing partner Nial Cain has taken to manufacturing crwths, and I mention him because I found an interview in which, questioned about the state of Welsh traditional music, he was able to give some very useful perspective:

> *"Later in the 19th century much damage was done to the tradition and a great deal was lost – when I say a great deal, I mean both music and the respect for traditional music. There were various factors at work here, but mention must be made of the enthusiastic takeup of Wesleyanism, and the doctrine that only hymns and religious music had*

legitimacy... bonfires of fiddles, the devil's instrument, and hymns sung around the house instead of folk songs. By the time the eisteddfodau got going, much of the folk music of Wales was being forced into respectability and clinging to legitimacy only as a competitive art-music. And to a large extent that is the profile it has enjoyed on the world stage ever since." [21]

9Bach are a young Welsh band trying to break the mould. In 2014 they signed with Real World records, and have released two albums with them which have really brought Welsh language music to world attention: Tincian (2014) and Anian (2016). 9Bach's vocalist, Lisa Jen Brown, was born and brought up in the village of Bethesda near Bangor speaking Welsh as a first language. Having founded 9Bach with Martin Hoyland, the two have since married and moved back to Bethesda, where they mix their albums in their small studio.

Tincian and Anian are the antithesis of Bragg's DIY music: these are sophisticated modern albums that require many hours in the studio mixing and arranging all the vocal and instrumental parts. Nor do they conform to any folk tradition: first and foremost they're creative works, mostly self-written, which take artistic inspiration from many places and genres. But there is a quality of Welshness that runs through them. It's present in the reverence that the band have for the language, the place, and yes, also the heritage of song on which they're seeking to build. **AMBELL HIRAETH** (Homesickness) is a stripped back number of great beauty and sensitivity. Lisa Jen tells us that it's "a combination of three Welsh folk songs that I've mashed into one. It's melancholic and talks about being ready for the grave."

To conclude this chapter, I'm going to look at a couple of artists who've dedicated their lives to preserving traditional song.

Fiona Hunter went to the Royal Conservatoire of Scotland

(then the Royal Scottish Academy of Music and Drama) to study traditional song with little idea of the scope of what she was about to take on. Her tutors, all respected singers, introduced her to a traditional song repertoire vaster than anything she'd imagined, and to travellers who had at their fingertips songs passed on through oral tradition. She was also taught ways of bringing the old songs back to life:

> *"The biggest lesson was probably the need to totally know a song, the background and historical relevance as much as the dynamics of when to be quiet or how to build it up dramatically... When you take on one of the big ballads, it's quite a project because you have to engage people with it through the different stages, make it live for them, and that's what I love about traditional songs because they're essentially stories." [22]*

She must have been a good learner because in 2004 she replaced Karine Polwart as lead female vocalist and cellist in Malinky, a band noted for the quality of their musicianship and their love of traditional song. Fiona enjoyed some good years with Malinky, but in the meantime she was still pursuing her academic career. She was now teaching music herself at the Conservatoire (she says she finds herself learning, or re-learning, almost as much as she imparts to her students).

MACCRIMMON'S LAMENT is one of those songs of which it helps to know the story. Donald Ban MacCrimmon came from a long line of pipers who were pipers to the MacLeods of Skye. In 1745 he served in the war against the Jacobites, and legend has it that he composed this song, with its premonitions of his own death, on the eve of battle. He did indeed die in battle a short time later, but it was a less than glorious end. An audacious attempt to capture Bonnie Prince Charlie ended up in panic and disarray after the lead piper was shot and killed. Fiona sings it on her debut solo album. She says in her liner notes, "the Gaelic words have been attributed to MacCrimmon's sister and the Scots translation I sing has been around since the early nineteenth century."

Originally this would have been a Ceòl Mòr for the bagpipe, but Jeannie Robertson sang it as a folk song without instrumental backing, and modern artists have followed her lead by having the vocals dominate. Here, the song opens with Fiona's strong, clear voice and gradually the song builds as a drone is added, and then strings. The result nicely captures the emotion and drama of the song.

I could describe Sam Lee as a fast-rising star of British folk, and technically that would be true, but it would actually tell you nothing of consequence about him. A Sam Lee album is not about personal fame, it's not even first and foremost about Sam Lee at all. Rather, it's a gateway to a disappearing culture. For Sam Lee's true vocation is to have become, in his 30s, Britain's leading folk song collector and a passionate advocate for the culture and the rights of Britain's travellers.

Sam had grown up in London, he wasn't part of any folk community. One day he heard an album by the Watersons and developed a fascination with learning more about where these old ballads came from. He began volunteering at Cecil Sharp House, the home of the English Folk Dance and Song Society, named after the man who 100 years earlier had been one of England's most important folk song collectors. He also began seeking out people who could teach him more about England's folk song heritage. This led him to Jeannie Robertson's nephew, Stanley Robertson (1940–2009).

"Our first meeting will never leave me… It was in a mighty gale, climbing the cliffs at Whitby. He reached the top, with me, nervously, following behind, waiting to introduce myself. Stanley was clutching a giant whale bone arch. I stopped him to say thank you for his songs in the concert…

he growled out in full proud drama 'I ken a thoosand ballads'. It was awesome, like a moment out of Tolkien... You just sensed this ancient magic about him and a power... he had such incredible psychic abilities. He would tell me everything about my life, even things I would deem very private... He'd just announce them as they hit him, usually in really inappropriate moments, too... To me it seemed real and indisputable, nothing was private and nothing could be hidden. That is the Travellers for you. They are a very gifted people." [23]

Having bonded, Sam devoted all the hours he could to learning from the veteran singer, travelling up to Scotland every month for the three years up to Robertson's death. "Every visit I sat in his living room for three days while he just sang and sang and sang, and I learned song after song from him. Sometimes we went out into the countryside, he showed me where the songs come from, where he had learned them, from which people, and where the Travellers lived." [24]

Sam wasn't just learning songs: he was discovering the vitality of traveller culture, which impacted on their lives and beliefs in many ways. He developed a strong admiration for these people who wore their heart on their sleeves and had a deep relationship to the land. Robertson's death only strengthened his conviction that he had a vital and urgent job to do. "The real tradition bearers in the community," he says, "the ones with the keys to unlock these treasure chests of song, there's not many of them left and they're all of a certain age and their life expectancy isn't good, so it's essential to seek them out now."

This led him to form the Song Collectors Collective, linking up with like-minded enthusiasts around an agreed set of objectives and way of working. As well as recording the songs and stories of the tradition bearers, the SCC is committed to sharing these as widely as possible (which it does through its website) and returning copies of the recordings to the individuals and communities who have contributed.

Freda Black probably knows more songs than any traveller alive in Britain. They're songs she learned from her parents and grandparents, and her husband's family. From the biography on the SCC website, she was born on Christmas Day, the "same hour as the Lord were born", to a gypsy family who roamed the country in their caravan. She's a mother to nine children, a grandmother and a great-grandmother.

> "Until the Song Collectors Collective conference in January 2013, Freda had never sung in public and never even for an audience. In fact, two of her daughters, Freda Bell and Kathleen, hadn't realised how gifted and knowledgeable a singer their mother truly is, and have since begun to learn some of her repertoire ensuring that it stays alive within the family, becoming another generation of tradition bearers." [25]

BONNY BUNCH OF ROSES is a 19th-century broadside ballad, and is an imaginary conversation between Napoleon II and his mother. It was Freda Black's rendition of the song that inspired Sam Lee to reinterpret it on his 2015 album, The Fade In Time. His version starts with a sample of an archive recording of an East European cantor singer. Then, as Sam's vocals cut in, the unusual drumbeat conjures up an image of marching cavalry. It's all rather interesting, and it works very well. This is fairly typical of how Sam Lee albums are put together. The songs are all traditional ones that he's heard sung by the traveller community. He reinterprets the songs using only his instincts as a guide, experimenting with a range of sounds and instruments. "Folk music," he argues, "is raw material. Lyrics and melody, that's all you've got, and even those are up for negotiation. After that, you can do what the hell you like." [26] Don't let this deceive you though. He wants us to listen to these songs, and to hear in them echoes of the way in which he'd heard them sung by the travellers. So the singing and the instrumentation are gentle and restrained, allowing the songs to breathe.

NOTES

1. Liner notes on the album, A Collection by Anne Briggs
2. David Burke – Singing Out: A Folk Narrative Of Maddy Prior, June Tabor and Linda Thompson (Soundcheck Books, 2015), p24
3. Liner notes on the album, Sing a Song For You, by Anne Briggs
4. http://ishotamaninrenobook.blogspot.co.uk/2008/08/update.html
5. https://www.theguardian.com/music/2007/aug/03/folk.shopping1
6. http://www.sting.com/news/article/5092
7. http://www.furious.com/perfect/shirleycollins2.html
8. http://thequietus.com/articles/18060-shirley-collins-interview
9. http://www.johnkirkpatrick.co.uk/wr_WhatEnglish.asp
10. http://www.scotsman.com/news/obituaries/obituary-ray-fisher-folksinger-1-1827892
11. http://www.dailyrecord.co.uk/entertainment/celebrity-interviews/capercaillie-singer-karen-matheson-went-3029906#ui4PBRBDcBRb7R5u.97
12. http://harpfestival.co.uk/latest-from-eihf/4671, retrieved June, 2016
13. http://www.ridge-records.com/artists_fred.htm
14. http://northings.com/2004/10/03/fred-morrison-2/
15. Recorded interview 25/10/13
16. https://www.irishtimes.com/news/social-affairs/liam-o-flynn-remembered-as-a-magical-musician-1.3429970
17. http://www.johnmcsherry.com/piping/
18. http://www.avclub.com/article/billy-bragg-13536
19. Kieran Cashell – More Relevance than Spotlight and Applause: Billy Bragg in the British Folk Tradition, in Ian Peddie (ed.), Popular Music and Human Rights, vol. I: British and American Music (Ashgate, 2011)
20. https://www.theguardian.com/music/2008/mar/11/folk.popandrock
21. https://americymru.net/ceri-shaw/blog/4149/oes-i-oes-an-interview-with-nial-cain-and-cass-meurig
22. http://www.heraldscotland.com/arts_ents/13156834.Hunter_out_to_unite_Scots_and_Gaelic_through_song/
23. http://www.uncut.co.uk/uncut-editors-diary/sam-lee-interviewed-66712

24. http://www.romea.cz/en/features-and-commentary/interviews/british-folk-singer-sam-lee-gypsies-are-our-indians
25. http://songcollectors.org/tradition-bearers/freda-black/
26. https://aeon.co/essays/for-britain-s-travellers-songs-can-still-summon-ghosts

VATICAN CITY

The world's tiniest country has music capable of enthralling people like few other places on earth.

The polyrhythmic melodies in **AD TE LEVAVI** are breathtaking: both the male and female vocal lines are ornamented, rising and falling in tandem. This has all the quality and complexity of an orchestral number, yet all of the sounds are produced by human voices. You don't need to understand the words to know that this is an intensely spiritual piece, a yearning for the divine.

It's also a historic first: the album, Cantate Domino (2015), is the first time that the Holy See has permitted recording to take place inside the Sistine Chapel itself. The Chapel was consecrated in 1483 with Michelangelo's awe-inspiring ceiling painted between 1508 and 1512. Most of the music on Cantate Domino was written specifically to be performed in the Sistine Chapel by 16th-century composers (Ad te levavi was written by Giovanni Pierluigi da Palestrina). The president of Deutsche Grammophon, Mark Wilkinson, could hardly contain his delight at being given the chance to record in this special place: "The Sistine sound is unique – richly resonant, vibrant and real. Our producer, Anna Barry, worked hand-in-hand with the Choir's director to ensure that the space was managed and arranged to maximum effect." [1]

AD TE LEVAVI   *Sistine Chapel Choir & Massimo Palombella*

In 2015, the choir achieved another first: its first British full-time member, baritone Mark Spyropoulos. Here Mark explains how the Sistine Chapel left its mark on musical terminology:

"You will have heard of the phrase 'a capella' singing. This literally refers to the Sistine Chapel (the 'capella'), and to the unaccompanied style in which the choir has been singing ever since it was installed in the world famous Cappella Sistina in the 15th century." [2]

Mark also says – and other sources bear this out – that the reputation of the Sistine Chapel Choir had been taking a few knocks before Pope Benedict appointed Massimo Palombella in 2010 as its new director. "The first thing Palombella did," Mark tells us, "was to electronically map the acoustic in the Sistine Chapel... so now, when we sing in the much larger space, we're amplified in a way that recreates the authentic Sistine acoustic and we can hold on to the choir's core repertoire – the many Renaissance masterpieces of early polyphony." There were many other changes: Palombella reportedly changed rehearsals from three hours a week to three hours a day and inculcated in the choir a deep reverence and understanding of Renaissance singing.

NOTES

1. http://www.classicfm.com/discover-music/latest/sistine-chapel-choir-pope-francis/
2. https://www.theguardian.com/music/2016/dec/29/mark-spyropoulos-sistine-chapel-choir-pope-vatican

ACKNOWLEDGEMENTS

This book was inspired by a love of world music, and while writing it there has rarely been a week gone by in which I've not found new inspiration. Some of the music I've listened to and the stories that I've read will stay with me all of my life. So to all the artists featured here, a very heartfelt thank you: you're an amazing group of people.

Particular thanks are due to the many who've given me their time – your wisdom, your support and the faith that you've shown in this project are greatly appreciated. I've tried to include you all in the lists below: if I've left anyone out I do apologise; please consider yourself thanked as well.

Those who gave me interviews (with special love to those who aren't native English speakers and those who helped with translations): Aaron Bebe Sukura, Alhousseini Anivolla, Andrea Konstankiewicz, Andrew Alamango, Andrey Vinogradov, Andy Patterson, April Verch, Attila Buzás, Boima Tucker, Conor Lamb, Damily, Daryana Antipova, Etsuko Takezawa, gamin, Gusztáv Balogh, Hanna Flock, Kimi Djabate, King Ayisoba, Kristi Stassinopoulou, Lakha Khan, Lisa Lestander, Louise Mulcahy, Marcus Gora, Mari Kalkun, Mariam Handani, Mariem Hassan, Marita Kruijswijk, Mark Humphrey, Msafiri Zawose, Nuru Kane, Pål Hægland, Pete Doolan, Petra Käppi, Raymond Ammann,

Saeid Shanbehzadeh, Sergei Starostin, Sibongiseni Shabalala, Sona Jobarteh, Steven Sogo, Temesgen, Terry Miller, Teta, Thomas Mapfumo, Wendy Cao Romero, Xavier Fethal, Yuval Ron.

Those who gave specific permission to publish music on my website: (record labels) Akcent, Amarrass Records, Asasi Records, Aztec Musique, Cobiana Records, Contrejour, Crammed, Cumbancha, Drag City, EMI/Virgin, Felmay, Fidjomusic, Filfla Records, Fire Museum Records, FM Records, FolkClub Ethnosuoni, Frequency Glide Enterprises, Fusion Embassy, iASO, Japan Overseas, JARO Medien, KKV, Lee Thorp Entertainment, Nubenegra, Ocora, Par les chemins productions, Rattle, Riverboat Records, Routes Nomades, Sahel Sounds, tanz raum, Yantra Productions, Zamzama; (other projects and organisations) The Amalgamation Project, Awesome Tapes from Africa, Bushman Music Initiative, Cambodian Living Arts, Maison Jephte (Togo), Raw Music International; (bands and artists) Annie Lou, Buttya, Di Naye Kapelye, Hudaki Village Band , Hüsch!, Marewrew, Pham Thi Hue, Sinan Celik, Suzanna Owiyo, Veja, Yuval Ron.

I'm very grateful to everyone who contributed to the crowdfunding campaign for this book; in particular, Kevin Donnellon, Harvey Duckers, David James, Richard Shield, Etsuko Takezawa, Catherine Wall and Sandra Wall.

This work has been brought to press without an agent or a publisher – yes, it can be done: it's a little bit scary, but there is support out there. So thank you to the people at Matador for their faith in the project, and for the many services that they were able to provide; to Forshaw Media for the crowdfunding video; and to my brilliant designer Makak Studios.

Finally, thank you to my parents Sandra and Terry for never stopping believing in me.